Joint Commission

# Preventing Adverse Events
# in Behavioral Health Care:

## A Systems Approach to Sentinel Events

## Joint Commission Mission

The mission of the Joint Commission on Accreditation of Healthcare Organizations is to improve the quality of care provided to the public through the provision of health care accreditation and related services that support performance improvement in health care organizations.

*Joint Commission educational programs and publications support, but are separate from, the accreditation activities of the Joint Commission. Attendees at Joint Commission educational programs and purchasers of Joint Commission publications receive no special consideration or treatment in, or confidential information about, the accreditation process.*

Printed in the U.S.A. 5 4 3 2 1

Requests for permission to reprint or make copies of any part of this book should be addressed to:

Permissions Editor
Joint Commission on Accreditation of Healthcare Organizations
One Renaissance Boulevard
Oakbrook Terrace, IL 60181

ISBN:    0-86688-640-0

Library of Congress Catalog Number: 99-73029

For more information about the Joint Commission, please visit our Web site at www.jcaho.org.

# CONTENTS

# Preface

Adverse events in behavioral health care organizations should trigger analysis and response to minimize the risk of recurrence. This requires understanding the root causes of the event and implementing improvement or redesign efforts to eliminate causative factors. It is clear that general knowledge about adverse events is limited, at best. Knowledge is even more limited in the area of proactive design or redesign of behavioral health care processes and systems to prevent, or at least minimize, the likelihood of future errors and protect individuals from the effects of errors when they do occur.

*Preventing Adverse Events in Behavioral Health Care: A Systems Approach to Sentinel Events* addresses this issue. This publication highlights adverse event prevention through proactive risk-reduction approaches or strategies. It is our hope that, even without the stimulus of an adverse event, organizations that provide behavioral health services will embrace the concept of prospective design and analysis of health care processes and systems to minimize the possibility of errors and protect individuals from adverse events.

Several examples included in this book demonstrate successful proactive risk reduction and prevention programs developed and implemented by behavioral health care organizations.

The publication also provides an overview of the types of errors and adverse events that have been reported in all types of health care organizations, ways organizations can respond to adverse events, and ways such events are investigated through root cause analysis, which uses a variety of traditional quality improvement tools.

*Preventing Adverse Events in Behavioral Health Care: A Systems Approach to Sentinel Events* is directed to the staff of *all* organizations providing behavioral health services. These include mental health, chemical dependency, forensic, and mental retardation/developmental disabilities (MR/DD) services. Hence, the audience includes the staff of inpatient, residential, and outpatient settings. Examples come from all types of settings where behavioral health care services are offered.

## Acknowledgments

We wish to acknowledge the enormous contribution made to the study of errors in medicine by James Reason, PhD, professor of psychology at the University of Manchester; Lucian L. Leape, MD, and his colleagues at Harvard; Donald M. Berwick, MD, MPP, president and chief executive officer of the Institute for Healthcare Improvement; and Marilyn Sue Bogner, PhD, of the Food and Drug Administration, among many others too numerous to cite individually here. These experts' work provided the foundation for this publication and is quoted extensively throughout the chapters.

We also wish to express profound thanks to our primary contacts at each organization providing proactive risk reduction examples for this book. These individuals invested many hours to give us the information needed to tell their stories in a way that would help their colleagues at other organizations. Our gratitude goes to Howard A. Savin, PhD, senior vice president of clinical affairs, Susan Soldivera Kiesling, national quality improvement coordinator, and Tom Shurer, a member of the information resource staff at the Devereux Foundation; Paul G. Quinnett, PhD, director of Greentree Behavioral Health; and Joyce Winters, MSN, clinical services director at Foundations Behavioral Health.

Finally, we are indebted to Nancy Gorham Haiman for her expertise in writing this book. Her thorough, diligent efforts significantly contributed to the excellence of this publication. Thank you, Nancy, for your outstanding efforts.

# Introduction

**D**espite remarkable advances in almost every field of health care, an age-old problem continues to haunt behavioral health care professionals—the occurrence of errors. When such errors lead to sentinel events—serious and undesirable occurrences—the problem is even more disturbing. Although the rate of errors and adverse events in behavioral health care is unknown (and may be unknowable), any error or adverse event is a cause for concern. Adverse events can result in tragedy for consumers and their families, add cost to an already overburdened health care system, and lead to wasteful litigation. They can also deeply affect behavioral health care professionals who are dedicated to helping their clients. Why do these things happen?

## A Changing Environment

Behavioral health care continues to experience dramatic change. As health care organizations become more complex, their systems and processes are increasingly interdependent and often interlocked or coupled. This makes the opportunity for error more frequent and recovery from error increasingly difficult. The rapid explosion of the health care knowledge base has made it more challenging for clinicians to stay up to date. Litigation concerns have created a climate characterized by fear and defensiveness. Moreover, the rigorous financial constraints imposed by managed care and the need to reduce health care expenditures have affected every type of health care organization. No organization is immune. Organization leaders are reassessing their workforces. Workloads are heavier, creating increased stress and fatigue for health care professionals. Caregivers are working in new settings and performing new functions, sometimes with minimal training. Skill mixes are shifting. In short, the health care environment is ripe for errors.

Instances of errors and adverse events within health care organizations have been reported in the media with increasing regularity. An 11-year-old client dies after an aide administers a chest-crushing therapeutic hold. A patient dies because of an incorrect drug administered during what should have been a routine procedure. These and other events raise questions about the public's trust in health care. People justifiably ask What's going on? A galvanized industry starts to respond. Governing boards of health care organizations invigorate their efforts to examine errors. Error detection, reduction, and prevention strategies receive needed new impetus. The health care industry begins to recognize that it has failed to make error reduction and prevention a common goal. Why?

## Accountability

Accountability in behavioral health care may provide part of the explanation. Accountability in any system demands the development of valid and reliable measures of quality, particularly outcomes measures. Traditionally, individual practitioners, operating independently as entrepreneurs, have been held responsible for their errors. Throughout most of the twentieth century, including the present decade, outcomes measures in all types of health care organizations have focused on individual errors. Not surprisingly, these are underreported because organizations continue to use sanctions and punishment as the "treatment" for errors.

Behavioral health care is a highly complex and technologically driven industry. In such an environment, systems, more than individuals, should be held responsible for errors and adverse events. In fact, some theorists suggest that as many as seven separate parties have accountability in a modern health care system: clients, clinicians, health care service organizations, health plans, investors, lawyers and the courts, and government entities. All parties are integrally related. All must balance the need to hold each other responsible for actions with the need to learn from errors that are made. All are interested in outcomes measurement, which is evolving rapidly as the first step in developing error-reduction strategies. After all, if you don't know the extent of the problem, how can you fix it or learn from it?

## A Word About Terminology

As described fully in Chapter 1, the terminology related to errors and adverse events in the health care world is far from fixed. A wide range of terms appears throughout the literature describing what are basically unwanted events. For the purposes of this publication, we use three terms extensively—*error, adverse event,* and *sentinel event* (*event* in the brief form). These terms are defined in Chapter 1. Other terms such as *adverse occurrence, adverse drug event, medical accident, medical mishap, medical mistake,* and *medication error* appear in this publication when we describe studies from the literature using such terms. Some of the terms (such as *medical mistake* and *medical mishap*) may be used interchangeably, whereas others may not (such as *medication error* and *adverse occurrence*). Readers are advised to consult the glossary at the end of the book for further clarification.

## How This Book Was Developed

In the development of this publication, we completed a thorough review of the literature devoted to errors and error prevention strategies and solicited practical examples of adverse events from organizations accredited by the Joint Commission. For Chapter 3, in-depth interviews with three behavioral health care organizations enabled us to provide profiles of successfully implemented risk-reduction approaches.

## Overview of Contents

*Preventing Adverse Events in Behavioral Health Care: A Systems Approach to Sentinel Events* provides organizations in the behavioral health services field with practical information on approaches to error reduction and prevention; the definition, measurement, and causation of errors and adverse events; and how to conduct a root cause analysis to evaluate the causes of a sentinel event.

*Chapter 1* provides an in-depth definition of adverse events, sentinel events, and errors in health care; describes how sentinel events stem from process variation; and provides background information on cognitive mechanisms and error, general taxonomies of error, and classification systems for health care errors. Chapter 1 also includes a discussion of issues involved in developing a comprehensive taxonomy for sentinel events.

*Chapter 2* describes the challenges of measuring errors and sentinel events. Challenges center on the lack of consensus regarding how errors or adverse events are defined and social views that deeply affect how errors are reported. The "myth of perfect performance" that is so prevalent among health care professionals is explored, as is the challenge of a measurement system based largely on self-reporting of errors. Surveillance mechanisms used to measure adverse events are described and compared. The chapter also presents the basic theories of error causation derived from human factors research and cognitive psychology. It explores how people contribute to organization error and how organizations contribute to human error. The chapter also describes the basic assumptions about error causation in the medical field and how they differ from those predominant in the engineering field. Finally, the chapter reviews selected performance and environmental factors, including fatigue, substance abuse, and workload, and how they influence error in the health care environment.

*Chapter 3* describes the practical strategies organizations may pursue to reduce and prevent adverse events. Proactive strategies include risk management and prevention; system design or redesign; sound hiring practices, education and training; and improvement of information management, teamwork, and in-depth self-assessment through performance measurement. Suicide risk reduction strategies, systems designed to reduce violence and the use of restraint and seclusion, and an award-winning performance measurement initiative for violence reduction within a psychiatric hospital are fully described. Three approaches to error reduction appear as profiles at the end of the chapter. They include the Suicide Risk Reduction Program from Greentree Behavioral Health in Spokane, Washington; an outcomes management initiative resulting in the reduced use of PRN (pro re nata or "as the occasion arises") behavioral medications, improved pre-employment screening, a major program to reduce suicidality, and reduced staff and client injuries at the Devereux Foundation of Villanova, Pennsylvania; and a major systems redesign initiative to reduce the use of restraint at Foundations Behavioral Health in Doylestown, Pennsylvania.

*Chapter 4* provides practical guidance on steps that organizations should take immediately following the occurrence of an adverse or sentinel event. These include providing prompt and appropriate care for the client, risk containment to minimize the possibility of a similar event recurring immediately with other clients, preservation of evidence so the organization can explore exactly what occurred and learn from the event, and notification of appropriate parties. Communication and disclosure by the behavior health care provider are discussed, including which mistakes require disclosure, the timing of disclosure, who should disclose the mistake, and the consequences of disclosure. The Joint Commission's Sentinel Event Policy and requirements are provided in full; requirements of other agencies are described briefly.

*Chapter 5* provides practical guidance on how to conduct a root cause analysis in response to a sentinel event. The chapter describes how to organize for the analysis, identify proximate causes and their underlying causes, design and implement interim changes, and identify the root cause of a sentinel event. Characteristics of a thorough and credible root cause analysis are outlined. Root causes identified by organizations that experienced client suicides and restraint deaths are outlined. The chapter also provides a brief description of helpful tools that organizations can use during root cause analysis. How-to information, as well as the benefits of each tool, are provided. Tools include flowcharts; cause-and-effect diagrams; Pareto charts; barrier analysis; change analysis; failure mode, effect, and criticality analysis; and fault tree analysis.

*Chapter 6* provides practical guidance on how to conduct the improvement portion of a root cause analysis. During this stage, an organization develops and implements improvement strategies to address underlying systems problems. Planning, designing and redesigning for improvement, implementing improvements, and measuring and assessing improvement efforts are described in detail. The chapter concludes with a discussion of a framework for a root cause analysis completed by an organization that experienced a pediatric suicide.

Finally, the Selected Bibliography guides readers to relevant literature, and the Glossary provides definitions of key terms used throughout the book.

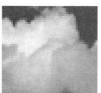

*Chapter One*
# Defining Sentinel Events and Errors in Health Care

*Chapter One*
# Defining Sentinel Events and Errors in Health Care

**R**ecent media coverage of tragic mistakes in health care organizations have captured national attention. A teenager dies after an aide improperly administers a therapeutic hold. An x-ray scanner tips over, injuring an elderly patient. A seriously mentally ill patient dies in seclusion after drowning in his own vomit. A 7-year-old boy dies of an incorrect drug administered during what should have been a routine procedure. An adolescent client in a psychiatric treatment program jumps out of an unsecured tenth-story window. A client with developmental disabilities is discovered to be pregnant as the result of rape by a caregiver. Whether called clinical errors, adverse events involving criminal behavior, medical mishaps, or sentinel events, these incidents have in common flawed care that reflects poorly on the health care organizations.

This chapter examines the foundation of sentinel events and errors—their definition and classification or taxonomy. Errors and events that occur in behavioral health care are not unique to the behavioral health care environment. They occur not only in *all* types of organizations providing behavioral health services, from hospitals to outpatient and community facilities, but in *all* types of organizations. The focus here is on errors, *wherever* they occur. With this foundation, readers can start the journey toward understanding error causation and developing a preventative approach.

## What Is a Sentinel Event?
The Joint Commission defines *sentinel event* as an unexpected occurrence involving death or serious physical or psychological injury, or the risk thereof. Serious injury specifically includes loss of limb or function. The phrase "or the risk thereof" includes any process variation for which a recurrence would carry a significant chance of a serious adverse outcome. Such events are called "sentinel" because they signal the need for immediate investigation and response. According to *Webster's Third New International Dictionary*, the word *sentinel* means "one who watches or

guards." An event is sentinel because it involves an unexpected variation in a process or an outcome and demands notice.

Sentinel events commonly result from errors of commission or omission. An error of *commission* occurs as a result of an action taken, for example, when an improper technique is used to restrain an individual, resulting in the individual's asphyxiation. An error of commission can also occur when the incorrect drug is administered or the correct drug is administered at the wrong time or in the wrong dosage.

An error of *omission* occurs as a result of an action *not* taken, for example, when a delay in monitoring a client in seclusion results in client injury, when a nurse omits a dose of a medication that should be administered, or when a client suicide is associated with a lapse in carrying out frequent observation. Errors of omission may or may not lead to adverse outcomes. For example, a client in seclusion is not monitored during the first two hours of seclusion. The staff corrects the situation by beginning regular observations as specified in organization policy. The possibility of error was present, however, and the mere fact that the staff did not follow organization policy regarding seclusion, and thereby violated acceptable professional standards, signals the occurrence of an error requiring study to ensure that it doesn't happen again. In this case, the error was insufficient monitoring. Had the individual suffered serious physical or psychological harm during seclusion, the sentinel event would have been the individual's adverse outcome. By definition, sentinel events require further investigation each time they occur.

Although the focus of this book is on *adverse* sentinel events, not all sentinel events are adverse. An unexpectedly successful outcome of a usually unsuccessful procedure is a *desirable* sentinel event because it constitutes an unexpected variation in a process. Process errors may unexpectedly have a positive outcome. For example, a client with physical and mental disabilities enters the facility's pool without the normally required flotation device. He is able to float on top of the water by himself until staff can reach him. Conventional wisdom may have indicated that the individual would not have fared well and may have drowned. However, subsequent analysis of this desirable sentinel event might help identify a subgroup of clients who can take swimming lessons and eventually use the pool without flotation devices. For the purposes of this volume, however, we will be using *sentinel event* to describe grave, undesirable, and adverse incidents that cause or could cause outcomes of death or injury.

The distribution of sentinel events reviewed by the Joint Commission between January 1995 and February 1999 indicates a wide range of event categories (see Sidebar 1–1, page 15). Those of particular pertinence to organizations providing behavioral health services include suicides, medication errors, deaths of clients in restraints, deaths immediately following elopement, deaths related to delay in treatment, assault/rape/homicide, fires, drug overdoses, and falls. A look at the settings in which these events occurred (see Sidebar 1–2, page 16) indicates that of those sentinel events reported to the Joint Commission, most occurred in general hospitals, followed by psychiatric hospitals and psychiatric units in hospitals. Of the 412 events, six occurred in outpatient behavioral health care settings. Of those six, five were suicides in 24-hour care settings and one was a rape of a client. Sidebar 1–3, page 17, provides a closer look at the sentinel events occurring in psychiatric hospitals and psychiatric units of general hospitals. Although suicide appears as the most frequently occurring type of sentinel event reported to the Joint Commission in both settings, *organizations should not assume that suicide is always the most frequently occurring event in health care.*

## Variation and Performance Improvement

According to *Webster's, variation* is a change in the form, position, state, or qualities of a thing. Although a sentinel event is the result of an unexpected variation in a process, variation is inherent in every process. To reduce the variation, its cause must first be determined. In fact, variation can be classified by cause.

*Common-cause variation,* which is inherent in every process, is a consequence of the way the process is designed to work. For example, perhaps a chemical dependency organization is examining the length of time required to produce a complete biopsychosocial assessment. Or perhaps a residential treatment facility is examining the length of time required to obtain a medication from a pharmacy. The time may vary depending on how busy the pharmacy is or how late the medication

**Sidebar 1–1:** *Sentinel Events Reviewed by the Joint Commission\**

| Type | Number |
| --- | --- |
| Patient suicide | 89 |
| Medication errors | 63 |
| Operative or postoperative complications | 33 |
| Wrong-site surgery | 28 |
| Delay in treatment | 26 |
| Patient death or injury while restrained | 23 |
| Patient elopement | 18 |
| Assault, rape, or homicide | 17 |
| Patient fall | 14 |
| Infant abduction | 13 |
| Transfusion error | 12 |
| Fire | 10 |
| Medical equipment-related event | 9 |
| Utility system failure | 7 |
| Death associated with transfer | 6 |
| Maternal death | 6 |
| Perinatal death | 5 |
| Infection-related death | 5 |
| Ventilator death | 4 |
| Dialysis-related event | 3 |
| Inpatient drug overdose | 2 |
| Other less frequent types | 19 |
| **Total** | **412** |

\*Distribution of sentinel events as reported to the Joint Commission between January 1995 and February 1999. These figures do not represent national data.

*Source:* Joint Commission on Accreditation of Healthcare Organizations, Oakbrook Terrace, IL. Used with permission.

is requested. On any particular day, many prescriptions may be received within a very short time frame. Or the medication may have been requested between midnight and 6AM when fewer pharmacists and pharmacist technicians are on duty. A process that varies only because of common causes is said to be *stable*. The level of performance of a stable process or the range of the common-cause variation in the process can be changed only by redesigning the process.

Another type of variation is called *special-cause variation*. This type of variation arises from unusual circumstances or events that may be difficult to anticipate and may result in marked variation and an *unstable* process. Human error and mechanical malfunction are examples of special causes that result in variation. All special causes should be identified and eliminated. However, removing a special cause will eliminate only that current aberrant performance in the process. It will not prevent the same special cause from recurring in the future. For example, firing an employee who failed to monitor a secluded client will do little to prevent the recurrence of the same error. Instead, organizations should probe, understand, and address underlying causes such as staff education, information management, and communication.

If special-cause variation—for example, mechanical breakdown of equipment that results in a sentinel event—could be corrected *only* each time it occurred, preventing the same sentinel event from recurring would be difficult. Fortunately, special causes in one process are usually the result of common causes in a larger system of which the process is a part. For example, repeated mechanical breakdowns may indicate a problem with an organization's preventive maintenance activities. Similarly, frequent assaults by staff against clients—from rough handling to sexual abuse—indicates a problem with the organization's hiring and training practices. Human resources practices need to be examined for common-cause problems involving the personnel screening and interview processes.

---

**Sidebar 1–2:** *Settings of the Sentinel Events Reviewed by the Joint Commission\**

| Type | Number |
|---|---|
| General hospital | 255 |
| Psychiatric hospital | 80 |
| Psychiatric unit in a general hospital | 30 |
| Long term care facility | 18 |
| Emergency department | 12 |
| Behavioral health facility | 6 |
| Home care service | 6 |
| Ambulatory care service | 3 |
| Clinical laboratory | 1 |
| Health care network | 1 |
| **Total** | **412** |

*Type of settings in which sentinel events were reported to the Joint Commission between January 1995 and February 1999. These figures do not represent national data.

*Source:* Joint Commission on Accreditation of Healthcare Organizations, Oakbrook Terrace, IL. Used with permission.

**Sidebar 1–3:** *Category of Sentinel Events Reviewed by the Joint Commission\**

**Psychiatric Hospitals**

| | |
|---|---|
| Patient suicide | 41 |
| Patient death or injury while in restraint | 13 |
| Patient elopement | 9 |
| Assault, rape, or homicide | 7 |
| Medication error | 3 |
| Patient fall | 2 |
| Other less frequent types | 5 |

**Psychiatric Units of General Hospitals**

| | |
|---|---|
| Patient suicide | 21 |
| Patient elopement | 4 |
| Medication error | 2 |
| Assault, rape, or homicide | 1 |
| Patient fall | 1 |
| Fire | 1 |

\*Distribution of sentinel events that occurred in psychiatric hospitals and psychiatric units in general hospitals as reported to the Joint Commission between January 1995 and February 1999. These figures do not represent national data.

*Source:* Joint Commission on Accreditation of Healthcare Organizations, Oakbrook Terrace, IL. Used with permission.

In health care, all clinical processes are part of larger systems in the organization. Therefore, special-cause variation in performance that occurs in consumer or patient care is frequently the result of common causes in organization systems. This provides an opportunity to reduce the risk of a special cause in one process by redesigning the larger system of which it is a part.

Any variation in performance, including a sentinel event, may be the result of either a common cause, a special cause, or both. In the case of a sentinel event, the direct or "proximate" special cause could be "uncontrollable" factors. For example, a client in a residential treatment center dies of smoke inhalation from a fire started by another client who "sneaked" a cigarette smoke in his room. This adverse outcome is clearly the result of a special cause in the organization that is not fully controllable by the staff. Staff members may not be able to prevent all future recurrences of a smoking policy breach. However, the breach and resulting death can also be viewed as the result of a common cause in the organization's system for preparing for and responding to fires and other emergencies. Perhaps fire drills were not conducted regularly in accordance with policy and regulations.

How can organizations providing behavioral health services prevent adverse events? What systems-oriented strategies can be implemented to decrease the likelihood of sentinel events? If an adverse event does occur, how should a behavioral health care organization respond to it? These topics are explored in depth in Chapters 3 through 6. In brief, however, in response to the final question, an organization begins by asking itself, "Is this event the result of a common cause or a special cause?" By definition, every occurrence of a sentinel event should be examined primarily upon the basis of its seriousness. It is possible to inadvertently design a process that intrinsically produces sentinel events—for example, an unsafe "take down" procedure for assaultive clients, which puts the staff at risk of being injured—thus generating a common cause for these injuries. A thorough investigation of the clinical decisions and processes linked to the event must always occur.

## What Is an Error?

An *error* is a deviation from that which is right or correct. Deviation implies variation from an expected norm. Such deviation may lead to bad outcomes or sentinel events. An error can be thought of as an unintended act, either of omission or commission, or one that does not achieve its intended outcome. Errors in the health care setting involve some kind of flawed process that may lead to injury. Hence, whereas sentinel events relate to *outcomes* or possible outcomes, errors relate to *processes*.

Errors, of course, are not the exclusive province of the health care field. To err is human. Errors are not planned or expected and generally cannot be predicted. They involve a behavioral or cognitive event, as well as an actual occurrence, with psychological or behavioral causes. Hence, the study of errors and their cause has taken place largely in the realm of cognitive psychology. Errors have also been studied extensively through *human factors research*—the study of the capabilities and limitations of human performance in relation to the design of machines, jobs, and other aspects of the physical environment. Research in both realms has helped in understanding why humans err and in developing a way of classifying errors, which is an important first step in the process of error detection and prevention.

## Cognition and Errors

Because many errors are the result of deviations or aberrations in mental functioning, it is helpful at the outset to understand the basics of normal human cognition. Psychologist James Reason provides a framework for cognitive theory.[1] He describes two types of cognitive mechanisms:

■ *Automatic mental functioning.* This is the effortless and rapid mental processing that takes place without conscious effort. For example, we are able to automatically perform the numerous tasks associated with starting the car and driving to the office without paying attention to each maneuver or decision along the way. Schemata or mental models allow us to perform recurrent tasks without attention to minute details.

■ *Problem solving or controlled mental functioning.* By contrast, this type of mental processing is slow, sequential, and difficult, and it requires conscious attention. It is activated to solve a new problem or to handle failures of automatic functioning. For example, the thought required to write a paper or compute a complex mathematical equation involves such functioning.

Errors involving either type of cognitive mechanism may contribute to adverse events.

## Taxonomies of Error

There are many different taxonomies of error. Some categorize the universe of error into *internal* causes that can be studied through behavioral or neurological approaches. Others look at *process* causes that can be analyzed and "cured" by engineering, design, societal, and procedural changes, or through psychological intervention and modification.[2] A definitive taxonomy and standard terminology for errors both have yet to be established. Presented here are the more commonly discussed classification schemes.

James Reason divides errors into two broad categories: *slips*, which involve errors in automatic mechanisms, and *mistakes*, which involve errors in problem-solving mechanisms.[3]

## Slips

Slips are lapses, trips, and fumbles—unintentional departures from otherwise adequate plans of actions. They are unconscious glitches in the automatic, skill-based activity stored by patterns of preprogrammed and mostly unconscious schemata or instructions. Such unintended actions occur when attention is diverted because of distraction or preoccupation. That in turn results in some change in either the planned procedure or the circumstances of its implementation. Many psychological, physiologic, or environmental factors can lead to preoccupation and diverted attention. For example, stress, fatigue, substance abuse, anger, noise, and temperature can all lead to slips.

A *capture slip* involves an error in which a more frequently used pattern takes over from a similar but less familiar one. For example, a person accustomed to driving straight home after work will automatically leave the office and turn the car toward home despite having a dentist appointment that requires driving in a different direction. Old learning interferes with new learning or new learning interferes with old learning. In a *description error*, the right action is performed on the wrong object, such as pouring coffee on cereal. *Association activation errors* result from mental associations of ideas, such as answering the phone when the doorbell rings. *Loss of activation errors*, typically caused by interruptions, involve temporary memory loss such as picking up the phone and not remembering who to call. The term *lapse* is generally used to describe failures of memory. Slips and lapses involve errors in the skill-based level of human performance. Human performance at this level is governed by stored patterns of preprogrammed instructions.[4]

## Mistakes

*Mistakes* are errors made in solving a problem—that is, departures from routine arising at the level of judgment, decision making, and problem solving. They involve inadequate plans of action and are either rule based or knowledge based. *Rule-based errors* result from misapplied expertise. Rule-based performance involves solving familiar problems according to stored rules such as "if X happens, then Y is appropriate." *Knowledge-based errors* may occur when individuals are confronting new problems for which they have no preprogrammed solution. Analytical processing and stored knowledge are called into play.

Knowledge-based mistakes may result from any of the following:

■ *Biased memory*—the tendency to base decision making on what is in our memory, which is biased toward overgeneralization and over-regularization of the commonplace.

- *Overemphasis on the discrepant*—the tendency for contradictory experiences to assume an exaggerated importance because our memory is also biased toward an overemphasis on discrepancies.
- *Availability heuristic*—the tendency to use the first information that comes to mind.
- *Confirmation bias*—the tendency to look for evidence that supports an early working hypothesis and ignore data that contradict it.
- *Overconfidence*—the tendency to believe in the validity of the chosen course of action and focus on evidence that favors it.
- *Focusing of attention*—the tendency in an emergency to concentrate on a single source of information.
- *Reversion under stress*—the tendency when under stress to revert to using older, more familiar patterns, even if inappropriate, rather than recently learned and more appropriate ones.

As with slips, mistakes may result from psychological, physiologic, or organizational characteristics or environmental factors. Mistakes generally are much harder to detect than slips and hence tend to be more dangerous.

Engineer John W. Senders offers another taxonomy of errors based on causal factors including psychological processes, location, and mode.[5] Senders draws his examples from the hospital environment, but they are retained here for illustrative purposes. According to Senders, psychological process errors include the following:

- *Input error or misperception.* The input data are incorrectly perceived; as a result, an incorrect intention is formed and the wrong action is performed. The action is other than what would have been intended had the input been correctly perceived. For example, the label "100.0 mg" on a drug may be read in error as "1000 mg." If administered as a bolus into a Y-port, a fatal overdose results.
- *Intention error or mistake.* The input data are correctly perceived, but an incorrect intention is formed; as a result, the wrong action is performed. The action is intended but is not what it should be given the correctly perceived input. For example, the label "1000 mg" may be read as "1000 mg." However, an individual incorrectly decides to administer it as one bolus into a Y-port, rather than as a drip, leading to a fatal overdose.
- *Execution error or slip.* The input data are perceived correctly, and the correct intention is formed; however, the wrong action is performed. The action is other than what was intended. For example, the label "1000 mg" is read correctly as "1000 mg." An individual correctly decides that it should be administered as a drip after dilution in a drip bag. However, the individual is distracted and, from habit, injects the contents as a bolus into a Y-port. A fatal overdose results.

Location errors include the following:

- *Endogenous errors*, which arise from physiologic, psychological, or neurologic processes in the individual. The aforementioned error resulting from distraction is an endogenous error.
- *Exogenous errors*, which arise from processes outside the individual. For example, the inconsistent use of an extraneous ".0" in the quantity "100" induces the false

interpretation of "100.0 mg" as "1000 mg" and could lead to an overdose. The custom of keeping both bolus and dilution syringes in the same area permits the substitution error. Elimination or reduction of such errors must involve engineering and design of objects and work environments.

Error modes, or particular appearances of error, may be classified as follows:

- *Omission.* Omission errors are characterized by leaving out an appropriate step in a process.
- *Insertion.* Insertion errors are characterized by adding an inappropriate step to a process.
- *Repetition.* Repetition errors are characterized by inappropriately using an appropriate step more than once.
- *Substitution.* Substitution errors are characterized by using an inappropriate object, action, place, or time rather than the appropriate object, action, place, or time.

## Taxonomies of Health Care Error

Numerous classification systems have been suggested for health care errors. Although no real consensus emerges from the literature, most systems rely on a general categorization of error by type, consequences to the patient, or what was done wrong. M.S. Bogner, PhD, categorizes what she calls "opportunities for errors."[6] These include medical decision making, laboratory reports, technology, medication, drug names, and situated environments such as the operating room and intensive care unit. Lucian L. Leape, MD, et al[7] categorize errors as belonging to one of five categories: performance, prevention, diagnosis, drug treatment, and system. Table 1–1, page 22, provides examples of each type.

R.L. Kravitz and colleagues[8] categorize errors based on malpractice claims review as three types of problems:

- Patient management problems, including diagnosis error, decision error, improper management, medication error, unnecessary treatment, and problem in communicating with patient;
- Technical performance problems (improper performance or unintentional iatrogenic injury); and
- Medical and nursing staff coordination problems, including equipment error, surgical foreign body or misidentification of patient, consultation or referral problem, problem in communication between providers, and patient falls.

Senders[9] mentions that it is common to report and label errors in health care settings only in terms of their adverse consequences, that is, what happened to the patient (for example, suicide, drug overdose). This practice has serious shortcomings because only those consequences that result in injury or death are noted.

Given the lack of consensus on the taxonomy of health care errors, we will briefly describe the following more common clinical categories of error experienced in health care organizations:

- Medication,
- Diagnosis,
- Use of medical equipment and devices, and
- Other errors.

**Table 1–1:** *Examples of Error by Type*

| | |
|---|---|
| **Performance Errors** | ■ Incomplete or inadequate patient/client assessment<br>■ Inadequate preparation of patient before procedure<br>■ Incorrect performance or procedures<br>■ Technical error<br>■ Inadequate monitoring of patient after procedure<br>■ Use of inappropriate or outmoded form of therapy<br>■ Avoidable delay in treatment<br>■ Physician or other professional practicing outside area of expertise |
| **Prevention Errors** | ■ Failure to take precautions to prevent accidental injury<br>■ Failure to use indicated tests<br>■ Failure to act on results of tests or findings<br>■ Use of inappropriate or outmoded diagnostics tests<br>■ Avoidable delay in treatment<br>■ Physician or other professional practicing outside area of expertise |
| **Diagnostic Errors** | ■ Failure to use indicated tests<br>■ Failure to act on results of tests or findings<br>■ Use of inappropriate or outmoded diagnostics tests<br>■ Avoidable delay in diagnosis<br>■ Physician or other professional practicing outside area of expertise |
| **Drug Treatment Errors** | ■ Error in dose or method of use<br>■ Failure to recognize possible antagonistic or complementary drug-drug interactions<br>■ Inadequate follow-up of therapy<br>■ Use of inappropriate drug<br>■ Avoidable delay in treatment<br>■ Physician or other professional practicing outside area of expertise |
| **Systems Errors** | ■ Defective equipment or supplies<br>■ Equipment or supplies not available<br>■ Inadequate monitoring system<br>■ Inadequate reporting or communications<br>■ Inadequate training or supervision of physician or other personnel<br>■ Delay in providing or scheduling service<br>■ Inadequate staffing<br>■ Inadequate functioning of service |

*Source:* Leape LL, et al: The nature of adverse events in hospitalized patients: Results of the Harvard Medical Practice Study. *N Engl J Med* 324:377-384, 1991. Used with permission.

## Medication Errors

Broadly defined, *medication errors* are "episodes in drug misadventuring that should be preventable through effective systems controls."[10] Medication errors in behavioral health care organizations are common and often serious. Multiple prescribers, multiple drugs for one client, and overdoses create a potential for adverse events. In residential or therapeutic foster homes, for example, recognition of adverse drug reactions which may be precipitated by drug or food interaction or other factors, may be delayed. Medications used in behavioral health institutions can lower seizure threshold, alter the gag reflex, and cause hypertension, agranulocytosis, or neuroleptic malignant syndrome (NMS).

Of course, not all medication errors lead to an adverse event. In fact, many medication errors are caught either before the client receives the drug or before the drug is dispensed. If a client does not receive a prescribed dose of an antidepressant, a medication error has occurred. Does this error result in harm or injury to the client? Probably not, yet the organization should assess rates and trends of these errors to improve its medication processes. If the error results or could result in therapy failure or harm, the event might be considered sentinel and investigated.

Diane D. Cousins, RPh, points out that physicians, nurses, and pharmacists have long been seen as the sole human causes of medication errors and that only in recent years have the broad multidisciplinary aspects of medication errors become recognized.[11] In fact, errors may be committed by any individual performing a part of the medication use function, whether an experienced health care professional or not. Even staff members who are not a part of the medication use function can contribute to errors. For example, missed medication dosages might occur when the staff of a residential treatment facility take residents off grounds for recreational purposes without checking with the nurse about medication schedules.

Medication errors generally are studied according to the stage in the continuum of the medication use process. This process commences with drug prescribing by the clinician and advances through drug preparation and dispensing by the pharmacist; drug administration by the nursing or clinical staff; and drug therapy monitoring by the nursing, clinical, and pharmacy staffs. One or more of these stages typically occurs within organizations providing behavioral health services.

When it comes to type of error, however, the drug use stages are frequently crossed. In their seminal study of adverse drug events with hospitalized patients, Leape and his colleagues at the Harvard School of Public Health identified 15 types of errors arranged by stage of drug ordering and delivery: wrong dose, wrong choice, wrong drug, known allergy, missed dose, wrong time, wrong frequency, wrong technique, drug-drug interaction, wrong route, extra dose, failure to act on a test, equipment failure, inadequate monitoring, and preparation error.[12] Wrong-dose errors occurred in the physician ordering and prescribing stage, the pharmacy dispensing stage, and the nurse administration stage. For example, errors in the latter stages might be the result of identity errors such as look-alike packaging and sound-alike names for drugs. Errors in the physician ordering stage might be the result of deficiencies of knowledge about the drug and how it should be used.

G.N. Fox describes four general categories of common prescribing errors:
- errors of drug selection;
- errors of drug dosing and calculations;
- errors of drug quantity or duration; and

- other errors such as those involving route, method, or technique of administration, dosage timing, poor handwriting, abbreviations, and wrong patient.[13]

In behavioral health care settings, drug selection errors can seriously harm clients and result in permanent injuries. For example, the use of once commonly prescribed neuroleptics or antipsychotic medications for clients with affective disorders can lead to tardive dyskinesia. Alternatively, prescribing an antidepressant medication rather than a mood stabilizer for clients with bipolar disorder could trigger manic reactions and could in turn cause clients to harm themselves or others.

W.N. Kelly defines nine types of errors in dispensing that have often led to morbidity or mortality[14]:

- Labeling problems;
- Trusting too much;
- Distributing "pharmacy only" products;
- Misreading or guessing at a prescription or an order;
- Not asking whether a drug, dosage, or large change in the dosage makes sense;
- Not using auxiliary labels;
- Lacking knowledge;
- Changing products; and
- Dispensing after hours.

Similar categorization exists for the administration and monitoring stages of the drug use process. The "five rights" of medication administration—the *right drug* to the *right patient* at the *right dose* by the *right route* at the *right time*—have been the focus of much of the research on medication administration errors. G.A. Pepper[15] suggests that the five rights overlook common errors such as omissions and improper rate and method of intravenous drug administration, which can lead to speed shock, cardiac arrhythmias, and other potentially serious adverse consequences. Many studies have focused on medication calculation errors. One study indicated that 81% of nurses surveyed were unable to calculate medication dosages accurately 90% of the time.[16] Failure to follow organization procedures, such as placing a zero before a decimal point for fractional dosages to prevent an overdose or clearly noting the end date of limited medication orders, is a source of errors that frequently lead to adverse outcomes.

Perhaps the most useful categorization of medication error types was developed by the American Society of Health-Systems Pharmacists (ASHP) in its "Guidelines on Preventing Medication Errors in Hospitals."[17] ASHP's categorization appears as Table 1–2, pages 25 and 26. Cousins provides case descriptions of actual medication errors in each category drawn from the U.S. Pharmacopeia's Medication Errors Reporting Program.[18] An example case study involving the death of a noncompliant patient following the injection of oral drugs (including an antidepressant) appears as Table 1–3, page 27.

### Diagnostic Errors

Diagnostician Stuart Levin, MD, once said, "There is no such thing as brilliant diagnosis, only lucky guesses and misses. The only truly astute diagnostic knowledge comes from the follow-up."[19] Nowhere is this more true than in the field of

**Table 1–2:** *Types of Medication Errors**

| | |
|---|---|
| **Prescribing Error** | Incorrect drug selection (based on indications, contraindications, known allergies, existing drug therapy, and other factors), dose, dosage form, quantity, route, concentration, rate of administration, or instructions for use of a drug product ordered or authorized by physician (or other legitimate prescriber); illegible prescriptions or medication orders that lead to errors that reach the patient |
| **Omission Error**[1] | The failure to administer an ordered dose to a patient before the next scheduled dose, if any |
| **Wrong-time Error** | Administration of medication outside a predefined time interval from its scheduled administration time (this interval should be established by each individual health care facility) |
| **Unauthorized Drug Error**[2] | Administration to the patient of medication not authorized by a legitimate prescriber for the patient |
| **Improper Dose Error**[3] | Administration to the patient of a dose that is greater than or less than the amount ordered by the prescriber or administration of duplicate doses to the patient, for example, one or more dosage units in addition to those that were ordered |
| **Wrong–Dosage Form Error**[4] | Administration to the patient of a drug product in a different dosage form than ordered by the prescriber |
| **Wrong–Drug Preparation Error**[5] | Drug product incorrectly formulated or manipulated before administration |
| **Wrong–Administration Technique Error**[6] | Inappropriate procedure or improper technique in the administration of a drug |
| **Deteriorated Drug Error**[7] | Administration of a drug that has expired or for which the physical or chemical dosage-form integrity has been compromised |
| **Monitoring Error** | Failure to review a prescribed regimen for appropriateness and detection of problems, or failure to use appropriate clinical or laboratory data for adequate assessment of patient response to prescribed therapy |
| **Compliance Error** | Inappropriate patient behavior regarding adherence to a prescribed medication regimen |
| **Other Medication Error** | Any medication that does not fall into one of the above predefined categories |

*Source:* Originally published in *American Journal of Hospital Pharmacy* 50(2):306, 1993. ©1993 American Society of Hospital Pharmacists, Inc. All rights reserved. Reprinted with permission (R9852).

*The categories may not be mutually exclusive because of the multidisciplinary and multifactorial nature of medication errors.
[1]Assumes no prescribing error. Excluded would be (1) a patient's refusal to take the medication or (2) a decision not to administer the dose because of recognized contraindications.

*(continued on next page)*

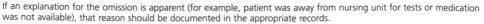

**Table 1–2:** *Types of Medication Error (continued)*

If an explanation for the omission is apparent (for example, patient was away from nursing unit for tests or medication was not available), that reason should be documented in the appropriate records.

[2]This would include, for example, a wrong drug, a dose given to the wrong patient, unordered drugs, and doses given outside a stated set of clinical guidelines or protocols.

[3]Excluded would be (1) allowable deviations based on preset ranges established by individual health care organizations in consideration of measuring devices routinely provided to those who administer drugs to patients (for example, not administering a dose based on patient's measured temperature or blood glucose level) or other factors such as conversion of doses expressed in the apothecary system to the metric system and (2) topical dosage forms for which medication orders are not expressed quantitatively.

[4]Excluded would be accepted protocols (established by the pharmacy and therapeutics committee or its equivalent) that authorize pharmacists to dispense alternate dosage forms for patients with special needs (for example, liquid formulations for patients with nasogastric tubes or those who have difficulty swallowing), as allowed by state regulations.

[5]This would include, for example, incorrect dilution or reconstitution, mixing drugs that are physically or chemically incompatible, and inadequate product packaging.

[6]This would include doses administered (1) via the wrong route (different from the route described), (2) via the correct route but at the wrong site (for example, left eye instead of right), and (3) at the wrong rate of administration.

[7]This would include, for example, administration of expired drugs and improperly stored drugs.

behavioral health care, where psychiatric diagnoses are difficult at best and often become the subject of heated debate by expert witnesses in courtroom settings. In other health care organizations, diagnostic errors account for a high percentage of all medical errors leading to adverse or sentinel events and a high percentage of malpractice claims and payments. Autopsy studies have indicated that rates of missed diagnosis causing death are as high as 35% to 45%.[20,21] The Department of Defense reported that approximately 40% of the sample liability claims involving military medicine in 1991 centered on allegations concerning difficulties in diagnosis.[22] These acts or omissions included the following:

- Failure to diagnose by concluding that the patient had no disease or condition;
- Misdiagnosis of an existing condition;
- Improper performance of a diagnostic test;
- Selection of inappropriate diagnostic or therapeutic procedures;
- Failure to perform certain diagnostic tests;
- Delay in diagnosis; and
- Failure to obtain informed consent for a diagnostic test or therapeutic procedure.

St. Paul Fire and Marine Insurance Company, a large commercial malpractice insurer, reports that diagnostic errors accounted for five of the ten most frequent malpractice allegations in 1995.[23] The occurrence of diagnostic errors is higher in hospital settings than in behavioral health care settings. However, failure to identify physical or sexual abuse or risk factors for suicide or homicide and assess suicide or homicide risk, at times because of diagnostic error, can lead to adverse events in all behavioral health care organizations.

### Errors Involving the Use of Medical Equipment and Devices

W.A. Hyman[24] indicates that problems with the use of medical equipment or devices are divided into two types:

- *Equipment malfunctions resulting from technical problems not caused by the user.* These malfunctions may be the result of an inherent defect in the design or manufacturing of the device, or they may result from the random failure of a component.

**Table 1–3:** *Sample Case Report from the U.S. Pharmacopoeia Medication Errors Reporting Program (USP MER)*

| **Wrong Route of Administration Error** | *Case Report.* An 83-year-old patient died after being injected with a solution of prescription drugs that she had refused to take orally. The nurse crushed tablets of Paxil® (paroxetine, an antidepressant), potassium chloride, and a multivitamin and combined them in sterile water. She then injected the mixture into the patient's central venous line. |
| --- | --- |
| | *Discussion.* Cases of wrong administration route are not as rare as one might think, nor are they as simplistic as an intramuscular drug being administered intravenously. In fact, the USP has received numerous cases like the one described here. Although the issue is clearly one of education, certain system changes can help prevent these errors. To avoid administering injections with oral syringes, amber-colored plastic syringes and an "oral" sticker on the barrel and/or plunger can clearly identify the correct match. Where possible, tubing and oral syringes with incompatible connections should be used. A labeling policy for all patient lines—such as color coding—should be developed to help emphasize correct routes. All crushing of tablets should be cleared with the pharmacy to avoid wrong route errors and also to prevent destruction of the drug release properties of enteric and time-release dosage forms. Crushed oral tablets should *never* be injected. |

*Source:* Reprinted with permission from Cousins DD: *Medication Use: A Systems Approach to Reducing Errors.* Oakbrook Terrace, IL: Joint Commission, 1998, p 46.

■ *User-caused or user-initiated malfunctions.* A technical failure can occur secondarily to the user's actions, or the objective of the device may be compromised by a user. For example, vests or jackets used as protective restraint devices might cause strangulation when used in combination with unprotected, split-side rails.

Users include not only the consumer in the care setting or home, family members, and direct care professionals, but also installers, engineers, maintenance personnel, housekeeping staff, and other employees who work around the equipment. In anesthesia services in the hospital environment, equipment problems caused by operators or users, particularly those occurring during the setup of the equipment, are a significant cause of adverse events.[25]

In behavioral health care settings, the use of vests, jackets, and other mechanical restraint devices have been implicated in numerous injuries and deaths from asphyxiation. In many cases, sentinel events have also occurred when the client was initially placed in a therapeutic hold or "taken down." For example, two adult men may have placed an 80-pound child in a therapeutic hold by placing a knee in the child's back, or the child may have been held face down with a soft object such as a pillow in the face. In other cases, an adult may have been held in restraint devices that had been misapplied, or the client may have been left unobserved and the restraint may have become constricting around the individual's head. In some of these cases, no supervisors were on the unit to oversee the application of restraint.

Pre-existing conditions such as asthma, cardiomyopathy, cocaine or other drug intoxication, pulmonary hypertension, or coronary artery disease can lead to sudden death of clients in restraint. Clients can also die of pulmonary embolism secondary to prolonged use of restraint or inactivity associated with restraint.

Human factor issues such as inadequate warning labels, difficult-to-read user instructions, and design deficiencies may contribute to the adverse events. Equipment may also be poorly designed or manufactured. User errors have been identified as a significant factor in adverse events involving medical devices. It would appear that many of these events are preventable if proper attention is focused on realistic evaluation of the user, the environment, the systems supporting device use within the organization, and the design of the equipment.

## Other Errors

Other errors, such as physical security failures and environment of care errors, have also led to adverse events, including improper security and physical safety assurance in psychiatric facilities. For example, non-breakaway hardware in showers and other areas has been associated with numerous client suicides in psychiatric hospitals and other behavioral health care settings. Although not relevant in the behavioral health care field, surgical errors, such as surgery at the wrong site, also account for a sizable proportion of all medical errors leading to adverse or sentinel events and malpractice claims.

## In Search of a Taxonomy

How do we understand how each of these errors affects the delivery of behavioral health care? Which of these events should be reported and to whom? There is a definite need for a taxonomy, or classification, of adverse events in behavioral health care. By using a taxonomy, a behavioral health care organization will be better able to objectively frame an adverse event so that an investigation into its causes can be initiated. The organization will be able to start with an understanding of what happened and the event's underlying causes.

It might be helpful for behavioral health care organizations to consider developing a taxonomy to gain an understanding of adverse events. Any taxonomy that is developed should consider the Joint Commission's definition of a sentinel event and be designed to help organizations better understand the root cause(s) of the event. Sentinel events can generally be classified on the basis of one or more of three critical factors:

- Process issues,
- Outcome, and
- Etiology.

The taxonomy should include *process issues*—that is, the type of sentinel event. Examples include medication errors, diagnosis errors, equipment errors, or even client elopement or abduction. The classification should also describe the possible *outcomes* of adverse events. Categories could include death, permanent harm, temporary harm, and no harm. Finally, the taxonomy should describe the *etiology*, or causality, of the event as assessed by the organization—its root cause. Examples may include lack of staff training or client supervision and improper medication use procedures.

## References

1. Reason J: *Human Error.* Cambridge, MA: Cambridge University Press, 1990.

2. Senders JW: Medical devices, errors, and accidents. In Bogner MS (ed): *Human Error in Medicine.* Hillsdale, NJ: Lawrence Erlbaum Associates, 1994.

3. Reason.

4. Rasmussen J, Jensen A: Mental procedures in real-life tasks: A case study of electronic troubleshooting. *Ergonomics* 17(3):293-307, 1974.

5. Senders JW: Detecting, correcting, and interrupting errors. *J Intraven Nurs* 18(1):28-32, 1995.

6. Bogner MS (ed): *Human Error in Medicine.* Hillsdale, NJ: Lawrence Erlbaum Associates, 1994, pp 6-10.

7. Leape LL, et al: The nature of adverse events in hospitalized patients: Results of the Harvard Medical Practice Study. *N Engl J Med* 324(6):377-384, 1991.

8. Kravitz RL, Rolph JE, McGuigan K: Malpractice claims data as a quality improvement tool: Epidemiology of error in four specialties. *JAMA* 266(15):2087-2092, 1991.

9. Senders, 1994, p 169.

10. American Society of Hospital Pharmacists: ASHP guidelines on preventing medication errors in hospitals. *Am J Hosp Pharm* 50(2):305-314, Feb 1993.

11. Cousins DD: *Medication Use: A Systems Approach to Reducing Errors.* Oakbrook Terrace, IL: Joint Commission, 1998, p 39.

12. Leape LL, et al: Systems analysis of adverse drug events. *JAMA* 274(1):35–43, 1995.

13. Fox GN: Minimizing prescribing errors in infants and children. *Am Fam Physician* 53(4):1319-1325, 1996.

14. Kelly WN: Pharmacy contributions to adverse medication events. *Am J Health Syst Pharm* 52(4):385-390, 1995.

15. Pepper GA: Errors in drug administration by nurses. *Am J Health Syst Pharm* 52(4):390-395, 1995.

16. Bindler R, Boyne T: Medication calculation ability of registered nurses. *Image* 23:221-224, 1991.

17. ASHP: Guidelines on preventing medication errors in hospitals. *Am J Hosp Pharm* 50(2): 306, 1993.

18. Cousins, p 41.

19. Dr. Stuart Levin, as quoted in Schiff GD: Commentary: Diagnosis tracking and health reform. *Am J Med Qual* 9(4):149–152, 1994.

20. Leape LL: Error in medicine. *JAMA* 272(23):1851–1857, 1994, p 1851.

21. Burton EC, Troxclair DA, Newmann WP: Autopsy diagnosis of malignant neoplasms: How often are clinical diagnoses incorrect? *JAMA* 280:1245-1248, 1998.

22. Granville RL, et al: Some characteristics of Department of Defense medical malpractice claims: An initial report. *Legal Medicine Open File,* 1992, pp 1-10.

23. St Paul Fire and Marine Insurance Co: Top 10 allegations by frequency and by cost, as cited in Gerber PC, Bijlefeld M: Watch out for these malpractice hot spots. *Physician's Management* 36(5):36-51, 1996, p 46.

24. Hyman WA: Errors in the use of medical equipment. In Bogner, p 327.

25. Cooper JB, Newbower RS, Ritz RJ: An analysis of major errors and equipment failures in anesthesia management—Considerations for prevention and detection. *Anesthesiology* 60(1):34-42, 1984.

*Chapter Two*
# The Measurement of Errors and Basic Causation Theories

*Chapter Two*

# The Measurement of Errors and Basic Causation Theories

How frequently do errors or adverse events occur? How are they detected and measured? How do we view errors? Why? What causes errors? Why do people err? How do they contribute to organizational errors? How do organizations contribute to human error? What are the basic premises about error causation in the health care field? How do these premises differ from those in the engineering field? What performance and environmental factors influence error? This chapter explores the responses to these questions. It also outlines the major approaches to surveillance for errors and presents basic theories on error causation, again deriving largely from human factors research and cognitive psychology.

## The Epidemiology of Errors and Sentinel Events

The epidemiology of errors leading to sentinel events is an inexact science at best. In fact, no one knows how frequently errors or sentinel events occur within various types of health care organizations. Perhaps at this stage of human progress, a true error rate is in fact unknowable. Why? The answer is twofold and relates to how errors are defined or classified and how errors are reported.

### Definition and Classification Issues

To date, studies of adverse events have focused primarily on events occurring in hospital settings because health care settings typically do not encourage reporting sentinel events. Consequently, information on sentinel events in areas other than hospitals is limited. Because much of the research regarding adverse events and error prevention has to date taken place in hospital settings, hospitals provide a good laboratory for error measurement as well as improvement activities.

Each study defines such events differently—so differently, in fact, one paper recently appearing in the literature is devoted exclusively to examining definitions and classifications of adverse events.[1] Some studies measure "complications" whereas others measure "adverse events," "potential risk events," "adverse effects," "iatrogenic illness," or "incidents." These terms are often interchangeable.

For example, H.B. Rubins and M.A. Moskowitz define a complication as "an unintended harmful occurrence or condition resulting from a diagnostic, prophylactic, or therapeutic intervention or an accidental injury occurring in the hospital setting."[2] L.I. Iezzoni and colleagues speak of "complications of care that were potentially preventable—complications that were avoided or minimized by improving the process of care…that raise concern about the quality of care based upon the rate of such occurrence at individual hospitals."[3]

The literature contains a variety of definitions of *adverse event*. The following are some examples:

- The Harvard Medical Practice Study defines an adverse event as one that (1) was caused at least in part by medical management and (2) required or prolonged hospitalization or led to disability after discharge. This definition requires physician review for determination of cause.[4]

- J.M. Geraci and colleagues define adverse events as complications potentially related to quality of care, resulting in a high likelihood of increased morbidity, subsequent intensive therapy, or prolonged hospital stay.[5]

- Fleming described adverse events as undesirable and unanticipated outcomes of care. In comparison, complication is defined as unexpected illness or injury caused by medical intervention or disease progression, and iatrogenesis is defined as unexpected illness or injury resulting from the medical intervention.[6]

The term *sentinel event* appears most frequently in the realm of occupational medicine, where it is described as an exposure to a hazardous material or situation. Many organizations use the term to imply a broader number of adverse incidents than would be included within the Joint Commission's definition of sentinel event (see Chapter 1, page 13). In summary, there appears to be little in the way of a common vocabulary for errors or sentinel events, and there has certainly been little in the way of comprehensive study of such events in behavioral health care settings.

## Major Research Findings

Most of the research on the frequency of errors occurring in health care has again focused on hospitalized patients and a specific type of error, namely medication errors. Error rates reported in the scientific and medical literature vary widely. The American Society of Health-Systems Pharmacists has estimated that roughly one out of every 100 doses of medication prescribed to hospitalized patients is administered in error.[7] Donald M. Berwick, president and chief executive officer of the Institute for Healthcare Improvement, cites significantly higher rates. Using observation as the measurement method, he cites that errors affect between 20% and 40% of all medication doses.[8]

Medication usage and errors have also been the focus of recent study of residents of long term care facilities. Many such residents have multiple chronic illnesses requiring regular treatment, principally in the form of prescription drugs. On average, long term care residents take eight prescription drugs per day.[9] The potential for drug-related errors is high with this population. This is also the case with behavioral health care clients who take multiple medications for psychiatric and medical treatment.

Highlighted in Sidebar 2–1, below, is a sample of major error frequency research initiatives, based primarily in hospital settings.

Certain agencies or organizations currently quantify and categorize sentinel events occurring in all health care organizations or as a result of the use of certain devices or procedures. For example, the Food and Drug Administration estimates that at least 100 deaths from improper use of restraint occur annually.[10] Experts suggest that many such deaths may never have been reported. Estimates commissioned by the *Hartford Courant* and completed by a research specialist at the Harvard Center for Risk Analysis corroborate such estimates and indicate that 50 to 150 such deaths may occur each year.[11]

## The Myth of Perfect Performance

Why is it so hard to get a fix on the rate of sentinel events and errors in health care organizations? In addition to the challenges of classification and reporting,

---

**Sidebar 2–1:** *Major Error Frequency Research Initiatives*

**California Feasibility Study.**[1] Conducted in the late 1970s, the California Medical Association's Medical Insurance Feasibility Study involved a large-scale effort to estimate the incidence of iatrogenic injury and substandard care…reviewing more than 20,000 records, researchers found a 4.6% rate of adverse events and a negligence rate of 0.8%.

**The Harvard Medical Practice Study.**[2] Before the early 1990s, information on the epidemiology of iatrogenic injury was mostly limited to small sample studies based on record reviews. To address the need for empirical information more current than the California Feasibility Study, the Harvard Medical Practice Study was undertaken with the goal of developing current and reliable estimates of the incidence of adverse events, defined as injuries caused by medical management rather than the underlying disease, and negligence in hospitalized patients. To estimate critical events, the interdisciplinary team reviewed more than 30,000 hospital records from 51 randomly selected acute care hospitals in New York State in 1984.

The team estimated the statewide incidence rate of adverse events to have been 3.7% (1,133 patients) and the rate of adverse events because of negligence to have been 1% (280 patients). Most adverse events (57%) resulted in minor impairments with complete recovery in a month. Others (14%) led to disabilities that lasted more than one but fewer than six months. However, 2.6% of the events caused permanent total disability and 1.7% caused death. Because 69% of adverse events were judged by physician reviewers to be due, at least in part, to an error in management, most of these events were presumably preventable. Adverse drug errors (ADEs) accounted for 19.4% of all disabling adverse events.[3]

Leape extrapolated these findings on a national basis to estimate an annual toll of medical injury to 1.3 million Americans who suffer injuries from treatment designed to help them, and 180,000 deaths "the equivalent of three jumbo jet crashes every two days." This number looks huge beside the annual automobile accident mortality of 45,000.[4] He also suggested that the problem of adverse events leading to injury may be more serious than indicated in the Harvard study, which looked only at hospitals and only at information obtained from medical records. In addition, the Harvard study looked at the results—adverse events themselves—and only those errors that resulted in injury or death. These rates cannot be used to estimate the actual number of errors.

*(continued on next page)*

**Sidebar 2–1:** *Major Error Frequency Research Initiatives (continued)*

*Brigham and Women's Hospital–Massachusetts General Hospital Study.*[5] Another major study coming out of Boston, reported in 1995, assessed the incidence and preventability of ADEs and potential ADEs. The prospective study covered admissions to 11 medical and surgical units in two tertiary care hospitals, Brigham and Women's Hospital and Massachusetts General Hospital, during a six-month period. Incidents were measured via self-reporting by nurses and pharmacists and by daily chart reviews by nurse investigators.

The study found that 6.5% of adult nonobstetrical patients (adjusted rates per 100 admissions) admitted to the two teaching hospitals suffered an ADE, which was defined as injury resulting from medical intervention related to a drug. In the case of an additional 5.5% of patients (also an extrapolated rate), a potential ADE was averted by chance or interception of the error. Of all the ADEs, 1% were fatal (none preventable), 12% life-threatening, 30% serious, and 57% significant. Of these, 28% were the result of errors that were judged preventable. Errors resulting in preventable ADEs occurred most often at the stages of ordering (56%) and administration (34%).

Although these studies reveal a lack of consensus about the magnitude of adverse drug errors, there is little doubt that it is significant.

### References

1. California Medical Association: *Report of the Medical Insurance Feasibility Study.* San Francisco: California Medical Association, 1977.

2. Brennan TA, et al: Incidence of adverse events and negligence in hospitalized patients. *N Engl J Med* 324(6):370-376, 1991.

3. Leape LL, et al: Preventing medical injury. *Qual Rev Bull* 19:144-149, 1993.

4. Leape LL: Errors in health care—Problems and challenges. Presented at the Examining Errors in Health Care Conference, Rancho Mirage, CA: Oct 13-15, 1996.

5. Bates DW, et al: Incidence of adverse drug events and potential adverse drug events. *JAMA* 274(1):29-34, 1995.

the answer also lies in our socialized views of error and how we, as individuals, respond to the errors we make. The following seemingly contradictory statements reveal the heart of the problem:

- "First do no harm" (the Hippocratic oath); and
- "If you haven't made any errors that have resulted in death or significant morbidity to one of your patients, you haven't been in practice very long."[12]

Precision predominates in medical school and residency training. D. Hilfiker writes: "In the large centers where doctors are trained, teams of physicians discuss the smallest details of cases; teaching is usually conducted to make it seem 'obvious' what decisions should have been made. And when a physician does make an important mistake, it is first whispered about in the halls, as if it were a sin."[13] The climate is little different in nursing schools. Indeed, health care professionals of all types are indoctrinated to believe that perfect performance is an attainable goal. Medical professionals embrace the Hippocratic oath as a moral duty. When faced with a deviation from what was intended, the individual's very foundation of self-esteem and worth is shaken. Hilfiker expresses it well: "Everyone, of course, makes mistakes, and no one enjoys the consequences. But the potential consequences of our medical mistakes are so overwhelming that it is almost impossible for practicing physicians to deal with their errors in a psychologically healthy fashion.

Most people—doctors and patients alike—harbor deep within themselves the expectation that the physician will be perfect. No one seems prepared to accept the simple fact of life that physicians, like anyone else, will make mistakes."[14] If harm occurs, guilt, shame, and anguish result.

Most studies of human error focus on physicians rather than other health care providers. In one study, J.F. Christensen and colleagues describe the profound emotional distress, sometimes continuing for a prolonged time, experienced by physicians after mistakes.[15] The cumulative effect of the mistakes had left some of the physicians participating in his study profoundly shaken in their confidence as caregivers. Albert F. Wu describes the emotional distress, including feelings of remorse, anger, guilt, and inadequacy, experienced by house officers after making mistakes during training in internal medicine. Despite the fact that virtually all students make medical mistakes during their training, only 54% of those surveyed discussed the mistake with their attending physician and only 24% told the patient or family.[16]

If the health care profession has little room for mistakes, health care organizations and society as a whole have even less. Because individuals expect perfect performance of themselves, the organizations for which they work do likewise. Much improvement activity at all kinds of health care organizations centers on eliminating error by requiring perfect performance. Writes Bogner, "The common reaction to an error in medical care is to blame the apparent perpetrator of the error. Blaming the person does not necessarily solve the problem; more likely, it merely changes the players in the error-conducive situation. The error will occur again, only to be associated with another provider. This will continue until the conditions that induce error are identified and changed."[17]

## The Challenge of Self-Reporting

Most physicians, nurses, and other health care professionals experience emotional difficulty in dealing with errors. In their judgment, mistakes are simply unacceptable. This pressure to be perfect, this need to be infallible, provides strong incentive to cover up mistakes rather than admit to them and deal with the consequences.

So too does the current tort system. Malpractice litigation is intended in part to promote better quality care by fixing economic sanctions on those who provide substandard care that leads to injuries.[18] However, the threat of malpractice provides strong incentives against disclosure or investigation of mistakes. A single error can ruin a practitioner's career and financial solvency. A practitioner must pay if "responsible" for an error. Leape calls this a "crime and punishment approach."[19] Hilfiker writes: "Even the word 'malpractice' carries the implication that one has done something more than make a natural mistake; it connotes guilt and sinfulness....But in our society, rather than establish a 'patient compensation fund' from which a deserving patient can be compensated for an injury that results from a legitimate mistake, we insist that the doctor be sued for malpractice, judged guilty, and forced to compensate the patient personally."[20] Simply stated, if health care practitioners present themselves as infallible, any errors constitute negligence.

Leape points to other "sanctions" meted out by society.[21] Regulators ask health care organizations to report sentinel events and then put the practitioners involved on probation. The media responds aggressively to a sentinel event and asks, "Whose head will roll?" So, should we really be surprised that errors are underreported—if they are reported at all?

## Surveillance Mechanisms

Measurement of performance lies at the heart and is the starting point of all improvement activities. Yet measurement of adverse events via self-reporting (for example, incident reports) continues to be the chief means by which errors are reported. Ineffective at best, this kind of reporting is likely to identify only a small portion of actual events. The Joint Commission's Sentinel Event Policy, described in Chapter 4, pages 140 through 147, encourages the voluntary reporting of errors to the Joint Commission. The goal is to learn about the relative frequencies and underlying causes of sentinel events, share "lessons learned" with other health care organizations, and reduce the risk of future sentinel event occurrences.

The literature suggests two major approaches to surveillance for adverse events: active and passive. *Active surveillance* is systematic and involves review of each case within a defined time frame. A variety of prospective or retrospective data sources or sampling techniques, denominator data, and methods of analysis are used. Methods for active surveillance range from concurrent incidence data collection (common in infection control) to periodic, retrospective claims data analysis by a third party. Active surveillance systems generally require more resources than passive surveillance systems do.

*Passive surveillance* is not systematic. Typically, physicians, nurses, and other health care professionals are expected to self-report their own incidents, incidents caused by others, or those of unknown etiology. Cases may be reported through written incident reports (mentioned earlier), verbal accounts at morning staff meetings, electronic transmission through on-line computer systems, or telephone hotlines, for example.

A look at the literature reveals four major surveillance approaches used to identify adverse events:
- Occurrence screening,
- Observational methods,
- Epidemiologic methods, and
- Passive incident reporting systems.

### Occurrence Screening

*Occurrence screening* is an active method, requiring systematic screening of a variety of data sources for potential adverse events. It often requires a second level of review to determine whether an adverse event actually took place and was related to the care provided. Data collection processes and data sources are discussed in Sidebar 2–2, page 39.

### The Observation Method

The *observation method* is also an active method of error surveillance. In this approach, a trained observer watches the care delivery process. The chief benefit of the method is more accurate measurement of events. A drawback is that it is not practical for very rare sentinel events because it is highly labor intensive.

K.N. Barker and E.L. Allen found a major discrepancy between the number of medication errors documented by incident reports in one year (36) and the number, extrapolated to one year after two weeks of data collection by observation (51,200).[22]

## The Epidemiologic Approach

A pure *epidemiologic approach* involves active surveillance targeting of events and mandatory internal reporting to those who need to know. Statistical analysis is often required because observations are based on a sample and inferences must be drawn to the entire population. Epidemiologists commonly use an active concurrent-incidence data collection system involving multiple data sources and requiring a trained practitioner. This concurrent screening is unlike occurrence screening, which is mostly retrospective. Major advantages of this method include timely

---

**Sidebar 2–2:** *Types of Occurrence Screening*

**Retrospective medical record review.** When they used this method with more than 3,000 records, Bates et al found that 11% of all patients admitted experienced an adverse event, and that 9% of those events were serious.[1] The Harvard Medical Practice Study (HMPS) found that 3.7% of all patients suffered an injury that prolonged their hospital stay or resulted in measurable disability.[2] A follow-up study by Localio et al found that 18% of the problems identified in the HMPS initial screen were likely caused by medical management.[3]

**Concurrent utilization review.** Occurrence screening performed during the utilization review process.

**Nurse monitoring.** Using nurse monitoring through daily chart review (that is, trained nurse investigators visited each unit on a daily basis to solicit voluntary reports), Leape et al found that 6.5% of adult nonobstetrical patients suffered an adverse drug event; 28% of these events were the result of errors.[4] Cullen and his colleagues reported that of the adverse drug events found by independent nurse investigators, only 6% resulted in the filing of an incident report by either the unit personnel or the pharmacy.[5]

**Computerized detection/monitoring systems.** Such systems include automated pharmacy drug-monitoring systems, laboratory report-monitoring systems, electronic algorithms that link lab and pharmacy data, and other computerized algorithms.

**Administrative and claims data analysis.** Administrative data, such as number of admissions and average lengths of stay, can be screened at the provider site or after being sent to a third-party payer. The detail and quality of the coding practices can limit the helpfulness of using administrative data to identify adverse events or complications.

**References**

1. Bates DW, et al: Evaluation of screening criteria for adverse events in medical patients. *Med Care* 33(55):452-462, 1995.

2. Brennan TA, et al: Incidence of adverse events and negligence in hospitalized patients. *N Engl J Med* 324(6): 370-376, 1991.

3. Localio AR, et al: Identifying adverse events caused by medical care: Degree of physician agreement in a retrospective chart review. *Ann Intern Med* 125(6):457-464, 1996.

4. Leape LL, et al: Systems analysis of adverse drug events. *JAMA* 274(1):35-43, 1995.

5. Cullen D, et al: The incident reporting system does not detect adverse drug events: A problem for quality improvement. *Jt Comm J Qual Improv* 21(10):541-548, 1995.

information, the avoidance of self-reporting bias of potentially litigious data, a continuous effort to record and report events without finding fault, prompt feedback, and demonstrated efficacy. The major disadvantage is that it is labor-intensive.

### Passive Surveillance Through Incident Reporting Systems

As discussed previously, *passive surveillance* is not systematic and involves a review of only reported cases. The literature is full of studies citing the failure of voluntarily submitted incident reports to capture the full extent of adverse events occurring in health care organizations. Hence, there is good reason to believe that self-reporting does not reliably capture the true nature or extent of adverse events.

Numerous studies suggest that passive surveillance systems identify far fewer adverse occurrences than active surveillance systems do. David Cullen and colleagues suggest the following reasons why incident reports may not be filed when indicated[23]:

- The observer is too busy to fill out the form when it calls for narrative response;
- Staff believe that reporting is of little value because feedback to those reporting is lacking;
- Staff fear disciplinary action against individuals responsible for the event or for reporting the event;
- Nonphysicians are reluctant to report incidents involving physicians;
- Staff are concerned that the report may subject the reporter or others to a lawsuit;
- Staff fail to recognize that an incident has occurred; and
- Staff lack understanding of what types of incidents should be reported.

Berwick cites a 0.2% adverse drug event rate in hospitals based on self-reporting. When a record review is performed, that rate increases to 0.7%. When computerized screening is used, the rate increases to 3.8%, and when chart review is combined with computerized screening, the rate rises to 10%.[24] K.N. Sanborn and his colleagues found a wide difference between the number of voluntarily reported and computer-detected intraoperative incidents in anesthesia. Only 4% of incidents found by electronic scanning of automated anesthesia records had matching voluntary reports.[25]

If we are unable to measure the rate of errors or adverse events efficiently and reliably, how are we to devise and monitor improvement strategies aimed at reducing the incidence of errors? This presents a major challenge for health care organizations.

## The Engineering Versus Medical Models of Error Causation

The pervasive view of errors in the engineering field is that humans err frequently and that the cause of an error is often beyond the individual's control. When designing systems and processes, engineers begin with the premise that anything can and will go wrong. Their role is a proactive one—to design accordingly. Because engineering-based industries do not expect individuals to perform flawlessly, they try to design systems that make it difficult for individuals to make mistakes. By compensating for less-than-perfect human performance, engineering systems achieve a high degree of reliability through backup systems and designed redundancy. A failure rate even as low as 1% is not tolerated. The emphasis is on systems rather than individuals.

In contrast, the still-pervasive view in the health care field is that errors are the result of individual human failure and that humans generally perform flawlessly.

Hence, processes in health care organizations tend to be designed based on the premise that nothing will go wrong. Education and training, which are more extensive in health care than in most other fields, focus on teaching professionals to do the right thing. The assumption is that properly educated and trained health care professionals will not make mistakes. Those who do are retrained, punished, or sanctioned. The immediate causes of errors are identified and corrected but not planned or designed for. Root causes are rarely identified. James Reason suggests the following: "Human error is one of a long-established list of 'causes' used by the press and accident investigators. But human error is a consequence, not a cause. Errors, as we have seen…are shaped and provoked by upstream workplace and organizational factors. Identifying an error is merely the beginning of the search for causes, not the end."[26]

## Causation and Latent Errors

A pioneer of human factors engineering, Reason proposes that human beings contribute to organization error in two ways. The first is by the commission of errors and violations—that is, *active failures*. These failures are difficult to anticipate and have an immediate adverse impact on safety by breaching, bypassing, or disabling existing defenses. The second is a consequence of management and organization processes—that is, *latent failures*. Latent conditions, or "pathogens," are present within existing systems and might lie dormant for a long time before they come into damaging contact with active failures and local triggers. *Local triggers* are intrinsic defects or atypical conditions that can create failures. The effects of latent conditions are delayed. They are, in essence, "accidents waiting to happen." They pose the greatest danger to complex systems. Latent failures cannot be foreseen but, if detected, can be corrected before they contribute to mishaps. Reason identifies two accident types:[27]

- *Accidents that happen to individuals.* These accidents happen frequently, they create little fallout in terms of consequences, they involve limited causes, and there are few defenses against them.
- *Accidents that happen to organizations.* These accidents happen infrequently, their consequences are widespread, they involve multiple causes, and there are many defenses against them.

According to Reason, accidents in health care tend to straddle both types.

To illustrate the random chance of multiple errors creating organizational accidents, Reason offers the image of slices of Swiss cheese sliding past one another. Latent failures are existing holes in the cheese. Active failures nibble away at the cheese, creating more holes here and there. When looking down at the block of cheese, the holes generally do not line up. However, if seen from the side, when active failures coincide with latent failures, the holes do line up, letting an error or damage occur. Something falls through the block of cheese. Although people can attempt to recover from active failures, they are often powerless to affect latent errors present within a system long before active errors occur.

The nuclear reactor disasters at Chernobyl and Three Mile Island represent cases involving multiple and interacting errors. Human errors, combined with latent failures in system design, created catastrophic disasters. The Three Mile Island accident occurred in 1979 when the core of a nuclear reactor started melting down, threatening to spill a massive quantity of radioactive contaminants. "The cause of the accident," writes Perrow, "is to be found in the complexity of the system. That is, each of the failures—design, equipment, operators, procedures, or environment— was trivial by itself. Each one had a backup system, or redundant path to tread if the main one were blocked. The failures became serious when they interacted."[28] Reason summarized the contributing conditions and latent failures at Three Mile Island and Chernobyl as a combination of management, maintenance, regulatory, design, procedural, operational, and training failures.

Diane Vaughan describes the 1986 Challenger space shuttle disaster in a similar fashion: "The Challenger tragedy was not an anomaly peculiar to NASA. It was a mistake resulting from factors common to all organizations. At NASA, organization history, culture, and structure contributed to the disastrous decision."[29] The go-ahead was given to launch the shuttle in spite of unprecedented cold weather. This resulted in the freezing of O-rings, triggering the disaster in which seven astronauts plunged to their deaths. Why did this happen? Simply stated, NASA engineers and managers relied on habits, routine, and rules in a situation to which they simply did not apply.

Vaughan suggests that the current health care environment is not so different from the environment in which NASA was operating before the Challenger disaster. Both involve highly complex, hierarchical organizations existing in different and often remote locations. Face-to-face communication is not always possible. Decision and action environments are highly charged with economic, political, and financial ramifications. Work is performed under conditions of uncertainty. Safety programs for both fields are error driven and retrospective.

Reason suggests that in highly complex environments, such as nuclear and chemical engineering, humans tend to inherit system defects created by poor design, faulty maintenance, and bad management decisions: "Their part is usually that of adding the final garnish to a lethal brew whose ingredients have already been long in the cooking."[30] According to Reason, numerous factors have contributed to the difficulty of controlling high-risk and high-complexity systems. These include

- the *automation* of systems that render human operators increasingly remote from the processes they nominally control;
- the *increasing complexity and danger* of systems that are highly interactive and tightly coupled;
- the *increasing number of defenses against failure*, which paradoxically are prey to latent human errors; and
- the *increasing opacity* of systems, which makes it difficult for people to understand the system and know what is happening within it.

These factors appear to apply within the modern health care environment.

## Lessons from Human Factors Research

Human factors research, as defined in Chapter 1, page 18, has contributed greatly to an understanding of error causation and the steps critical to error prevention.

Leape identifies six major lessons:[31]

- *Errors are common.* Normal humans make multiple errors every day.
- *The causes of errors are known.* Errors are not things that just happen. They are rooted in human cognitive functions.
- *Errors are by-products of useful cognitive functions.* The human ability to organize complex tasks into automatic functions frees up the mind for other tasks; at the same time, it sets us up for slips and lapses when our attention is not focused. Our ability to rapidly change our focus of attention enables us to respond to multiple stimuli; it also makes us prone to distraction. Our aptitude to generalize from past experience when encountering a new situation helps us process new situations; it also carries with it biased memory and the tendency for oversimplification and overconfidence. Errors, in effect, are the "flip side" of positive attributes of mental functions.
- *Many errors are caused by activities that rely on weak aspects of cognition.* Challenges may include reliance on memory, reliance on vigilance, nonstandard processes, long work hours, and excessive workloads. For example, short-term memory and attention are two weak aspects of cognition. A clinician may err in remembering the proper drug dosage. A distracted nurse dealing with multiple interruptions may err by forgetting to give a client necessary medication. A behavioral health care staff member may forget to check on an individual in seclusion.
- *Errors can be prevented by designing tasks and processes that minimize dependence on weak cognitive functions.* Basic human factor principles include avoiding reliance on memory, simplifying processes, standardizing processes, using "forcing functions" (such as computerized systems for medication orders that are designed so a physician cannot enter an order for a lethal overdose of a drug), improving information access, and specializing. Prevention strategies are described in Chapter 3, pages 51 through 59.
- *Systems failures are the "root causes" of most errors.* To prevent errors, systems failures must be corrected. Errors are the symptoms of system diseases. Just as physicians are taught to treat the patient's disease rather than just its symptoms, we need to treat the system's disease, not just its symptoms.

## Human and Environmental Factors and Error Causation

The literature is full of research studies measuring human and environmental factors as causative in health care errors. The roles of human performance factors—fatigue, stress, substance abuse, boredom, heavy or uneven workloads—and working environments have each been studied in depth. Like the human factors research, these studies conclude that systems failures are the root cause of most errors created by performance and environmental factors. System improvements can eradicate or reduce such errors. Selected factors are described here, however, to provide a sense of the breadth and depth of human performance and environmental factors discussed in error causation studies.

### Fatigue and Circadian Disruptions

Health care must be available 24 hours a day, 365 days a year. So too must medical technology and supporting services such as laboratories and information systems be available. This requirement presents a challenge to human caregivers and supporting workers, who require sleep. Adults generally do not function at their peak levels of mental performance with fewer than five to eight hours of sleep per 24-hour period. Nonstandard work schedules, such as those often encountered in some types of behavioral health care settings, disrupt workers' circadian rhythms. Human performance can be adversely affected, leading to an increased risk of error.

The effects of sleep deprivation and fatigue in health care personnel have been studied in depth. Much of the research focuses on physicians, specifically physicians in training whose on-call periods of duty commonly last for 24 to 36 hours, and anesthesiologists, whose long stints in the operating room require uninterrupted vigilance in monitoring heart rates and other vital signs. Tasks that require vigilance are sensitive to the performance-impairing effects of sleep deprivation and fatigue. Vigilance can also be eroded by illness, drugs, lack of motivation, and attitudes of invulnerability. In contrast, it appears tasks requiring short-term memory and manual dexterity are reasonably maintained in the face of sleep deprivation.[32]

D.M. Gaba writes, "Despite the lack of clear evidence that fatigue impairs anesthesia care, it is widely believed that there is a limit to how long safe performance can be maintained. Public attention has recently turned to questions of physician fatigue and work scheduling...still, the interaction of circadian rhythms with work schedules may be more important than fatigue itself in delineating causes of poor work performance."[33]

M.R. Rosekind suggests that there is no single solution to eliminate human fatigue in health care or other 24-hour operational settings.[34] Instead, he recommends an integrated approach that addresses the multiple factors affecting fatigue, sleep, circadian rhythms, and performance. Instead of trying to eliminate fatigue, the objective should be to manage human alertness and performance. He identifies six factors for an integrated approach to managing fatigue:

- Education and training about fatigue and circadian principles directed at those addressing these issues in the workplace;
- Work hours that incorporate recent scientific data and reflect the requirements of the setting;
- Scheduling policies that incorporate recent scientific data weighed against operational demand and flexibility;
- Fatigue countermeasures, including preventive strategies (such as teaching good sleep habits) and operational strategies to maintain or improve alertness and performance (such as physical activity and strategic naps);
- Design and technology measures, including such things as the level of light in operating rooms and the design of on-call staff sleep rooms; and
- Continued research on sleep, circadian physiology, and fatigue.

## Substance Abuse and Dependence

Substance abuse and dependence undoubtedly contribute to errors in health care. Intoxicated health care professionals suffer diminution in skills and make mistakes that in turn result in adverse events, injured patients or clients, increased costs, and erosion of the public trust regarding the safety of the health care system.

Alcoholism and other chemical dependencies affect at least 10% of adults at some point in their lives. Health care workers are no exception. The data indicate that the prevalence is either the same or slightly greater for physicians.[35] As evidence of pharmacist impairment, T. Tommasello[36] offers such items as unreasonable behavior, inaccessibility to patients and employers, prescription errors, patient complaints, filling of illegal prescriptions, lessening of ethical values, and decreased work performance. He writes: "It is clear that when a nurse diverts narcotic analgesics from a patient for personal use, the patient literally suffers. When a physician doesn't answer a page because of substance intoxication or its pursuit, the delay in treatment could be critical. When hangover effects cause irritability and staff conflicts emerge, the patient's care is compromised."[37]

The magnitude of errors created by individuals with substance abuse and dependence problems is largely unknown. Self-reporting of an impairment problem is unlikely in the current health care environment, which punishes both impairment and the errors it creates.

### Workload and Environmental Factors

People function best with optimal workloads. If workloads are too heavy, errors are more likely to occur; if workloads are too light, individuals can lose focus and make mistakes. If individuals work in environments where they are frequently interrupted or where there is a lot of talk about matters unrelated to the task at hand, there is a chance they will make errors. If the work flow is not logical or the work space is inadequate, there is a higher chance for error.[38]

Studies reported in the nursing literature indicate that medication errors tend to increase with double-patient assignments, with the number of patient days per month, and with the number of shifts worked by temporary nursing staff.[39] In addition to workload, seasonal changes in daylight have been shown to affect the work performance of hospital nursing staff, with impairment and increased errors most frequently occurring in midwinter months.

In summary, there is little doubt that environmental and human performance factors affect the rate of errors in health care. How these factors are addressed can have a significant impact on care and outcomes.

## References

1. Fleming ST: Complications, adverse events, and iatrogenesis. *Clin Perform Qual Health Care* 4(3):137-147, 1996.

2. Rubins HB, Moskowitz MA: Complications of care in a medical intensive-care unit. *J Gen Intern Med* 55(2):104-109, 1990.

3. Iezzoni LI, et al: Using administrative data to screen hospitals for high complication rates. *Inquiry* 31(1):40-55, 1994.

4. Brennan TA, et al: Incidence of adverse events and negligence in hospitalized patients. *N Engl J Med* 324(6):370-376, 1991.

5. Geraci JM, et al: Predicting the occurrence of adverse events after coronary artery bypass surgery. *Ann Intern Med* 118(1):18-24, 1992.

6. Fleming, p 138.

7. Gobis JL: Medication errors: Learn from your colleagues' mistakes. *RN* 58(12):59-63, 1995.

8. Berwick DM, et al: Reducing adverse drug events and medical errors. Presented at the National Forum on Quality Improvement in Health Care Conference, New Orleans, LA: Dec 4-7, 1996.

9. American Society of Consultant Pharmacists: A Model Long Term Care *Pharmacy Benefit.* Alexandria, VA: ASCP, 1996, p 3.

10. Food and Drug Administration: Safe use of physical restraint devices. *FDA Backgrounder,* Jul, 1992.

11. Weiss EM: A nationwide pattern of death. T*he Hartford Courant,* Oct 11, 1998.

12. Lipp MR: *Respectful Treatment: A Practical Handbook of Patient Care.* New York: Elsevier, 1986.

13. Hilfiker D: Facing our mistakes. *N Engl J Med* 310(2):118-122, 1984.

14. Hilfiker, p 119.

15. Christensen JF, Levinson W, Dunn PM: The heart of darkness: The impact of perceived mistakes on physicians. *J Gen Intern Med* 7(4):424-431, 1992.

16. Wu AW, et al: How house officers cope with their mistakes. *West J Med* 159(5):565-569, 1993.

17. Bogner MS (ed): *Human Error in Medicine.* Hillsdale, NJ: Lawrence Erlbaum Associates, 1994, p 1.

18. Brennan, et al.

19. Leape LL: Error in medicine. *JAMA* 272(23):1851-1857, 1994, p 1852.

20. Hilfiker, p 121.

21. Leape LL: Errors in health care—Problems and challenges. Presented at the Examining Errors in Health Care Conference, Rancho Mirage, CA: Oct 13-15, 1996.

22. Barker KN, Allan EL: Research on drug-use–system errors. *Am J Health Syst Pharm* 52(4):400-403, 1995.

23. Cullen D, et al.

24. Berwick DM, et al.

25. Sanborn KV, et al: Detection of intraoperative incidents by electronic scanning of computerized anesthesia records. *Anesthesiology* 85(5):977-987, 1996.

26. Reason JT: *Managing the Risks of Organizational Accidents.* Aldershot, UK: Ashgate, 1977.

27. Reason JT: Human and organizational factors: Lessons from other domains. Presented at the Examining Errors in Health Care Conference, Rancho Mirage, CA: Oct 13-15, 1996.

28. Perrow C: *Normal Accidents: Living with High-Risk Technologies.* New York: Basic Books, 1984, p 7.

29. Vaughan D: The social organization of mistake: Lessons from the Challenger disaster. Presented at the Examining Errors in Health Care Conference, Rancho Mirage, CA: Oct 13-15, 1996.

30. Reason J: *Human Error.* Cambridge, MA: Cambridge University Press, 1990, p 173.

31. Leape LL: Error in medicine. *JAMA* 292(23):1851-1857, 1994.

32. Howard SK: Fatigue studies in medical personnel. Presented at the Examining Errors in Health Care Conference, Rancho Mirage, CA: Oct 13-15, 1996.

33. Gaba DM: Human error in anesthetic mishaps. In Lebowitz PW (ed): *International Anesthesiology Clinics.* Boston: Little Brown, 1989, pp 137-147.

34. Rosekind MR: Fatigue countermeasures: An integrated operational approach. Presented at the Examining Errors in Health Care Conference, Rancho Mirage, CA: Oct 13-15, 1996.

35. Brewster JM: Prevalence of alcohol and other drug problems among physicians. *JAMA* 255(14):1913-1919, 1986.

36. Tommasello T: Clues to impairment in pharmacists. *Maryland Pharmacist* 68(5):21, 1992.

37. Tommasello T: Do substance abuse and dependence contribute to errors in health care? Presented at the Examining Errors in Health Care Conference, Rancho Mirage, CA: Oct 13-15, 1996.

38. Davis NM: Performance lapses as a cause of medication errors. *Hosp Pharm* 31(12): 1524-1527, 1996.

39. Roseman C, Booker JM: Workload and environmental factors in hospital medication errors. *Nurs Res* 44(4):1226-1230, 1995.

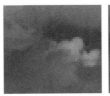

*Chapter Three*
## Approaches to Error Reduction and Prevention

*Chapter Three*

# Approaches to Error Reduction and Prevention

When errors do occur in organizations, what should be done so that the organization can learn from them and decrease the probability of their happening again? More importantly, what proactive techniques can organizations use to reduce the likelihood that adverse events will occur in the first place?

Whereas Chapters 4 through 6 will help organizations answer the first question, this chapter will focus on answering the second question—how organizations can prepare proactive strategies to prevent adverse events from occurring. Because systems are at the root of the majority of errors and adverse events in the health care environment, design or redesign initiatives aimed at system improvements can be productive. Efforts to enhance education and training, teamwork, self-assessment or performance measurement, and information management can also be productive.

Proactive efforts in each of these areas have been shown to reduce and prevent errors. Each approach is described in this chapter, along with information on the basic risk-management strategies suggested by error prevention leaders. At the end of this chapter, profiles from three organizations that provide behavioral health services highlight the use of proactive, systems-based methods to reduce and prevent errors.

Throughout this chapter, the Joint Commission advocates a learning-based approach to error reduction and prevention and systems improvement. This approach asks Why? What? and How? about errors and uses data for learning and to find and implement the best solutions to a problem.[1]

In contrast, a judgment-based approach asks Who? and seeks improvements by finding and eliminating the bad apples. The judgment-based approach is fundamentally flawed and unproductive. In fact, the judgmental approach to errors offers the largest barrier to doing anything about errors.

## Risk Management and Prevention

Donald Berwick and Lucian Leape have each offered concepts, outlined in this section, to reduce errors in health care. Some overlap; others do not. Because these concepts cut across the error reduction and prevention approaches outlined in this chapter, they are presented here at the chapter's beginning.

Berwick's concepts (see Table 3–1, below) to reduce errors in medical care are based on the premise that achieving error reduction requires a system for achieving such reduction. Leaders are responsible for creating, tending, and improving such a system. The concepts are also based on the belief that medical errors can be reduced only if organizations and their leaders intend to do so. Improvement requires aim.[2]

Leape itemizes several mechanisms of health care delivery systems that could be redesigned to significantly reduce the likelihood of error. Excerpts of these appear as Table 3–2, page 54.[3] For example, to minimize clinical judgment errors, clinicians may wish to list alternative diagnoses and seek evidence for each. Studies indicate that clinicians arrive at the most accurate diagnoses later than do less

---

**Table 3–1:** *Berwick's Ten Concepts to Reduce Errors in Medical Care*

- **Simplify.** Reduce the number of steps and hand-offs in work processes. Reduce nonessential elements of equipment, software, and rules of procedure.

- **Standardize.** Limit unneeded variety in drugs, equipment, supplies, rules, and processes of work.

- **Stratify.** Identify strata of need, and "mass customize" to each stratum. Avoid "one size fits all." Substitute "five sizes fit 80%."

- **Improve auditory communication patterns.** Use repetition, standard vocabularies, and unmitigated communication.

- **Support communication against the authority gradient.** Use lessons from "cockpit resource management" (crew resource management). Train for team communication. Huddle. Use nominal group methods and other group processes that increase exchange.

- **Use defaults properly.** Design processes so that the safe channel is the one requiring the lowest energy. Make "doing the right thing" the easiest thing to do.

- **Automate cautiously.** Avoid overautomating systems and equipment. Make sure that operators can know the true state of the system, can override automation effectively, and can maintain proper vigilance. Make the system visible to the user.

- **Use affordances and natural mapping.** Let the environment and equipment "speak," informing the user about proper use. Use visual controls. Minimize translation steps between instructions and their effects. Design physical shapes and flows to guide proper use. Increase "knowledge in the world" so as to reduce reliance on "knowledge in the head."

- **Respect limits on vigilance and attention.** When designing tasks and work systems, keep in mind issues of stress, workload, circadian rhythm, time pressure, limits to memory, and properties of human vigilance. Design for normal human behavior and capacity.

- **Encourage reporting of errors and hazardous conditions.** Assume the requirement of anonymity until proven otherwise. Reward reports. Build a culture that celebrates the increase of knowledge on the basis of which error rates can be reduced and risks mitigated.

*Source:* Berwick DM: *Taking action: Leading the reduction of error.* Presented at the Examining Errors in Health Care Conference, Rancho Mirage, CA: Oct 13-15, 1996.

accurate clinicians. Clinicians may also wish to question their memory. Studies show that clinicians forget previous symptoms that are inconsistent with the final diagnosis, so keeping a reference list of the symptoms is helpful.

In recommending error prevention strategies, Leape has also taken a look at the aviation industry and compared it to the health care industry.[4] Both industries rely on high-technology equipment and highly proficient and trained professionals functioning as teams within life-threatening environments. The aviation industry designs for safety; the health care industry often does not.

Leape suggests four safety design characteristics of aviation that could, with some modification, prove useful in improving safety in the health care industry:

- *Built-in multiple buffers,* automation, and redundancy. The design systems assume that errors and failures are inevitable and should be absorbed. Instrumentation in airplane cockpits includes multiple and purposely redundant monitoring instruments.
- *Standardized procedures.* Mandatory protocols exist for operating and maintaining airplanes.
- *A highly developed and rigidly enforced training, examination, and certification process.* Pilots take proficiency exams every six months.
- *Institutionalized safety.* The airline industry reports directly to two agencies, the Federal Aviation Administration (FAA), which regulates all aspects of flying and prescribes safety procedures, and the National Transportation Safety Board, which investigates all accidents. A confidential safety reporting system established by the FAA in 1975, called the Air Safety Reporting System, enables pilots, controllers, or others to report dangerous situations, including errors they have made, to a third party without penalty. This program greatly increased error reporting in aviation, resulting in enhanced communication and prompt problem solving.

As noted in Table 3–2, page 54, an error prevention strategy for the health care industry must include the design of systems to absorb errors, standardization of tasks and processes to minimize reliance on weak aspects of cognition, testing of professional performance, and institutionalized safety through "near miss" and nonpunitive reporting. For example, clinical practice guidelines and organization policies and protocols designed to reduce variation in the care provided by practitioners can help to reduce the likelihood of errors. An example of how one state uses procedures to help ensure the safe recording, storage, and administration of medications in community psychiatric rehabilitation programs appears as Table 3–3, pages 55 through 57.

### Example: Suicide Risk Reduction

Nearly 90 Americans commit suicide every day, making suicide the eighth leading cause of death in the United States. Approximately 31,000 people take their lives each year. Another estimated 775,000 others attempt suicide. In 1995, the number of suicides (31,284) exceeded the number of homicides (22,552).[5] Suicide has become an acute problem among black teenage males and other groups, including American Indians, gays and lesbians, the elderly, and the mentally and physically ill. Nonetheless, as U.S. Surgeon General David Satcher, MD, points out, "Suicide is

---

**Table 3–2:** *Leape's Mechanisms to Reduce the Likelihood of Error*

**Reduce reliance on memory**

Work should be designed to minimize the requirements for human functions that are known to be particularly fallible, such as short-term memory and vigilance. Checklists, protocols, and computerized decision aids could be used more widely. For example, physicians should not have to rely on their memories to retrieve a laboratory test result, and nurses should not have to remember the time a medication dose is due. These are tasks computers do much more reliably than humans.

**Improve information access**

Develop ways to make information more readily available and display it where it is needed, when it is needed, and in a form that permits easy access.

**Error-proof**

Where possible, critical tasks should be structured so that errors cannot be made. "Forcing functions" can be helpful. For example, a computerized system for medication orders can be designed so that a physician cannot enter an order for a lethal overdose of a drug.

**Standardize**

The advantages, in efficiency as well as in error reduction, of standardizing drug doses and times of administration are obvious. Other candidates for standardization include information displays, methods for common practices (such as applying surgical dressings), and the geographic location of equipment and supplies in patient care units.

**Train**

Instruction of physicians, nurses, and pharmacists in procedures or problem solving should include greater emphasis on possible errors and how to prevent them.

**Absorb errors**

Because it is impossible to prevent all error, buffers should be built into each system so that errors are absorbed before they can cause harm to patients. At a minimum, systems should be designed so that errors can be identified in time to be intercepted. Critical systems (such as life-support equipment and monitors) should be provided in duplicate in those situations in which a mechanical failure could lead to patient injury.

*Source:* Leape LL: Error in medicine. *JAMA* 272(23):1851-1857, 1994.

---

an overlooked area of health care." Says Satcher, "Many suicides are already preventable. Even more suicides could be prevented if this country better focused its resources and its attention on this problem."[6]

Suicide is a particularly pressing issue for organizations providing behavioral health care services. Although only 2% to 6% of suicides in the United States are committed by individuals who are receiving treatment from health care professionals in a hospital setting, suicidal behaviors are far more common among consumers receiving behavioral health care services than in the population at large. Studies show that of those persons completing a suicide, 50% of them saw a mental health provider at some time in their lives and 17% were in treatment with a mental health provider at the time of their suicide. Not all suicidal behaviors result in death or serious physical or psychological injury—which is the outcome of a sentinel event according to the Joint Commission's definition (see Chapter 1, page 13). Many organizations providing behavioral health community or outpatient services refer

**Table 3–3:** *Title 9 —Department of Mental Health, State of Missouri*

**Division 30—Certification Standards**

**Chapter 4—Mental Health Programs**

**9 CSR 30–4.041 Medication Procedures at Community Psychiatric Rehabilitation Programs**

PURPOSE: This rule sets out procedures to safely record, store and administer medications at a community psychiatric rehabilitation program facility site or in off-site situations.

(1) The community psychiatric rehabilitation (CPR) provider shall implement policies and procedures for the storage, preparation and dispensation of medications consistent with United States Pharmacopeia Standards.

(2) The CPR provider shall implement policies on how medication, including that brought to the CPR Program by clients, is to be dispensed and administered.

(A) The CPR provider shall assure that staff authorized by the CPR Program and by law to conduct medical, nursing and pharmaceutical services do so using sound clinical practices and following all applicable state and federal laws.

(B) The CPR provider shall have written policies and procedures for recording client intake of medication, to include client name, medication, dose of medication, date, frequency of intake and the name of the staff who observed the medication intake.

(C) Staff shall report adverse drug reactions and medication errors immediately to the physician responsible for the client.

(D) The CPR provider's policies shall address the administration of medications in emergency situations.

(E) The CPR provider shall establish a mechanism for the positive identification of individual clients at the time medication is dispensed or administered.

(F) The CPR provider shall implement policies that prevent the
 1. Use of medications as punishment, for the convenience of staff, as a substitute for services or other treatment or in quantities that interfere with the client's rehabilitation program;
 2. Issuance of standing or pro re nata (PRN) medication orders; and
 3. The issuance of chemical restraints, except in emergency situations.

(G) The CPR provider shall train all staff in the dispensing and administration of medications and observation for adverse drug reactions and medication errors as is consistent with each staff person's job duties.
 1. The CPR provider shall review staff job duties and training needs at least semiannually to assure staff competence and compliance with applicable standards.
 2. The CPR provider shall make available to all staff, consultation with a registered nurse or physician to check medication procedures.

(3) The CPR provider shall provide each client (or family member or caretaker, if appropriate) with medication education as needed, by enrollment in a medication awareness group or by receipt of individualized instruction concerning medication.

(4) The CPR provider shall implement written policies and procedures on how medications are to be prescribed.

*(continued on next page)*

**Table 3–3:** *Title 9 —Department of Mental Health, State of Missouri (continued)*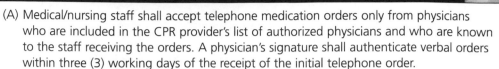

(A) Medical/nursing staff shall accept telephone medication orders only from physicians who are included in the CPR provider's list of authorized physicians and who are known to the staff receiving the orders. A physician's signature shall authenticate verbal orders within three (3) working days of the receipt of the initial telephone order.

(B) A physician shall review and evaluate medications at least every six (6) months, except as specified in the client's individualized treatment plan. Face-to-face contact with the client and review of relevant documentation in the client record, such as progress notes and treatment plan reviews, shall constitute the review and evaluation.

(C) For each client receiving a neuroleptic medication, appropriately trained staff under a physician's supervision, shall screen the client using the Abnormal Involuntary Movement Scale.

  1. The screening shall occur at least every six (6) months.

  2. Staff shall enter the scale into the clinical record, which shall be signed and dated by the responsible physician.

  3. In cases of abnormal findings, staff shall refer the client for a medication/neurological evaluation as indicated.

(D) The client's clinical record shall include a medication profile based on evaluation of the client's drug history and current therapy, including

  l. name;

  2. age;

  3. weight;

  4. current diagnosis;

  5. current drug therapy;

  6. allergies;

  7. history of compliance; and

  8. other pertinent information related to the client's drug regimen.

(5) The CPR provider shall implement written policies and procedures on how medications are to be stored.

(A) The CPR provider shall establish a locked storage area for all medications that provides suitable conditions regarding sanitation, ventilation, lighting and moisture.

(B) The CPR provider shall store ingestible medications separately from noningestible medications and other substances.

(C) The CPR provider shall maintain a list of personnel who have been authorized access to the locked medication area and who are qualified to administer medications.

(D) All medications shall be properly labeled. Labeling for each medication shall include

  1. drug name;

  2. strength;

  3. amount dispensed;

  4. directions for administration;

  5. expiration date;

  6. name of client;

  7. name of physician; and

  8. name of dispensing individual.

*(continued on next page)*

**Table 3–3:** *Title 9 —Department of Mental Health, State of Missouri (continued)*

(6) The CPR provider shall develop all medication policies and procedures in conjunction with a psychiatrist.

(7) The CPR provider shall assure that all policies and procedures regarding medication are consistent with relevant rules issued by the department.

AUTHORITY: section 630.655, RSMo (1994).* Original rule filed Jan. 19, 1989, effective April 15, 1989. Amended: Filed Dec. 13, 1994, effective July 30, 1995.

*Original authority 1980.*

their clients with a high risk of suicide and suicidal behavior to inpatient settings. However, these community organizations still consider suicidal behavior by clients in the community a major risk and take steps to monitor and reduce such risks. Hence, suicide risk-reduction strategies are critical to the prevention of sentinel events and "near misses" in all types of organizations providing behavioral health services.

On November 6, 1998, the Joint Commission released aggregated information regarding 65 cases of inpatient suicide reviewed by the Joint Commission's Board of Commissioners since enactment of the Joint Commission's Sentinel Event Policy in 1996.[7] A description of that policy appears in Chapter 4, pages 140 through 145. Data from the Joint Commission's review of suicides appears as Table 3–4, page 58. Most of the suicides occurred in psychiatric hospitals (34), followed by general hospitals (27) and residential care facilities (4). Of those cases in general hospitals, 14 occurred in psychiatric units, 12 in medical/surgical units, and one in the emergency room. In 75% of the cases, the method of suicide was a hanging in a bathroom, bedroom, or closet. Twenty percent of the suicides resulted from patients jumping from a roof or window.

Along with the data, the Joint Commission offers risk-reduction strategies recommended by the organizations that experienced the suicides. Strategies include

- revising suicide risk assessment/reassessment procedures (for example, by using a standardized procedure);
- updating the staffing model to ensure adequate staffing levels and competency review or credentialing;
- enhancing staff orientation/education regarding suicide risk factors;
- updating policies and procedures for patient observation;
- monitoring the consistency of the implementation of observation procedures;
- revising procedures for contraband detection and engaging family and friends in the process;
- identifying and removing or replacing non-breakaway hardware;
- weight-testing all breakaway hardware;
- redesigning, retrofitting or introducing security measures (for example, locking mechanisms, patient monitors and alarms);
- revising information transfer procedures; and
- implementing education for family/friends regarding suicide risk factors.

**Table 3–4:** *Joint Commission Aggregate Information from Review of Inpatient Suicides*

**Suicides reviewed          65**

**Settings in which the suicide occurred**

| | |
|---|---|
| *Psychiatric hospital* | 34 |
| *General hospital* | |
| Psychiactric unit | 14 |
| Medical/surgical unit | 12 |
| Emergency | 1 |
| *Residential care* | 4 |

**Source of notification to Joint Commission**

| | |
|---|---|
| *Self-reported* | 25 |
| *Media* | 20 |
| *Discovered on survey* | 10 |
| *Reported by state* | 9 |
| *Reported by family* | 1 |

**Method of suicide**

| | |
|---|---|
| *Hanging* | 75% |
| *Jump (roof or window)* | 20% |

**Site of hanging**

| | |
|---|---|
| *Bathroom* | 62% |
| *Bedroom* | 23% |
| *Closet* | 15% |

*Source:* Joint Commission on Accreditation of Healthcare Organizations, Oakbrook Terrace, IL. Used with permission.

John Oldham, MD, director of the New York State Psychiatric Institute in New York City, emphasizes that good patient care is the first step in preventing inpatient suicides. Organizations should also examine their environment of care to make sure that patients do not have access to items that could be considered harmful to them. Oldham recommends that facilities adopt the following practices:

- Make sure that items that can harm patients in the facility are addressed (for example, install appropriate shower heads, shower bars, and closet bars that do not easily suggest such a use; do not leave open doors that should be closed; and do not give patients access to sharp objects and other potentially harmful items such as cleaning solvents).

- Institute professional practice guidelines that are helpful in administering appropriate medications and dosages and appropriate combinations of medications to treat conditions that contribute to the risk of suicide.

- Pay particular attention to patients who have multiple diagnoses that can in combination increase the risk of suicide (for example, a combination of depression and substance abuse).

- Institute policies about passes and privileges for patients who are considered a suicide risk (for example, exercise special caution when patients have their first unaccompanied pass to an activity in the facility or a trip outside the facility).[8]

Organizations should assess the degree of suicidal risk on admission, with the intent to place those patients with the highest risk on constant observation, according to William Tucker, MD, director of the Bureau of Psychiatric Services in the New York State Office of Mental Health in New York City. Staff members who provide any level of observation should inquire at least once per shift regarding suicidal intent, and more frequently if a positive response is obtained or suspicion is high. "Avoid reliance on 'pacts' with patients that they will not act on suicidal impulses," Tucker explains. "Also, maintain a high level of suspicion if perturbation is present, or paradoxically, if symptoms lighten."[9]

A description of one thorough, systems-based approach to reducing the risk of suicide, emanating from Greentree Behavioral Health in Spokane, Washington, appears as an example at the end of this chapter, pages 83 through 90.

## Systems Design or Redesign

The main thesis of this book is that errors and adverse events can best be addressed through a systems rather than an individual human approach. What is a system, and what does a systems approach involve?

### Overview of Health Care Delivery as a System

A *system* can be thought of as any collection of components and the relationships among them, whether the components are human or not, when the components have been brought together for a well-defined goal or purpose.[10] Health care delivery is perhaps the largest, most complex, and most expensive system in existence. Comprised of autonomous yet communicating subsystems, it includes such diverse elements as community treatment centers, outpatient psychiatric facilities, hospitals, ambulance services, medical devices and instruments, pharmacies, testing laboratories, home care agencies, physicians' offices, and many, many others. Each element has a distinct culture with its own unique goals, values, and norms of behavior. Coordination among the subsystems is accomplished by informal networking, custom, and regulation. Change across such a decentralized system is accomplished at a slow speed and often with unpredictable outcomes, which provides increased opportunity for error.[11]

Bogner suggests that the systems approach to human error must consider medical care delivery settings as discrete systems with constituent subsystems.[12] Each subsystem must be divided into smaller subsystems to analyze and take action with productive error reduction and prevention measures. For example, a hospital is a system with subsystem components including the patient care units, services such as radiology and pharmacy, operating and emergency room units, and others. Bogner writes, "The systems approach is to analyze the situation, decompose it to the level at which the function associated with the error occurred, identify those factors that precipitated the error, bring those factors to the attention of the appropriate responsible party for action to remove or alter those factors, and evaluate the impact of the resultant action on the future incidence of error."[13]

Figure 3–1, page 60, suggests a hierarchical, systems-oriented approach to design and analysis. In the inner regions of the diagram, errors are more local in scope and the steps needed to reduce and control them are localized. As one moves outward,

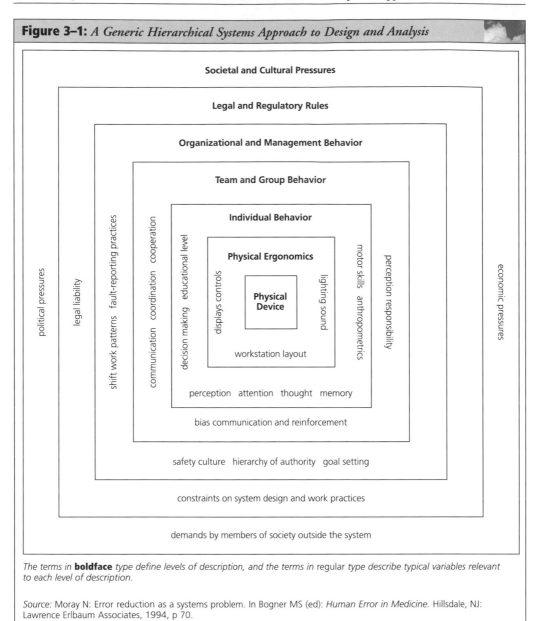

**Figure 3–1:** *A Generic Hierarchical Systems Approach to Design and Analysis*

The terms in **boldface** type define levels of description, and the terms in regular type describe typical variables relevant to each level of description.

*Source:* Moray N: Error reduction as a systems problem. In Bogner MS (ed): *Human Error in Medicine.* Hillsdale, NJ: Lawrence Erlbaum Associates, 1994, p 70.

the causes of error become more global in scope. Actions taken to solve these errors tend to be pervasive throughout the system and hence have a greater payoff.

N. Moray outlines the hierarchical structure (see Figure 3–1, above).[14] At the center of the system is *physical ergonomics*, the physical design of equipment and the work environment. In the health care system, this would include such things as the noise level in working environments that may render communication impossible or the legibility of labels on bottles. At the next level is *individual human behavior*. This includes slips and mistakes, which are discussed in detail in Chapter 1, pages 18 through 21. *Team and group behavior* create errors when a team dissolves into an informal group, for example, undermining the formal patterns of authority and responsibility. The structure of authority in teams is important in reducing error.

At the level of *organization and management*, behavior can have a major effect on the probability of error. For example, the setting of policy for shift work and hours of work can deeply affect individual performance, as can managerial decisions regarding the kind of equipment purchased for a facility. Finally, at the level of *legal and societal pressures*, the probability of error can be exacerbated by such things as economic pressures and cultural beliefs.

## Systems Design or Redesign for Safety

Because there are so many mechanisms and causes of error, as shown from the core of Figure 3–1, page 60, to its periphery, the task of reducing errors and sentinel events is not simple. Leape writes, "Creating a safe process, whether it be flying an airplane, running a hospital, or performing cardiac surgery, requires attention to methods of error reduction at each stage of system development: design, construction, maintenance, allocation of resources, training, and development of operational procedures."[15] If errors are made, if deficiencies are discovered, individuals at each stage must revisit previous decisions and redesign or reorganize the process.

Designing for safety means making it difficult for humans to err. However, those designing systems must recognize that errors will occur and that recovery or correction should be built in to the system. If this is not possible, errors must be promptly detectable so that humans have time to take corrective actions. *Risk points*—specific points in a process that are susceptible to error or system breakdown—must be eliminated through design or redesign efforts. Risk points generally result from a flaw in the initial process design, a high degree of dependence on communication, nonstandardized processes, and failure or absence of backup. For example, the risk of inadequate staffing levels is higher during evenings, nights, holidays and weekends, as is the risk of temporary staff and on-call physicians or pharmacists who may not be familiar with the clients.

As described earlier, built-in buffers and redundancy, task and process simplification and standardization, and training are all appropriate design mechanisms to reduce the likelihood of error at risk points and elsewhere.

The field of anesthesiology has pioneered systems-oriented solutions for patient safety. Why this field? Accidents arising from errors in anesthesiology can be dramatic and can result in death or serious brain injury to patients. Bogner describes both the operating room and the intensive care unit as "hotbeds for human error."[16] The environments are complex and dynamic, with constant change and time pressures. High-technology equipment is used extensively, as are potentially lethal drugs. Situational or environmental factors, including long working hours, boredom, and intensive technology, impinge on human performance. Procedures require the effort of physicians and nurses working smoothly as a team. An anesthesiologist works with severe time pressures and within a tightly coupled system that does not provide much slack or the opportunity for recovery. Perrow describes the difference between such a tightly coupled system and its counterpart, a loosely coupled system (see Table 3–5, page 62).[17]

Hence, the study of human error in anesthesiology commenced comparatively early, catalyzed by the first malpractice crisis of the 1970s. According to Ellison

**Table 3–5:** *Tight and Loose Coupling Tendencies*

| Tight Coupling | • Delays in processing not possible<br>• Invariant sequences<br>• Only one method to achieve goal<br>• Little slack possible in supplies, equipment, personnel<br>• Buffers and redundancies designed in, deliberate<br>• Substitutions of supplies, equipment, personnel limited and designed in |
|---|---|
| Loose Coupling | • Processing delays possible<br>• Order of sequences can be changed<br>• Alternative methods available<br>• Slack in resources possible<br>• Buffers and redundancies fortuitously available<br>• Substitutions fortuitously available |

*Source:* Perrow C: *Normal Accidents: Living with High-Risk Technologies.* New York: Basic Books, 1984, p 96.

Pierce, the founding and current president of the Anesthesia Patient Safety Foundation (APSF), anesthesiology "has undergone a cultural evolution in patient safety" in which "events and forces have created an environment that openly addresses issues of human error and has adopted patient safety as equivalent in importance to traditional medical teaching and training."[18]

The results have been dramatic. In the early 1980s, anesthesia mortality was approximately two deaths per 10,000 anesthetics administered. Today, the rate is one death per 200,000 to 300,000 anesthetics. The APSF, a nonprofit organization including physicians, nurses, pharmaceutical and device manufacturers, administrators, insurers, and biomedical engineers, deserves much of the credit. It has funded more than $1 million of research, much of it in the area of human factors—the study of the interaction of people and machines—and human performance.[19] The research

- pioneered the use of "complete environment realistic simulators and computer screen simulators" to evaluate decision making and performance of trainees and practitioners;
- identified error modes of anesthesiologists in simple and complex situations;
- developed techniques to measure vigilance and monitoring performance of clinical personnel;
- investigated the role of sleepiness and fatigue in contributing to errors by clinicians; and
- developed new display technologies to minimize errors and maximize data transfer during complex patient care.

The organization also helped persuade manufacturers to improve safeguards on anesthesia devices and simplify drug labeling. Moreover, it helped rewrite anesthesiology's standards of care. First appearing in 1986 and addressing minimal requirements for monitoring during anesthesia,[20] the standards were adopted in a similar form by the American Society of Anesthesiologists.

## Example: Designing Systems to Reduce Violence and the Use of Restraint and Seclusion

Violence by clients against fellow clients and health care staff is not common, but it does represent a significant problem in all health care facilities, particularly those providing behavioral health services. Violence is an occupational risk to staff in psychiatric hospitals and other facilities, with injury rates for nursing staff exceeding those from such high-risk industries as lumber, heavy construction, and mining.

Agitated or aggressive patients are helped by a variety of techniques including verbal de-escalation. However, seclusion or mechanical restraint is sometimes necessary. Physical restraint is dangerous when used improperly and can lead to death or serious injury.

Part of the process for using restraint or seclusion may include conducting a postevent feedback session with the client and staff. The feedback session is one way of improving the staff's ability to respond to clients who may show evidence of potential violence in the future. It should also be a way to get feedback from clients as to how they were feeling and what could be done in the future by both clients and staff to avoid restraint or seclusion use.

So how does a behavioral health care organization design a system that will reduce the likelihood of aggressive behavior by clients or patients and hence the need for the use of restraint and other aggression management techniques? A review of the literature indicates that organizations with a lower incidence of violence and of restraint and seclusion use share several key attributes[21, 22] :

■ Leaders clearly advocate a treatment philosophy;
■ At admission, clients are assessed for risk;
■ Staff are well trained in aggression management;
■ Staff practices encourage maximum use of de-escalation techniques and minimal use of restraint and seclusion;
■ Increased activities for clients correlate with decreased rates of restraint and seclusion use;
■ The need for restraint or seclusion is based on an evaluation of the individual case and situation; and
■ The staff follow well-defined policies and procedures.

The system designed by a public psychiatric hospital for children in Virginia is described by Suzanne Goren and her colleagues in an article in the psychiatric literature.[23] The hospital used strategies involving practice-based research, organization development, and changes in practice. The strategies included:

■ Conducting practice-based nursing research to probe how organization norms and staff behavior influence violence among psychiatric patients;
■ Communicating to the staff the findings of that research which indicated that the hospital was inadvertently maintaining, rather than decreasing, aggressive symptoms;
■ Assessing the agency climate;
■ Creating an aggression-free task force whose efforts and recommendations resulted in the commitment of organization leaders, improvement of staff-patient ratios, improvement of the physical environment, improved coordination regarding admissions, and development of strategies to improve interdisciplinary communication;

- Changing the mind-set about the use of seclusion and restraint through education and improved intrastaff communication;
- Revising and standardizing the behavior modification program to ensure organizationwide consistency;
- Revising policies and procedures related to crisis episodes; and
- Developing a family-focused approach to treatment.

Through organizationwide systems-based efforts including education, improved staff communication, policy revision, and program development, the hospital achieved impressive results. It was able to change a climate characterized by violence, nearly eliminate the use of restraints organizationwide, significantly reduce the use of PRN medication, and decrease the seclusion use rate by 50%.

Another comprehensive systems-based approach to reducing the use of restraint, which is used by Foundations Behavioral Health in Doylestown, Pennsylvania, appears as an example at the end of this chapter, pages 101 through 126.

---

**Table 3–6:** *Joint Commission Data on Cases of Restraint-Related Deaths*

From the time the Joint Commission began tracking sentinel events in 1996 until November 18, 1998, the Accreditation Committee of the Joint Commission's Board of Commissioners reviewed 20 cases related to deaths of individuals who were being physically restrained. Most of the events occurred in psychiatric hospitals (12), followed by general hospitals (6), and long-term care facilities (2).

In 40% of the cases, the cause of death was asphyxiation. Asphyxiation was related to factors such as:
- putting excessive weight on the back of the patient in a prone position;
- placing a towel or sheet over the patient's head to protect against spitting or biting; or
- obstructing the airway when pulling the patient's arms across the neck area.

The remaining cases were caused by strangulation, cardiac arrest, or fire. All the victims of strangulation death were geriatric patients who had been placed in a vest restraint. All the victims of death by fire were male patients who were attempting to smoke or using a cigarette lighter to burn off the restraint.

Two-point, four-point or five-point restraints were used on extremities in 40% of the cases of restraint-related deaths. A therapeutic hold was used in 30% of the cases, a restraint vest was used in 20%, and a waist restraint was used in 10%.

Joint Commission analysis identified the following factors that may contribute to an increased risk of deaths:
- Restraining a patient who smokes;
- Restraining a patient with deformities that preclude proper application of the restraining device (especially a vest restraint);
- Restraining a patient in the supine position (may predispose the patient to aspiration);
- Restraining a patient in the prone position (may predispose the patient to suffocation); and
- Restraining a patient in a room that is not under continuous observation by staff.

*Source:* Joint Commission on Accreditation of Healthcare Organizations, Oakbrook Terrace, IL. Used with permission.

In *Sentinel Event Alert:* * *Issue Eight,* the Joint Commission offers the following: aggregated information on the cases reviewed by the Joint Commission between 1996 and 1998 of an individual's death while being physically restrained; factors that may contribute to an increased risk of death while in restraint (see Table 3–6, page 64); and strategies recommended by organizations that experienced restraint-related deaths for reducing the risk of adverse events.[24] The strategies, some risk management oriented and some systems-redesign oriented, follow:

- Redouble efforts to reduce the use of physical restraint and therapeutic hold through the use of risk assessment and early intervention with less restrictive measures.
- Revise procedures for assessing the medical condition of psychiatric patients.
- Enhance staff orientation and education regarding alternatives to physical restraint and proper application of restraint or therapeutic holding.
- Consider a patient's age, sex, and gender when setting therapeutic hold policies.
- Revise the staffing model.
- Develop structured procedures for consistent application of restraint.
- Continuously observe any client or patient who is restrained.
- If an individual must be restrained in the supine position, ensure that the airway is unobstructed at all times (for example, do not cover or "bury" the individual's face). Also ensure that expansion of the individual's lungs is not restricted by excessive pressure on the individual's back (special caution is required for children, elderly individuals, and very obese individuals).
- Never place a towel, bag, or other cover over an individual's face as part of the therapeutic holding process.
- Do not restrain an individual in a bed with unprotected split-side rails.
- Discontinue use of certain types of restraints, such as high vests and waist restraint devices.
- Ensure that all smoking materials are removed from patients' access and from the access of their family and friends.

Jack Zusman, MD, a psychiatrist who teaches at the Florida Mental Health Institute of the University of South Florida in Tampa, says that a facility can have alternatives to restraint. For example, an organization can create special rooms open to clients, such as a quiet area for clients who are feeling upset or a room with punching bags or treadmills where clients can work off energy without threatening others. Zusman recommends that psychiatric hospitals or psychiatric units of general hospitals train staff in de-escalation techniques. This training involves using interpersonal skills to calm and relax patients in a difficult situation involving conflict or potential conflict. Says Zusman, "All frontline staff should be trained in de-escalation and the application of restraints. Supervisors also should be trained in team leadership in dealing with these situations."[25]

In response to the *Hartford Courant's* October 1998 report on the use of physical restraint in psychiatric facilities, the National Alliance for the Mentally Ill (NAMI) proposed five legislative remedies. These remedies appear as Sidebar 3–1, page 66.

---

* *Sentinel Event Alert* is published by the Joint Commission to share "lessons learned" with health care organizations and provide clarifications about the Joint Commission Sentinel Event Policy. *Sentinel Event Alert* may be obtained from the Joint Commission Web site at www.jcaho.org or by calling the Sentinel Event hotline at 630-792-3700.

---

**Sidebar 3–1:** *Legislative Remedies Proposed by the National Alliance for the Mentally Ill to Address Inappropriate Use of Physical Restraint in Psychiatric Facilities*

- Independent, third-party entities should be established to conduct thorough and immediate investigations into all deaths and serious injuries that occur during psychiatric treatment. When necessary, these entities should be vested with the authority to recommend and institute changes and practices to prevent further abuses.

- The U.S. Department of Justice and the U.S. Department of Health and Human Services should launch a thorough national investigation to determine the magnitude of abusive and harmful seclusion and restraint practices in psychiatric treatment facilities and programs throughout the country.

- States should adopt laws authorizing the establishment of third-party independent monitoring groups to conduct unannounced inspections of psychiatric facilities. Active participation by consumers and family members should be required.

- States should allocate funds for the express purpose of training individuals who work with psychiatric patients on the appropriate use of physical restraints.

- National standards on the appropriate use of restraints representing best clinical practices should be developed and enforced by the Health Care Finance Administration (HCFA). Commercial insurance payers should adopt these HCFA standards to apply to private-pay patients.

*Source:* National Alliance for the Mentally Ill: NAMI calls for major reforms in use of physical restraints in psychiatric facilities. Press release, Oct. 16, 1998.

---

## Other Concepts from the Engineering Literature

Systems engineering literature includes numerous other design concepts that could be useful tools to prevent errors and sentinel events in health care organizations. *Redundancy* is one such concept familiar to the aerospace and nuclear power industries, where systems have backups and even the backups normally have backups. System reliability can be increased by introducing redundancy into system design. However, the cost of designing in redundancy is an issue in most environments.

*Fail-safe design* is also a concept familiar to high-reliability industries, including aerospace and nuclear engineering. The design may be fail passive, fail operational, or fail active. For example, a circuit breaker is a *fail-passive* device that opens when a dangerous situation occurs, thereby making an electrical system safe. A destruct system on a satellite or an air-to-air missile is an example of a *fail-active* device. If the satellite or missile misses its target within a set time, the destruct system blows the satellite or missile apart to halt its flight and limit any damage it might cause by falling to the ground.

## Sound Hiring Practices, Education and Training

### Hiring with Care

Assaults against consumers and patients—from rough handling to rape and homicide—are occurring with alarming frequency in health care facilities. Furthermore, the number of unreported assaults may actually be several times the number of known incidents. Mental health consumers and those with developmental disabilities may be at increased risk of assault from staff, visitors, other consumers, or a trespassing intruder. How have violence-prone or disturbed individuals become part of a health care organization's staff? The answer may be negligent hiring.

To reduce the risk of hiring a violence-prone individual, organizations can follow some rather simple rules and make some inquiries. Writes Russell Colling, a health care security consultant, "Due diligence in hiring can save large amounts of money by avoiding high 'after-hire' costs, including wasted training and supervisory expenditures, program setbacks, unemployment and workers' compensation claims, and litigation expense."[26] Colling recommends looking for clues that signal a need for more in-depth inquiry during the screening and interview process. Sources of information include the following:

- *The application form.* Incomplete or missing information on the application form can indicate that an applicant is withholding information or is ill-prepared. Frequent changes of address could also be a source of concern.
- *Past employers.* Clues in what is said and not said by past employers can be helpful in verifying information provided by the applicant. For example, an applicant may indicate working for a past employer from 1995 to 1999; the employer may indicate that the dates of employment were 1996 to 1998. Or a past employer may answer the question, Did the applicant get along with his colleagues? by saying "His strength was getting his work done on time."
- *Official records.* Discharge papers, licenses, and credentials verify applicants' claims. If they can be obtained, criminal justice records also may be helpful.
- *Previous coworkers.* These individuals often possess a wealth of information on an applicant and may be less inhibited than former employers in sharing information.

Behavioral health care organizations may wish to consider drug screening, criminal background checks, and sexual abuse registry checks for staff with client contact. Sexual misconduct by staff towards a client is a serious problem. In some cases, staff members have prior histories of similar misconduct while in another jurisdiction or when working at another facility. Organizations should consider obtaining a thorough background check on staff members who deal one on one with clients. "Hiring of professionals can't be complacent," says Colling. "The goal is to render an informed decision, through diligent effort, to hire or not to hire."[27]

## Education and Training Objectives

Education and training provide the foundation of professional competence. Health care professionals are trained extensively before assuming care functions. But after initial training, their performance is expected to be flawless. Education and training constitute traditional proactive and reactive initiatives to reduce and prevent errors. Unfortunately, these initiatives feed into the notion of perfect performance and the belief that flawed human performance is the root cause of errors. Efforts to retrain personnel following the occurrence of errors or adverse events focus on eliminating human error. Also, such efforts often take the place of a substantive effort to identify, study, and eradicate systems problems. Sometimes called "blame and train," these efforts begin with the assumptions that human error is the source of the problem and that this error is due to the inattentiveness or insufficiency of practitioners.[28]

There *are* effective educational and training approaches that emphasize systems rather than humans as causative factors for errors and the critical preventive role performed by humans. One such approach is the simulated training method used in anesthesiology that has been described previously; another is the Crew Resource Management approach (see page 72 for more information). Yet even these approaches are not without flaws. How can one simulate events that have not yet happened, but could happen? Or how can someone simulate events that have not been foreseen?[29]

After researching trainees' attempts to learn a word processing program, James Reason developed four error management principles that can be applied to other training situations. Those with appropriate controls to ensure consumer safety—such as simulated environments—are particularly suited to his approach:

- Training should teach and support an active exploratory approach. Trainees should be encouraged to develop their own mental models of the system.
- Error training should form an integral part of the overall training process. Trainees should have the opportunity to make errors and recover from them.
- The heuristics of error should be changed from "mistakes are undesirable" to "it is good to make mistakes; they help learning."
- Error training should be introduced at the appropriate point, midway through a training program. Early in the learning process, trainees are struggling with every step and are unlikely to benefit from error feedback. Later, they are better equipped to learn from such feedback.[30]

Leape indicates that education and training efforts in the health care industry should address three critical components[31]:

- *Training for safety.* Health care professionals must also be trained how not to do things rather than just how to do things. Professionals can be taught how to avoid errors. For example, in the behavioral health care arena, staff must be educated in identifying behaviors that may require the use of physical restraint, available alternatives, and if necessary, how and when to apply the appropriate, least-restrictive, physical restraint device.[32]
- *Training for teamwork.* Physicians and other health care professionals must be trained to work in teams. Although autonomy traditionally has been sought by physicians, the complexity of the medical environment makes professionals interdependent and teamwork vital.
- *Training for errors.* Physicians and other health care professionals must be taught how to handle errors, their reactions to errors, and communication with the patient and others following an error.

Many organizations face challenges while trying to introduce new kinds of training programs, such as those centered on team coordination or improving communication. The challenges derive from the amount of time and financial support required by training programs. If staff members are expected to volunteer unpaid time to attend courses, they tend to resist and resent the obligation. Some suggest that the most effective way to introduce training programs is to provide tangible incentives for staff to work more efficiently and use the time gained for additional training.[33]

## Resident and Student Training

J. Gosbee and R. Stahlhut describe a groundbreaking effort to teach medical students and residents about errors in health care.[34] At Michigan State University Kalamazoo Center for Medical Studies, they developed a curriculum designed to change the "blame and train" mind-set in medical education. The program also helped expand error medicine research, encourage human-centered design of medical technology, and institute organizationwide quality improvement efforts. "Many of the students/residents commented that this was the first time they understood why they might be involved in quality improvement efforts at the hospital or clinic…almost all of the students breathe a sigh of relief when they see the theory behind the mistakes they make, how some of the errors are facilitated by poor design, and the potential for properly designed information systems to help them."[35] There is little doubt that medical education needs to embrace "error education."

## Risk-Management Education

Risk-management education for physicians and other health care professionals presumes that controllable events in medical practice render a health care professional more or less vulnerable to malpractice claims and that educational efforts focused on such events and changing practitioner behavior can reduce injury and subsequent claims.[36]

Insurance companies have been proactive in sponsoring loss prevention/risk-management activities, including seminars and formal education programs, research studies identifying areas of loss, and site evaluations or office audits aimed at identifying poor clinical and business practices in physicians' offices that can lead to claims experience.

An innovative and award-winning suicide risk-reduction program that was developed by Greentree Behavioral Health of Spokane, Washington, is profiled at the end of this chapter, pages 83 to 90. In an integrated and comprehensive approach focused on education, this program recognizes the need to protect behavioral health care provider organizations and their practitioners from allegations of malpractice by improving internal standards of care.

## Consumer Education

Educational initiatives have not been limited to health care practitioners. Awareness of the value of educating the consumer to reduce and prevent errors is growing. Consumers can play a particularly vital role in preventing medication errors across all health care settings. By providing consumers with information about the drugs they are receiving, the correct dosages, and the administration times and frequency, health care organizations can incorporate consumers into their error prevention programs. Extensive private and publicly funded efforts are currently being made in this area.

For example, Partners for Patients, Inc, a Virginia-based nonprofit organization, believes that the public can and should improve the quality of medical care in the United States. It has developed booklets to be distributed to patients by physicians and hospitals and has delivered lectures around the country. The information is geared toward empowering patients to detect problems in their care. Checklists of ideas provide practical patient education information. For example, the "Before Surgery" checklist provides information on getting a second opinion, storage of the patient's own blood, questions to ask about what will happen after the surgery so that patients can prepare their homes, and special instructions before and after surgery. The organization's goal is to help change the paradigm of what it means to be a patient from the notion of the "patient as object" to the view of the "patient as participant."[37]

The National Council on Patient Information and Education (NCPIE) is a government-supported umbrella organization founded around the single issue of improving health professionals' communication with patients about prescription medicines. Through brochures and other written information, public service announcements, and multimedia materials, NCPIE aims to improve the information consumers receive about medications. Much of their efforts are focused on drug information in ambulatory settings.

## Improving Information Management

Impaired access to information has been found to be at the root of many systems failures in the health care environment. Hence, it would stand to reason that

| **Table 3–7:** *The Impact of Information Technology (IT) on Process Innovation* | |
|---|---|
| **Automational** | IT is able to eliminate human labor from a process. |
| **Informational** | IT can be used within a process to capture data about process performance, which can then be analyzed for the purpose of increased understanding. |
| **Sequential** | IT can allow changes in the sequence of processor or transform a process from sequential to parallel in order to achieve process cycle–time reductions. |
| **Tracking** | IT can be used to closely monitor the status of a process. |
| **Analytical** | In processes that involve analysis of information and decision making, IT can offer sophisticated analytical resources that permit more data to be incorporated into and analyzed during the decision-making process. |
| **Geographical** | IT can coordinate processes across distances. |
| **Integrative** | IT can provide coordination between tasks and processes. |
| **Intellectual** | IT can capture and distribute expert knowledge and experience across a setting. |
| **Disintermediating** | IT can eliminate human intermediaries from a process. |

Davenport TH: *Process Innovation: Reengineering Work Through Information Technology.* Boston: Harvard Business School Press, 1993, pp 50-55.

improved information management would reduce and prevent errors and improve health care systems and processes.

## Information Technology

Davenport describes nine different categories in which information technology can support process innovation (see Table 3–7, page 70) in the proactive creation of high-quality processes.[38]

Information plays a major supportive role in the efficiency and effectiveness of health care processes. It can be used to measure and monitor process performance, integrate existing processes, and facilitate planning. Health care professionals need ready access to extensive information to provide their services safely. Information on drug side effects, interactions, and so on is vital to a physician's provision of medications to consumers, for example. Nurses and technicians need to be similarly equipped. Computers provide one tool.

## The Role of Computers

Computers are being used increasingly in the provision of health care information. For example, computers can reduce medication prescription errors resulting from illegible handwriting, and they can check the consistency of drug and dosage. Berwick, et al suggest that computerized physician order entry systems can reduce the likelihood of errors by

- providing information when needed,
- providing doses and frequencies,
- eliminating transcription errors, and
- eliminating handwriting errors.[39]

Such systems can also increase the likelihood of intercepting errors, including drug-drug interactions, allergies, out-of-range doses, and contraindications. A recent study by D.W. Bates and colleagues[40] indicates that when a hospital used a physician computer order entry system, the rate of ordering errors decreased by 19%, transcription errors fell by 84%, dispensing errors declined by 68%, allergy errors decreased by 23%, and administration errors fell by 59%.

Although computerized information systems have been repeatedly tested and computerized medical records have received considerable media attention because of recent health reform initiatives, few health care organizations have workable systems for collecting and retrieving clinical information. Leape et al observe, "Few (organizations) are able to present information in a manner that facilitates bedside use. Even fewer have the capability to pull (medication) data from different systems and present it at the time of ordering when it can have the greatest impact."[41] The findings of the adverse drug error study conducted at Harvard "make a compelling case for accelerating the computerization of both drug and clinical information to make it available to all who need it, at each stage of the process, in a form that is easy to use and understand."[42] Another study cites the critical need for laboratory and pharmacy computers to talk to each other to reduce potentially lethal drug errors.[43]

Indeed, organizationwide computerized information systems are vital to an error prevention and reduction program. Whether collected, retrieved, or analyzed with automated or manual systems, however, information is key to identifying, reducing, and preventing errors. Identifying and reducing the incidence of error without analyzing the context within which the error occurred is a condition characterized by "one hand clapping." Bogner writes, "To identify and define the other hand to participate in the clapping, to explore the operational context for the error, it is necessary to have information about the elemental unit of the provider, the patient, and whatever medical treatment devices or medication were used at the time of the error."[44] All organizations need to be moving in the direction of enhanced and computerized information management systems.

## Teamwork

The effectiveness of individuals working as a team to reduce and prevent errors has been studied in great depth in the airline industry. Crew Resource Management (CRM) is used extensively by airlines as a tool to improve performance with flight, cabin, ground, and maintenance crews. Its success in improving morale, teamwork, coordination, and communication to reduce and prevent errors has been significant.

The CRM technique views crews as a resource for solving problems and gives such crews experience in handling crisis situations via simulation, role playing, and other strategies. Write Cook and Woods, "Unlike blame-and-train methods that seek to regiment human performance to eliminate human error, CRM implicitly views human performance as the critical resource in dealing with novel, threatening situations and focuses on developing in pilots and engineers the ability to work together as a coordinated team."[45] CRM training covers self-critique, communication skills, personality assessments, distraction avoidance, interpersonal relationships, leadership-followership issues, and overall technical proficiency and crew effectiveness.

Traditionally, teamwork has *not* been stressed in the health care environment. Clinicians, placing a high degree of value on autonomy, are trained to think as individuals rather than as team members. Interactions among the individuals caring for a client are mostly informal and are usually not codified.[46] Communication problems are a major source of errors. Team performance has been studied most extensively for its error-reducing and prevention capabilities in the operating and emergency room settings.[47] Like airline crews, medical professionals operating in these environments are highly technically trained, and they must respond quickly in emergencies, work within a task-interdependent environment, and participate in teams whose composition changes frequently.

As part of a comprehensive error reduction and prevention strategy, behavioral health care organizations need to recognize the importance of groups functioning as teams and create interdisciplinary teams or task forces charged with improving organization performance. Teamwork is important not only in complex and dynamic environments, but also throughout care functions and processes. "Rounding teams" by including representatives from all disciplines can direct consumer care. Organized teamwork can and should provide the impetus for the bulk of organizational performance improvement initiatives. Small teams, ranging in size from five to ten individuals, that meet regularly and are empowered by the organization's leaders, can

■ identify performance improvement opportunities,

- recommend and implement appropriate action plans and thereby,
- have a significant positive impact on organizational effectiveness and error prevention.

## Self-Assessment Through Performance Measurement

Organizationwide self-assessment through performance measurement is potentially one of the most effective proactive strategies for reducing and preventing errors. Assessment of organizational performance is a systematic process for understanding the work an organization does and how well it does that work. Information that emerges from such an assessment provides a foundation for informed judgments about how the organization is performing.[48] Knowledge about areas of *strong* performance can be used to support learning about why and how successes were achieved. Knowledge about areas of *weak* performance can be used to support informed decision making about priorities for performance improvement. Through performance improvement initiatives, effective error reduction and prevention programs can be shaped.

Organization assessment involves collecting and analyzing data to measure dimensions of performance. The Joint Commission identifies the dimensions of performance as the degree to which what is done is efficacious and appropriate for the individual client or consumer and the degree to which it is available in a timely manner, effective, continuous with other care, safe, efficient, and caring and respectful of the consumer. Performance measurement allows behavioral health and other health care organizations to

- have continuous access to objective data that supports claims of quality;
- receive and respond to early warnings of performance problems;
- verify the effectiveness of corrective actions;
- highlight areas of outstanding performance; and
- compare performance to that of peer organizations using the same measures within the same performance measurement system.

Readers may wish to consult the Joint Commission's publication, *Using Performance Measurement to Improve Outcomes in Behavioral Health Care,*[49] as a reference on performance and outcomes measurement in the behavioral health care setting.

To improve performance and design effective error prevention programs, data collection must be systematically and prospectively focused on specific important issues and trended over time. The pre-established objective must be to identify interventions or proactive strategies likely to have sustained impacts on performance improvement. A fictitious example of the use of measurement to improve aggression management appears as Sidebar 3–2, pages 74 and 75. An actual example of a forensic state psychiatric hospital's use of data to improve health outcomes by reducing violent events appears as Sidebar 3–3, pages 76 and 77. This initiative by Atascadero State Hospital in Atascadero, California, received a 1998 Ernest A. Codman Award in recognition of excellence in the use of performance measures to achieve health care quality improvement.

Data collection may be based on an accepted set of performance guidelines such as the Joint Commission standards or the Baldrige criteria. Many organizations develop their own assessment tools, often based on professional standards

**Sidebar 3–2:** *Using Measurement to Improve Aggression Management: An Example*

The New Morning Center* is a behavioral health care facility that provides crisis stabilization and acute inpatient, partial hospital, and outpatient services to adults. In alignment with the organization's treatment philosophy of providing the most comprehensive and appropriate care in the least restrictive manner, managers and staff were interested in improving the management of aggressive behavior.

A multidisciplinary performance improvement team was convened to tackle this issue. The team was chaired by the program director of the inpatient unit, who was a clinical psychologist. Members of the team included a staff nurse and licensed clinical social worker, from the crisis stabilization unit and an occupational therapist from the inpatient unit. The medical director of the intensive treatment unit, who is a psychiatrist, served as an ad hoc member. The team was facilitated by a clinical care coordinator from the utilization/quality management area.

At the outset of this aggression management improvement project, critical operational definitions were developed. Aggression was defined as client behaviors such as verbal threats and gestures, menacing behaviors, and attempts to harm self or others. Aggression management was defined as early assessment of impending aggression and progressively restrictive de-escalating interventions, such as "talking down," time-outs, administration of medications as required, and use of seclusion and leather restraints.

To understand current performance, the center collected baseline data about aggressive episodes and aggression management interventions. Measures included the following:

1. The total number of aggressive occurrences by service per week;

2. The number(s) of specific aggressive incidents (verbal threats, threatening gestures, menacing behaviors, self-harm attempts, and attempts to harm others) by service per week;

3. The total number of de-escalating interventions conducted by service per week; and

4. The number(s), type(s), and; reason(s) for provision of specific de-escalating interventions (verbal interventions, time-outs, administration of medications as required, and use of seclusion and leather restraint devices) by service per week.

The current performance data showed an unacceptably high rate of seclusion and leather restraint use on the 16-bed intensive treatment unit. (During the past month seclusion had been used an average of 22 times per week and leather restraint devices had been applied an average of 15 times per week.) Seclusion and restraint were typically used in response to menacing behaviors and physical aggression toward other clients or staff. In addition, the use of medications administered on an as-needed basis was steadily increasing from an average of 5 times per day to 11 times per day, with the greatest increase occurring on the evening shift. The most commonly documented reason for administration of medications on an as-needed basis was for verbal threats.

A root cause analysis revealed unstable staffing on the intensive treatment unit. Many of the unit staff were new to the organization and had not received any formal training in aggression prevention, assessment, and management. In addition, temporary staff from external agencies were frequently used to fill several vacancies resulting from staff attrition, illness, and other issues. The root cause analysis also uncovered an outdated aggression management protocol that focused on the use of medications administered as required and rapid tranquilization and failed to emphasize the importance of early assessment and prevention of impending aggression.

*Source:* Joint Commission on Accreditation of Healthcare Organizations, Oakbrook Terrace, IL. Used with permission.

* The New Morning Center is a fictional facility. Any resemblance to an actual organization is coincidental.

*(continued on next page)*

**Sidebar 3–2:** *Using Measurement to Improve Aggression Management: An Example (continued)*

After considering these findings, the improvement team brainstormed several potential improvements and recommended the use of additional performance indicators.

One suggested improvement action was the development and delivery of a comprehensive aggression management staff education program. After implementation of this training, improvement in aggression management would be verified and demonstrated by collecting performance data using the same measures that were initially used to assess performance. The team defined improved performance as the prevention of aggression, as evidenced by an overall decrease in the occurrence of aggressive behaviors, as well as a decreased use of more restrictive interventions such as restraint and seclusion, and an increased use of less restrictive interventions such as verbal de-escalation and reduction-of-stimulation techniques.

### Table. Aggression Management Protocol

| Client Behavior | Staff Intervention |
| --- | --- |
| Controlled verbal expression of anger and hostility | One-to-one exploration of feelings |
| Uncontrolled verbal expression of anger and hostility | One-to-one exploration of feelings, "talking down," time-out |
| Verbal threats and/or gestures and/or menacing behaviors | Talking down, limit setting, time-out, medications as required |
| Intimidating behaviors | Limit setting, time-out, medications as required, seclusion |
| Attempts to harm self or others | Medications as required, seclusion, restraints |

A second suggested improvement was to revise and update the existing aggression management protocol to include progressively more restrictive interventions for escalating behaviors (see above). The measure for performance control that derives from this protocol is the occurrence of each of the defined client behaviors.

Additional assessment/improvement indicators recommended by the improvement team included the following:

1. Rate of aggressive behaviors by diagnosis;

2. Rate of aggressive behaviors by client length of stay in the intensive treatment unit;

3. Rate of aggressive behaviors by ratio of permanent to temporary staff; and

4. Average length of time for which temporary staff had worked on the service.

The same or similar measures may be used for different purposes (assessment, improvement, or control).

and literature and customized to reflect the unique characteristics of the organization. The Joint Commission accreditation process is, in fact, a highly effective assessment strategy. Performance measurement for organization improvement is integrated in Joint Commission standards. See Table 3–8, page 78, for the relevant standards from the *1999–2000 Comprehensive Accreditation Manual for Behavioral Health Care.*

**Sidebar 3–3:** *The Atascadero State Hospital Mealtime Quality Action Project: Using Performance Measures to Improve Health Care Quality*

Atascadero State Hospital (ASH) is a 1,000-bed maximum security, forensic psychiatric hospital for men. With a staff of 1,650, including more than 800 psychiatric nurses, ASH is located on 900 acres of the central California coast and surrounded by vineyards and horse ranches. ASH received Accreditation with Commendation from the Joint Commission in both 1993 and 1996.

The hospital's mission is threefold: public protection from criminally insane patients, evaluation of those patients, and treatment of those patients. More than 80% of ASH patients have committed violent criminal offenses such as rape, armed robbery, and murder and have been remanded by the California Department of Corrections, parole board, or the criminal justice courts to ASH for psychiatric treatment. The average length of stay at ASH is nearly 800 days, with a range of 300 to 2,400 days.

"Since the best predictor of violence is a history of violence, ASH is an excellent laboratory for studying violence," says Colleen Carney Love, DNSc, RN, ASH's director of the Clinical Safety Project, a clinical and research-based branch of ASH's Environment of Care Process Management Team. As in most public sector psychiatric settings, violence poses a significant hazard to workers and patients at ASH. Since 1988, ASH has averaged four violent special incident reports a day, ranging from an annual high of 1,682 (1988) to a low of 988 (1997). Violent events, including battery injuries and containment injuries, are recorded through the filing of a Special Incident Report (SIR). Violent behavior is unevenly distributed across the hospital with 20% of the patients responsible for more than 50% of all reported violent incidents. Although ASH patients are in a high-risk category for future violence, half of the patients leave the facility without ever having been involved in a reported violent event.

As a recipient of the Codman Award, ASH was recognized for its collection, analysis, and use of data throughout the organization to reduce violence, thereby improving the quality of patient care and services. "Monitoring and preventing violence in psychiatric settings are essential to the creation of a therapeutic environment where effective treatment can take place," mention both Love and Melvin E. Hunter, JD, MPA, the Clinical Safety Project's co-director and director of the Forensic Services Department.

One initiative, outlined in the hospital's application for the award, was to examine the hospital's mealtime procedures to reduce the number of violent events during mealtimes, reduce weapon use in the dining rooms, and enhance the therapeutic benefits of mealtime activities for ASH patients. Although the hospital had numerous performance improvement and specific violence prevention initiatives underway, ASH chose the mealtime violence reduction initiative because, according to Jon DeMorales, ASH's executive director, "It clearly illustrates the use of data, the team approach, and performance improvement concepts and principles used throughout the organization."

The Mealtime Violence Quality Action Team (MV-QAT), commissioned by the hospital's Quality Council in 1993, collected and analyzed data about mealtime processes from numerous sources. A key source was the SIR database, which provides information regarding trends and patterns of violent events through accurate data and narrative descriptions of incidents. Following careful data analysis, the team recommended eliminating the use of silverware in the patient dining rooms (replacing it with plasticware), training food service workers in techniques for communicating effectively with the mentally ill, opening additional areas to patients for recreation following meals, and playing music during mealtimes.

*Source:* Adapted from *The Joint Commission Annual Report on Excellence: Ernest A. Codman 1998 Award Winners.* Oakbrook Terrace, IL: Joint Commission, 1999.

*(continued on next page)*

---

**Sidebar 3–3:** *The Atascadero State Hospital Mealtime Quality Action Project: Using Performance Measures to Improve Health Care Quality (continued)*

In the year following implementation of the team's recommendations, the initiative succeeded in:

■ contributing to reducing violent events in the dining rooms by 40%;

■ decreasing Workers' Compensation and industrial disability leave expenditures by 24% (in combination with the numerous other hospital-wide violence prevention strategies);

■ eliminating weapon attacks with silverware;

■ decreasing the time patients spent waiting at mealtimes by 15 minutes; and

■ saving 78 nursing staff hours each day, hours that previously were devoted to mealtime procedures.

As a result of the MV-QAT improvement initiative, eating utensils have been completely eliminated as a weapon of opportunity. Since the switch to plasticware, no eating utensil assaults have occurred. In addition, eliminating the cumbersome silverware control procedures saved approximately 70 nursing staff hours each day—the equivalent of 14.5 full-time nursing positions each year. The time savings has allowed the staff to focus more attention on other treatment and security concerns. The classes provided to food service workers were well received. The overall dining room milieu has been enhanced, crowding has decreased, more flexible procedures have been created, and the amount of time spent by patients in the dining rooms has been reduced.

Ongoing monitoring of mealtime processes indicates that the improvements achieved through this initiative have been sustained during the subsequent four years.

---

Many examples of performance measures are pertinent to behavioral health care settings. Some measures are clinical, whereas others may be administrative or operational. Patrice Spath, ART, a health care consultant, delineated performance measures or indicators that could be used to evaluate the quality of important functions and activities in behavioral health care organizations. They include the following:

■ Percentage of cases lacking appropriate informed consent;

■ Percentage of discharge summaries that include all required documentation;

■ Percentage of clients for whom a follow-up appointment is scheduled within two weeks of discharge;

■ Percentage of cases in which the family/significant other was involved at the appropriate stage of therapy;

■ Percentage of children with serious emotional disturbances who were placed outside the home for at least one month during the year; and

■ Substance abuse treatment completion rate for clients completing at least two face-to-face treatment contacts[50];

In 1996, the Maryland Quality Indicator Project identified four indicators for use by freestanding psychiatric hospitals and psychiatric acute care units in general hospitals. The measures capture data regarding the occurrence of

**Table 3–8:** *Performance Measurement Standards from the 1999–2000 Comprehensive Accreditation Manual for Behavioral Health Care*

- The performance of new and modified processes is measured.

- Data is collected to monitor the stability of existing processes, identify opportunities for improvement, identify changes that will lead to improvement, and sustain improvement.

- The organization collects data to monitor its performance.

- The organization collects data to monitor the performance of processes that involve risks or may result in sentinel events.

- The organization collects data to monitor performance of areas targeted for further study.

- The organization collects data to monitor improvements in performance.

- Data is systematically aggregated and analyzed on an ongoing basis.

- The organization compares its performance over time with other sources of information.

- Undesirable patterns or trends in performance and sentinel events are intensively analyzed.

- The organization identifies changes that will lead to improved performance and reduce the risk of sentinel events.

*Source:* Joint Commission on Accreditation of Healthcare Organizations, Oakbrook Terrace, IL. Used with permission.

specified critical incidents in relation to the total client population. The indicators are as follows:

- Injurious behaviors;
- Unplanned departures resulting in discharge;
- Transfers to an acute care (medical) unit; and
- Readmission within 15 days of discharge.[51]

A multiagency outcomes evaluation of children's services in Pennsylvania provides an excellent summary of the important principles and observations to be gleaned from outcomes and performance measurement. These include

- involving stakeholders in the development of all aspects of the measurement system, including selection of outcomes.
- fostering continued commitment to the long development process through any means possible, including group meetings, newsletters, communications regarding mandates for outcomes, and early products.
- measuring a few things well, keeping it simple, and building on what providers are already measuring. The involvement of many stakeholders in the development will naturally result in a system that is initially somewhat complicated and burdensome; however, through testing and refinement, simplicity will result.
- designing a system for agency self-evaluation that is built into ongoing program operations and requires agency staff to routinely collect information for midstream correction. Moving towards a culture of outcome account-ability requires that providers embrace self-evaluation as part of their program models.

- selecting outcomes that are based on social validation and immediately understandable and socially significant for both internal and external audiences. Such an emphasis will produce a greater reliance on functional outcomes.

- using rigorous testing procedures in the development of outcomes measures but recognizing that naturalistic settings often require great flexibility in research design and methodology. It should also be recognized that providers must be involved in product testing.

- working toward multiagency adoption of common outcomes measures. The power of outcomes is the aggregate of many cases; thus, outcomes measurement should increasingly focus on multiagency, multisystem data pools that can provide benchmarks for comparisons and answers to fundamental questions of children's services: which services work better than others, for which children, and at what cost.[52]

As with other organization efforts, executive leadership must reassure both management and staff that performance data derived from assessment and measurement efforts will not be used for disciplinary or punitive actions. Cesarone writes, "Revelation of performance problems must be embraced as a step in the process of improving organizational performance."[53] Assessment initiatives can be powerful tools in the effort to reduce and prevent errors, but only if they occur within a truly blame-free environment.

## References

1.  James BC: Establishing accountability for errors: Who, how, with what impact? Presented at the Examining Errors in Health Care Conference, Rancho Mirage, CA: Oct 13-15, 1996.

2.  Berwick DM: Taking action: Leading the reduction of error. Presented at the Examining Errors in Health Care Conference, Rancho Mirage, CA: Oct 13-15, 1996.

3.  Leape LL: Error in medicine. *JAMA* 272(23):1851-1857, 1994.

4.  Leape, 1994, p 1855.

5.  AAS: National suicide statistics. American Association of Suicidology, June 1997.

6.  Satcher D: Press conference on suicide prevention, Atlanta, Oct 23, 1998.

7.  Joint Commission: Inpatient suicides: recommendations for prevention. *Sentinel Event Alert,* Issue 7, Nov 6, 1998.

8.  *Sentinel Event Alert,* Issue 7.

9.  *Sentinel Event Alert,* Issue 7.

10. Moray N: Error reduction as a systems problem. In Bogner MS (ed): *Human Error in Medicine.* Hillsdale, NJ: Lawrence Erlbaum Associates, 1994, pp 70-71.

11. Van Cott H: Human errors: Their causes and reduction. In Bogner, p 55.

12. Bogner MS (ed): *Human Error in Medicine.* Hillsdale, NJ: Lawrence Erlbaum Associates, 1994, p 378.

13. Bogner, p 378.

14. Moray, pp 70-83.

15. Leape, 1994, p 1854.

16. Bogner, p 9.

17. Perrow C: *Normal Accidents: Living with High-Risk Technologies.* New York: Basic Books, 1984, p 96.

18. Pierce EC, Cooper JB, Gaba DM: From human error to patient safety in anesthesia: Pioneering strategies for the rest of health care. Presented at the Examining Errors in Health Care Conference, Rancho Mirage, CA: Oct 13-15, 1996.

19. Pierce, Cooper, Gaba.

20. Eichhorn JH, et al: Standards for patient monitoring during general anesthesia at Harvard Medical School. *JAMA* 256(8):1017-1020, 1986.

21. NYS Commission of Quality of Care: Restraint and seclusion practices in New York State psychiatric facilities, Sep 1994.

22. American Psychiatric Association: APA task force reports: Seclusion and restraint.

23. Goren S, Abraham I, Doyle N: Reducing violence in a child psychiatric hospital through planned organizational change. *J Child Adolesc Psychopharmacol* 9(2):27-37.

24. Joint Commission on Accreditation of Healthcare Organizations: Preventing restraint deaths. *Sentinel Event Alert,* Issue 8, Nov 1998.

25. *Sentinel Event Alert,* Issue 8.

26. Colling R: Protect your patients: Hire with care. *Jt Comm Envir of Care News,* July/Aug 1998, pp 10-11.

27. Colling.

28. Cook RI, Woods DD: Operating at the sharp end: The complexity of human error. In Bogner, p 290.

29. Reason J: *Human Error.* Cambridge: Cambridge University Press, 1990, pp 245-246.

30. Reason, pp 245-246.

31. Leape LL: Errors in health care—Problems and challenges. Presented at the Examining Errors in Health Care Conference, Rancho Mirage, CA: Oct 13-15, 1996.

32. Firestone T: Physical restraints: Meeting the standards/improving the outcomes. *Med Surg Nurs* 7(2)121-123.

33. Helmreigh RL: Team performance in the operating room. In Bogner, p 229.

34. Gosbee J, Stahlhut R: Teaching medical students and residents about errors in health care. Presented at the Examining Errors in Health Care Conference, Rancho Mirage, CA: Oct 13-15, 1996.

35. Gosbee, Stahlhut.

36. Frisch PR, et al: The role of previous claims and specialty on the effectiveness of risk management education for office-based physicians. Presented at the Examining Errors in Health Care Conference, Rancho Mirage, CA: Oct 13_15, 1996.

37. Gosden FF: Partners for Patients, Inc. Presented at the Examining Errors in Health Care Conference, Rancho Mirage, CA: Oct 13-15, 1996.

38. Davenport TH: *Process Innovation: Reengineering Work Through Information Technology.* Boston: Harvard Business School Press, 1993, pp 50-55.

39. Berwick D, et al: Reducing adverse drug events and medical errors. Presented at the National Forum on Quality Improvement in Health Care Conference, New Orleans, LA: Dec 4-7, 1996.

40. Bates DW et al: Effect of computerized physician order entry and a team intervention on prevention of serious medication errors. *JAMA* 280(15):1311-1316, 1998.

41. Leape LL, et al: Systems analysis of adverse drug events. *JAMA* 274(1):35-43, 1995.

42. Leape LL, et al, 1995, p 42.

43. Schiff G: The critical need for lab and pharmacy computers to talk to each other: The case of K⁺. Presented at the Examining Errors in Health Care Conference, Rancho Mirage, CA: Oct 13-15, 1996.

44. Bogner, p 379.

45. Cook, Woods, p 301.

46. Xiao Y: Informal teams. Presented at the Examining Errors in Health Care Conference, Rancho Mirage, CA: Oct 13-15, 1996.

47. Gaba DM, DeAnda A: The response of anesthesia trainees to simulated critical incidents. *Anesth Analg* 68(4):444-451, 1989, p 449.

48. Cesarone D: *Assess for Success: Achieving Excellence with Joint Commission Standards and Baldrige Criteria.* Oakbrook Terrace, IL: Joint Commission, 1997, p 19.

49. Joint Commission on Accreditation of Healthcare Organizations: *Using Performance Measurement to Improve Outcomes in Behavioral Health Care.* Oakbrook Terrace: Joint Commission, 1998.

50. Spath PL: Performance measurement in behavioral health. Brown-Spath & Associates, July, 1998.

51. Morrissey J: Quality project expands to psych care. *Modern Healthcare* 26:49, Mar 1996.

52. Beck SA, et al: Multiagency outcome evaluation of children's services: A case study. *Behav Health Serv Res* 25(2):163-176.

53. Cesarone, p 30.

# PROGRAM PROFILE

## *The Suicide Risk Reduction Program*

### Greentree Behavioral Health

## *About the Organization*

Greentree Behavioral Health (GBH), located in Spokane, Washington, provides outpatient services, employee assistance programs, and national training programs. A division of the not-for-profit organization Spokane Mental Health (SMH), GBH sees approximately 700 clients per year on an outpatient basis and has a multidisciplinary staff of five clinical professionals, all of whom specialize in suicide prevention. Suicidologist Paul G. Quinnett, PhD, founder of the prevention program described here, assumed GBH's directorship three years ago, bringing with him more than 20 years of experience at SMH. His responsibilities there included managing a volunteer crisis response and community information hotline and training volunteers to work with suicidal callers, directing the urgent care system, completing sentinel event death reviews for all completed suicides experienced by the agency over the years, and counseling high-risk suicidal patients.

GBH's parent organization, SMH, is one of the largest publicly funded mental health providers in the state of Washington. SMH serves more than 11,000 consumers each year on an outpatient basis and has a clinical staff of more than 220 professionals. SMH's range of services includes crisis intervention; individual, family, and group therapy; multicultural services; case management; medication management; vocational rehabilitation; foster care placement; and residential placement. In addition to its own 12 service sites throughout Spokane County, SMH provides services at community locations, including the county jail, detention center, community centers, and area schools. Its services include urgent care; services for children and families adults, and the elderly; and prevention and early intervention services. With annual revenue approaching $20 million, SMH receives more than half its funding from state and local grants, approximately one-third through federal sources, and less than 10% through patient service fees.

## *Program Development*

Quinnett and his colleagues started developing Greentree Behavioral Health's Suicide Risk Reduction Program in the mid-1990s. Says Quinnett, "Suicide is a reality in our culture. Unfortunately, in the present health care environment, it results in liability and malpractice exposure for providers of behavioral health care services." In fact, as Quinnett cites, suicide malpractice claims are the number one cause of suits against behavioral health practitioners, including psychiatrists, psychologists, social workers, and nurses.

The answer, according to Quinnett, would be a program that could improve standards of care for suicide prevention, intervention, and postvention while simultaneously enhancing client or consumer safety and reducing professional liability exposure. The goal was a community-based program that would provide a comprehensive, integrated, and programmatic approach to suicide risk reduction.

In 1996, Quinnett started developing such a program for application at SMH. SMH's chief executive officer, David Pankens explains, "We wanted to use GBH's Suicide Risk Reduction Program because it enhances quality of care. The program not only reduces the risk of suicidal behaviors among consumers by creating a safer, more knowledgeable, and caring treatment environment but also helps protect staff from the trauma of losing a patient to suicide for lack of skill or knowledge."

As a first step, Quinnett and his team presented a broad education and training plan to SMH's Quality Improvement (QI) Committee. The committee included line staff, supervisors, and case managers from every SMH program. With input from the committee, he identified and fine-tuned a description of staff and client education and training needs. Quinnett describes, "From the very beginning, we thought of this as a *suicide risk reduction* rather than strictly a *suicide prevention* program. The fact is that we are not going to prevent every suicide. Rather, if we are successful in identifying those at risk for suicide and getting them into treatment, we would actually experience more suicides as an organization. A large mental health center which has not experienced any suicides probably is not reaching or treating those most in need."

Early phases of the program involved routine screening of all clients for suicidal ideation at intake, outreach to family members of completed suicides to offer support and assessment services at no cost, and assistance in the funding and volunteer staffing for a community-based suicide survivors group. Staff also served on the Governor's State Task Force for Youth Suicide Prevention and a national suicide prevention board called the Suicide Prevention Advocacy Network.

The program's developmental process included the following steps:

- A QI subcommittee wrote, published, and distributed suicide-specific clinical policies and procedures to address suicide prevention, suicide intervention/risk assessment and management, documentation, supervision/consultation, training requirements for all staff, postvention, and death review. These were reviewed by SMH's medical director, all clinical directors, and legal counsel.
- GBH staff developed three postgraduate training modules to address issues of suicide risk assessment, suicide and chemical dependency, and suicide postvention.
- *QPR: Question, Persuade, and Refer* gatekeeper training (a one-hour public health education program) was offered to consumers, their family members, and concerned citizens.
- Two 24-page booklets *(QPR: Question, Persuade, and Refer* and *Helping Someone Survive a Suicide Crisis)* for public and family education about suicide prevention were distributed to each trainee.
- A collection of books, journal articles, and suicidology literature was made available to all staff through the library.
- A combined research and program evaluation project was initiated with the Washington Institute for Mental Illness Research and Training.

The entire program was reviewed by counsel for content and exposure risk.

The program was developed and fully implemented at SMH within an impressively short time frame. Mandatory training commenced for all SMH staff in the fall of 1997, one year after presentation of the original plan. Clinical and support staff members alike are currently trained in QPR. A suicide risk assessment, which is a key program component, is included in the medical records of every client. "Just as patients routinely receive blood pressure checks during intake assessment, every client now also receives a routine suicide risk assessment," states Quinnett.

## Program Description

Greentree Behavioral Health Suicide Risk Reduction Program is a comprehensive educational program that addresses both the training needs of clinicians providing services to at-risk populations and the educational and network communication needs of consumers, their friends, and family members. "Because suicide is always multidetermined and multidimensional, we had to take a multilevel approach to loss control," mentions Quinnett. The educational initiatives offered in the areas of prevention, intervention, and postvention to the program's audiences, including consumers, family members, providers, and administrators, appear in a Suicide Risk Reduction Program matrix, Figure 3-2, page 86.

The program is policy driven. Policy and procedures drive clinical protocols for routine questioning of consumers for suicidal thoughts, feelings, and past behaviors. If these are present, a standardized, automatic, guided suicide risk assessment is triggered, leading to a suicide risk-management safety plan. The safety plan is family-centric. For example, consumers and their loved ones assist the clinician in establishing a safety plan and monitoring a network of supportive others. These individuals can, if a crisis worsens or reappears, activate a suicide prevention/intervention effort.

Training modules address suicide risk assessment, management and treatment (question, persuade, refer and/or treat—the QPRT module), suicide and chemical dependency (QPR-CD), and postvention in the aftermath of suicide. Says Quinnett of the QPR gatekeeper training program, "Training has to be interactive because our research indicates that for every 13 gatekeepers we train, we have one immediate referral from someone at risk or a person who knows someone at risk. And, out of every 52 consumers we train, at least one will have lost a

**Figure 3-2:** *Greentree Behavioral Health – Suicide Risk Reduction Program Matrix "Prevention Through Education"*

| | Prevention | Intervention | Postvention |
|---|---|---|---|
| **Consumer** | ■ Public awareness campaign<br>■ Public education/QPR training<br>■ Hotline/resource numbers<br>■ Recommended reading<br>■ Depression screening | ■ Clinical assessment/diagnosis<br>■ QPRT interview and safety plan<br>■ Specialty consultation<br>■ Community referral<br>■ Aggressive treatment | ■ Respect for confidentiality<br>■ Multidisciplinary comprehensive chart review<br>■ Recommendations for review |
| **Family** | ■ Public awareness campaign<br>■ Public education/QPR training<br>■ Referral information<br>■ Depression screening<br>■ Recommended reading | ■ Family interview (if possible)<br>■ Family-centric education<br>■ Booklet: *How to Help Someone Survive a Suicide Crisis*<br>■ Referral resources | ■ Outreach and free postvention services<br>■ Free assessment and referral<br>■ Referral for community support<br>■ Reading list |
| **Provider** | ■ Enhanced risk factor awareness<br>■ Postgraduate education<br>■ Supervisor support<br>■ AAS affiliation/membership<br>■ Specialty certifications<br>■ Library/literature support | ■ Clinical assessment protocols, including chemical dependency<br>■ QPRT format<br>■ Consultation protocols<br>■ Risk-benefit analysis<br>■ Knowledge of community resources | ■ Postvention training<br>■ Critical incident debriefing<br>■ Empathic supervisory support<br>■ EAP specialist referral |
| **Administration** | ■ Mission statement for prevention<br>■ Commitment to risk reduction program<br>■ Policies and procedures<br>■ QPR training for staff<br>■ AAS institutional membership | ■ Provide staff training<br>■ Written QI protocols<br>■ Periodic quality review<br>■ Annual evaluation of risk reduction program | ■ Formal response to provider and family/survivors<br>■ QI death review<br>■ Directors' review<br>■ Adjustments to policy and procedures |

*Source:* Greentree Behavioral Health, Spokane, WA. Used with permission.

**Abbreviations:**
AAS    American Association of Suicidology
QPR    Question, Persuade, Refer, Community Psychiatric Rehabilitation for Suicide Prevention
QPRT   Question, Persuade, Refer and/or Treat Suicide Risk Assessment Inventory
EAP    Employee Assistance Professional
QI     Quality Improvement.

loved one to suicide and may need postvention services." Training components are designed to fit into any service delivery system at any locale and hence are uniquely portable. The videos, training guides, forms, and educational booklets are generic by nature and can be customized to fit any community, institution, or service delivery system.

GBH is making the program available to other behavioral health care organizations across the country. Portions of the program, including the QPRT module, are being implemented in a large residential and outpatient mental health facility in Tacoma, Washington, and a hospital version of the program, QPRT-H Suicide Risk Inventory, currently is being implemented at a Spokane-area hospital. The hospital program assists hospital staff and treatment teams in assessing and documenting suicidality and determining safety levels for the patient. The QPRT-H inventory form helps to collect data that leads to a decision about appropriate monitoring levels for the client. Because research indicates that a large proportion of suicides among inpatients occur while the patient is on an authorized pass or shortly after discharge from the unit, the protocols call for reassessment at such times. A pediatric version of the program is also available. This risk assessment inventory includes checklists for known risk factors for suicide by children and age-appropriate questions for children, and takes a family-centric approach. A parent or caregiver is present during the risk assessment and commits to a collaborative safety plan.

The QPRT module for adults was developed to help those who assist, evaluate, manage, council, or treat suicidal people and to better assess and aggressively manage those who are at elevated risk for suicidal behavior. It fills practicing clinicians' need for a structured risk assessment interview tool. The interview guide helps the practitioner gain critical information about the nature, urgency, and context of a suicidal crisis and the current level of immediate risk. A one-page QPRT Suicide Risk Management Inventory (see Figure 3–3, page 88) is used by the practitioner to document the interview. The data gathered from the QPRT flow into a decision tree and invite the suicidal person and the person's family to develop and implement a crisis management plan. The goal of this plan is to reduce the risk of a suicide attempt or completion.

In the "Q" (question) portion of the QRPT interview, the practitioner begins by asking the client about any suicidal tendencies. Sample questions that will detect the presence of suicidal thoughts or feelings are provided. One such question is Suicidal thoughts are a common symptom of depression; have you had those thoughts lately? In the event the client says no, the QPRT provides a carefully worded statement that may be an important protection against a claim of malpractice. If the practitioner gets an affirmative answer to the question about suicide, the QPRT guides the client through critical questions to ask about current dynamics, contributing factors in the crisis, and present risk status. Questions include What is wrong? Why now? With what? Where and when? When and with what in the past? Who is involved? and Why not now? Additional questions and specific instructions for using the inventory are included in a staff user manual.

The "P" (persuade) portion of the interview, persuading the person to accept help, follows. The goal is to form a therapeutic alliance and confirm that the client is willing to accept help and find life-affirming solutions. The "R" (referral) and "T" (treat) portions of the interview include a "no suicide" agreement and the patient's agreement to a safety or risk-management plan. Guidelines for periodic monitoring are provided along with information on malpractice documentation and limitations.

GBH's Suicide Risk Reduction Program improves quality of care by

- requiring routine suicide risk detection questioning at intake;
- requiring standardized, comprehensive assessment of suicide risk, if present;
- requiring monitoring and reassessment of suicide risk at treatment transitions, periods of high stress, and other times associated with increased suicide attempts and completions;
- establishing a consumer-shared safety plan as part of the treatment alliance and plan;
- matching level of care to level of assessed risk;
- improving the skill and knowledge of clinical providers; and
- educating consumers, families, and concerned others about how they can respond in a helpful fashion when someone they care about is suicidal.

**Figure 3–3:** *QPRT—Suicide Risk Management Inventory*

Patient Name _____ Case Number _____ Date _____

Questioned the patient about thoughts of death or suicide: Yes_____ No_____

Suicidal thoughts/feelings present: Yes _____ No_____ If no, review and initial statement on following page.

If YES, document:
What is wrong?

Why now?

With what?

Where and when?

When and with what in the past?

Who is involved?

Why not now?

**Persuaded patient to accept help/treatment**
_____ Risk low, patient commits to safety plan.
_____ Risk moderate, commits to safety & referral plan.

**Patient not persuaded to accept help/treatment**
_____ Risk high, initiate emergency room evaluation/(in)voluntary hospitalization procedure.

**Referral. Patient agrees to remain with current provider and/or**
_____ Accepts a referral to Community Mental Health_____
_____ Accepts a referral to _____

**Risk Management Plan. Patient verbally agrees**
_____ to remain clean and sober until crisis passes.
_____ to follow medical advice, including medication regimen (if prescribed).
_____ to remove (or see to the removal of) the means of suicide.
_____ to not harm or kill self accidentally or on purpose.
_____ to call and talk to office, hotline, mental health provider, or other responsible person in case of crisis.
_____ to accept responsibility for this safety plan.

**Quote patient's statement of agreement to safety**
_____ Patient/family educated about access to (in)voluntary psychiatric hospitalization and community resources.
_____ Patient/family accepts literature on suicide prevention and agrees to return for follow-up.
_____ Appropriate releases signed (if necessary).

*Source:* Greentree Behavioral Health, Spokane, WA. Used with permission.

In short, enhanced quality of care in the areas of prevention, intervention, and postvention greatly reduces the risk of accusations of malpractice.

## Implementation Challenges

GBH's Suicide Risk Reduction Program still has its share of implementation challenges. Initially, some staff members resisted the training program, believing that they "already knew this stuff" and that the program would create more paperwork. Preprogram tests given to clinician participants to test their knowledge of suicide risk factors made the resistant "pop little beads of sweat when they couldn't answer questions reflecting a basic knowledge base about the population they worked with," describes Quinnett. Testing is an important quality improvement component of the program.

Another challenge faced, not at SMH, but potentially at other organizations interested in adopting the program, is organization resistance to raising the standards of practice. Quinnett explains: "If an organization is forthright and says that part of its mission is to reduce mortality and morbidity due to suicide and suicide attempts by consumers of services, then the organization may be taking on a whole new responsibility. Many organizations have no real experience in this arena. In fact, if you travel around the country visiting mental health centers and asking them, 'What are your suicide prevention efforts?' they will answer that they have a hotline. The problem with this approach is that the people most in need of help will not use a hotline—they simply don't self-refer. This approach is not a comprehensive solution to the identification and treatment of people at risk for suicide. If an organization's mission is to reduce morbidity and mortality due to suicide and suicide attempts, then the organization may need to obtain technical assistance to determine how it is going to do this. There are expenses associated with mandatory staff training and most organizations don't have a line item budget for this type of work. However, it's part of the cost of doing business." Quinnett urges behavioral health care leaders to assume a more proactive approach to reducing the risk of suicide in their organizations.

## Program Results

The results of implementation of the Greentree Behavioral Health Suicide Risk Reduction Program at Spokane Mental Health have been significant. One measure of progress is staff knowledge about suicide risk factors, assessment, and management. The staff's competence in this area was evaluated before and after program implementation. The results indicate that QPRT training significantly improves the knowledge base of staff participants. The average number of correct items on the pretest was 16 out of 27; on the post-test, the number of correct items rose to 21 out of 27.

Another measure of progress is staff satisfaction with the training. Training evaluations indicate high staff appreciation for a standardized and effective procedure for suicide risk assessment. Still another measure is the satisfaction of consumers seeking urgent care. Consumers interviewed with the QPRT Suicide Risk Management Survey are being surveyed on an ongoing basis to determine satisfaction with the interview format and final outcomes.

Yet another measure is the quality of the data collected through the QPRT Suicide Risk Management Inventory and whether that data and information have led to better treatment planning. Whereas data were historically collected and documented in a tiny portion of an intake form, a one-page form now facilitates thorough data collection. GBH is studying the effect of this documentation on level-of-care triage decisions.

The program's reach into the community has been broad and deep. More than 7,000 people in the Spokane area have received QPR gatekeeper training to date. "Of course, we're also trying to measure whether the program has helped to reduce our exposure to suicide malpractice, and we won't know about this unless we're sued," says Quinnett. Yet, GBH's attorneys indicate that the program does an excellent job documenting what needs to be documented. "This documentation is critical to having a good defense to a malpractice action. Having the QPRT in place demonstrates that an agency has thought about screening for suicide potential in a systematic manner," writes attorney Barbara Weiner. Attorney Brain Rekofkfe concurs. "The QPRT program provides a concrete, systematic approach to raising the issue of suicide with the patient and documenting the response. Documentation is absolutely essential in the defense of any medical negligence action, but particularly important in the area of suicide. This is because a typical suicide malpractice case presents with the psychiatrist or mental health professional determining that a patient isn't suicidal, only to have a suicide occur shortly thereafter. This factual scenario provides a plaintiff with a tremendous hindsight argument that the assessment of the suicide potential was inaccurate and substandard, as the patient ultimately committed suicide," says Rekofkfe.

Quinnett says, "We believe that our QPRT suicide risk assessment, intervention, and management approach, when integrated into an already high standard of care, provides state-of-the-art risk assessment and management services to our consumers. This program not only reduces malpractice exposure by raising the standard of care for consumer safety but also leads to improved professionalism and morale of those who work with at-risk individuals. By eliminating systemic organizational inadequacies through state-of-the-art education and protective policies, procedures, and protocols, tragedies can be avoided."

In 1998, the Greentree Behavioral Health Suicide Risk Reduction Program received the President's Award for Excellence in Risk Management (The Negley Award) from The Mental Health Risk Retention Group, which was founded by the Mental Health Corporation of America.

# PROGRAM PROFILE

*Outcomes Management*

The Devereux Foundation

## About the Organization

Devereux is the nation's largest independent, nonprofit provider of treatment services for individuals with emotional, behaviorial, and developmental disabilities. Through a staff of approximately 5,000 professionals, Devereux provides services to more than 15,000 individuals on an annual basis. Clients include

- at-risk children with serious emotional disturbances, their families, communities, and schools;
- adolescents with behavior disorders and involvement in the criminal justice system;
- children and adolescents with multiple diagnoses and other emotional and behavioral health complications; and
- adults with mental illness, mental retardation, and/or developmental disabilities.

With headquarters in Villanova, Pennsylvania, Devereux has 14 major treatment centers located in Arizona, California, Connecticut, Florida, Georgia, Maryland, Massachusetts, New Jersey, New York, Pennsylvania, Illinois, Texas, and Washington, D.C. Specialty programs include chemical dependency treatment; intensive residential treatment for children, adolescents, young adults, and adults; and outpatient services providing mental health resources for clients of all ages. Six of the facilities, which provide services to more than 50% of Devereux's clients, are independently accredited by the Joint Commission.

## The Outcomes Management Initiative: Phase 1

Self-assessment through performance measurement and outcomes management are integral to Devereux's operations organizationwide. Approximately five years ago, a multidisciplinary team that included representatives from the treatment centers and corporate headquarters developed a comprehensive list of indicators to be tracked by the centers and the organization as a whole.

Fifteen indicators addressing functional areas such as individual rights and organization ethics, continuum of care, care of the individual/treatment, management of human resources, and so forth were identified. Each indicator is either process or outcome oriented. For example, one indicator for care of the individual measures the use of behavior management techniques and special treatment procedures. Another measures the number of facility-administered medication errors. Indicators for the management of human resources track staff turnover, staff development, and staff injury rates.

The Devereux Quality Indicator Report describes each indicator, the data elements, the calculation method, the sample size, and the population studied. Susan Soldivera Kiesling, national quality improvement coordinator for Devereux, states: "We tried to standardize the indicators so that we could ensure data integrity. Each of the centers had representatives who provided feedback to the team. It was a grassroots effort." Sample pages from the report appear as Figure 3–4, page 93.

To supplement the effort, the team reviewed how the industry defines selected indicators. As data were obtained, the team identified problems in how indicators were being measured. Staff revised, modified, or clarified the indicators and their descriptions to ensure standardized data collection and analysis. The team spent six months developing the indicators, which have been in place for approximately three years. The process of revising and improving them is ongoing.

The Devereux Quality Indicator Report enables the organization to review aggregated data on the performance of the organization as a whole on a quarterly basis. Says Kiesling, "The centers use the indicator reports for internal benchmarking over time." For example, when the data on staff or client injuries at one center are disproportionate to the data from the larger organization, the smaller center has a focus for its improvement initiatives. "Like the instruments on the dashboard of a car," describes Howard A. Savin, PhD, senior vice president of clinical affairs, "the indicator report enables us to look at performance closely and start performance improvement initiatives, wherever needed."

Savin provides an example: Data indicated that injury rates were much higher in a situation where only one staff member was available to apply restraint. "This finding helped us to change our whole approach to restraint use," says Savin. "Through ensuring the application of restraint

**Figure 3–4:** *Devereux Quality Indicator Report*

**Function:**     *Care of the Individual/Treatment*

*Indicator #5:* **The number of facility-administered medication errors.**

Definition of a medication error is any occurrence in which the medication actually reached the individual and should be counted as a medication error. Additionally, documentation errors are those that are detected by a subsequent shift after they are administered. The new definition includes the following: wrong medication, wrong route, wrong dose, dose omitted, wrong time and prescribing concern (such as medications prescribed by a physician that reach the individual that are questioned by other professional staff regarding their appropriateness and are subsequently modified). This excludes self-medication and ambulatory services; however, it is suggested that centers track this where applicable. In addition, medication refusals are not considered errors.

**Calculation:**
*Data elements*
Total # of errors for the quarter

# of medication errors by type for the quarter

# of administered doses for the quarter (pharmacy order [# of pills] less any that had to be destroyed, not # of administered)

Total # of individuals receiving meds during the quarter

*Formula*
Ratio of medication errors:

$$\frac{\text{\# of errors for the quarter}}{\text{Administered doses for the quarter}}$$

**Sample Size:** All errors submitted
**Population:** All programs (excludes self-administered and ambulatory services)

*Indicator #6:* **Use of behavior management techniques/special treatment procedures.**

Special treatment procedures (STPs) include seclusion, mechanical restraint and personal hold (exclusions of escorts). Seclusion should be defined according to individual state requirements for monitoring, such as a locked room or any area from which there is no egress. PRNs will be a separately calculated category that includes only medications administered for behavioral control.

Injuries are defined as level 2 or greater, for example, external medical attention (clinic or hospital remedies) or head, neck, or back injuries.

**Calculation:**
*Data elements*
# of individuals receiving STPs
# seclusions per policy definition for the quarter
# mechanical restraints for the quarter
# personal holds (excluding escorts) for the quarter
Average Daily Census for the quarter
# of client injuries secondary to STP for the quarter
# of staff injuries secondary to STP for the quarter

*Source:* The Devereux Foundation, Villanova, PA. Used with permission.

*(continued on next page)*

**Figure 3–4:** *Devereux Quality Indicator Report (continued)*

*Formulas*

Ratio of STP occurrence:

$$\frac{\text{\# of seclusions + \# mechanical restraints + \# personal holds}}{\text{Average Daily Census for the quarter}}$$

% of individuals receiving STPs:

$$\frac{\text{\# of individuals receiving STPs}}{\text{Average Daily Census for the quarter}}$$

% of client injuries secondary to STP:

$$\frac{\text{\# of client injuries related to STP}}{\text{(Total number of STP occurrences - seclusions)}}$$

% of staff injuries secondary to STP:

$$\frac{\text{\# of staff injuries related to STP}}{\text{(Total number of STP occurrences - seclusions)}}$$

**Sample Size:** All occurrences
**Population:** All programs

---

only when multiple staff members were available, we were able to reduce rates of restraint-related injury to below benchmark levels." Centers have used the data to support positive programming, thereby reducing required restraint use. Kiesling explains, "Using the indicator data, we are able to measure the effectiveness of programs or initiatives on reducing restraint use."

A description of other performance improvement initiatives spawned by the Quality Indicator Report and Devereux's approach to outcomes management follows.

## Data-Driven Performance Improvement Initiatives

### Reducing Behavioral PRNs

In analyzing data on special treatment procedures, the treatment team in Devereux's Florida facility observed that the use of PRN medications to control behavior in the facility had been drifting upwards. The facility treats 42 developmentally disabled residents and severely emotionally and behaviorally disturbed children with mental health diagnoses in two locked units. Two years ago, that facility's staff implemented a performance improvement initiative aimed at reducing the use of "behavioral PRNs" to as close to zero as possible.

The facility houses extremely aggressive, self-injurious, and disruptive children who are frequently dangerous to themselves, others, and property. "Aggressive behavior frequently escalated, triggering a crisis prevention approach to controlling the behavior," describes Savin. Restraint and seclusion procedures were used frequently as were PRNs. "In general, preventing PRNs, where possible, is a good thing," mentions Savin. Many consider behavioral PRNs chemical restraint that is equally or more restrictive than mechanical restraint. As restraint use increases, so does the risk of sentinel events.

A team of behavior analysts and psychologists at the facility developed a strong behavior management system in which high frequency reinforcement is used to eliminate the need for chemical interventions. Through program redesign, the team established an enriched environment focused on reducing challenging behaviors and teaching socially appropriate replacement behaviors. "Through positive programming, the staff was able to redirect behavior and keep maladaptive behavior from occurring in the first place," describes Savin.

Donna N. Strickland, MS, CBA, Andy Vega, BS, CBA, and Frank Carrera III, MD, the principal architects of the initiative, describe the effort: Point systems were revised. Clients would start with zero points and earn points through the absence of inappropriate behaviors and display of appropriate alternatives. Staff were trained in "token economy"—in the proper and frequent delivery of social and tangible reinforcers and in identification of appropriate choices for the children. Behavioral consequences were designed to be shorter to maximize the child's opportunities to engage in correct responses and increase opportunity for reinforcement. Replacement behaviors taught on the units to help control acute behavior included progressive relaxation (where the child learns to request time alone), planned ignoring (where the child is reinforced for ignoring inappropriate behaviors of peers), engaging in appropriate social skills (which is reinforced throughout settings and situations), and verbal and nonverbal communication to express wants and needs. Following implementation of the behavioral management system, children spent significantly more time in programs and planned activities.

Concurrently, a check and balance procedure for the approval of behavioral PRNs was developed and implemented. A variety of interventions had to have been tried and have failed, and a series of supervisors had to have been contacted before PRNs could be used.

The results were impressive. The use of restraint and seclusion was reduced significantly as was the use of behavioral PRNs. PRN use declined quickly from an average of 40 to 60 per month in one unit to near zero three months later (see Figure 3–5, below). Both units have maintained low to no PRN use rates since April 1997.

### Pre-employment Screening

Analysis of the Devereux Quality Indicator Report also provided impetus to a major new human resources initiative—pre-employment screening. Data on turnover rates for frontline staff, staff and client injuries during the use of restraint, and allegations of abuse between staff and clients triggered the organization to explore methods to more scientifically screen out undesirable applicants during the application and interview process.

"To ensure that such individuals don't get hired in the first place," describes Savin, "we researched and reviewed pre-employment screening instruments and selected one used

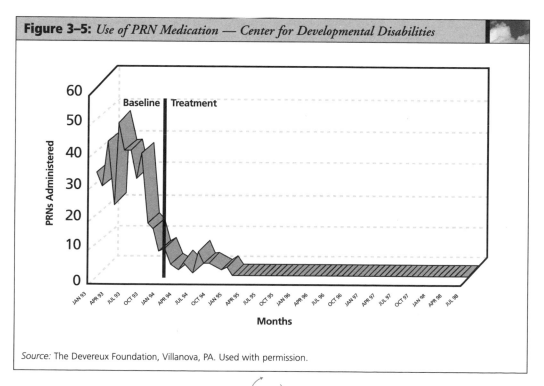

**Figure 3–5:** *Use of PRN Medication — Center for Developmental Disabilities*

*Source:* The Devereux Foundation, Villanova, PA. Used with permission.

by numerous Fortune 500 companies." Called the Employee Reliability Inventory (ERI®) System and developed by a psychologist at Harvard University, the instrument assesses a number of productive job behaviors, including freedom from disruptive alcohol and substance use, courteous job performance, emotional maturity, conscientiousness, trustworthiness, long-term job commitment, and safe job performance. "There's an excellent rate of prediction with these characteristics," mentions Savin.

The screening test is administered to applicants directly on-line or in a paper-and-pencil format. Scoring is instantaneous, thereby enabling the individual who is interviewing the applicant to use the results during the interview for assistance in making an accept or reject decision.

Devereux is pilot-testing the tool in a cross section of both mental health and mental retardation/developmental disabilities treatment centers in early 1999. A cohort of applicants screened with the tool will be compared to a sample of applicants hired but not screened. "We will be looking at indicators such as turnover rates, use of sick days, initiation of workers compensation claims, and voluntary versus involuntary discharge. Within 120 days, we'll have a good sense for whether or not the tool is effectively screening applicants. If it is, we'll start using the tool in all of our facilities nationwide," says Savin. With more than 4,000 full-time employees, Devereux views pre-employment screening as a vital tool for performance improvement and error or adverse event reduction.

### Reducing Suicidality

During the past two years, the staff of Devereux's Institute of Clinical Training and Research and the Devereux Suicide Prevention and Intervention Best Practices work group have been studying Devereux's organizational capacity to reduce suicidality among its clients. "Even one suicide is too many," cites Savin, the Institute's director.

Following an extensive review of the literature on the state of professional knowledge concerning risk factors, assessment, and intervention in youth suicide, the work group developed a set of practice guidelines to enhance Devereux's capacity to prevent and respond to individual suicide gestures and completions. Kiesling, a member of the work group, describes, "We wanted to generate specific recommendations for how to approach prevention, intervention, and postvention within each of our programs." According to the report generated by the work group, the guidelines are not designed to be all-inclusive prescriptions for developing prevention, intervention, and postvention procedures and strategies. Rather, they are designed to offer key considerations for development of such procedures and strategies.

Suggested systemwide practice guidelines address five major topics: a crisis response plan, assessment, intervention, documentation, and staff training. The crisis response plan guidelines, for example, suggest developing a plan that clearly defines roles, responsibilities, and responses to be implemented in the event of a completed suicide or life-threatening suicide attempt. A sample outline for the plan appears as Figure 3–6, page 97. The staff training guidelines suggest annual in-service training programs for all staff.

The work group is now developing a curriculum to support implementation of the guidelines at all Devereux facilities. The curriculum will be competency based according to the level of care provided by staff members. For example, an administrator's training would be different than the training provided to direct care staff. However, all staff will receive core training in suicidality. The work group is reviewing existing curricula for application to Devereux environments. Staff training is due to start in early 1999.

"We are taking great pains to ensure that our suicide prevention, intervention, and postvention programs are implemented properly," mentions Savin. "This initiative will be implemented organizationwide and everyone must 'get it.'"

### Reducing Staff and Client Injuries

Analysis of data across all Devereux's programs indicated a relationship between the method used for crisis intervention and the levels of injuries sustained by both clients and staff members. Further, Devereux centers that had fully implemented the Devereux Crisis Prevention/Intervention (CPI) program demonstrated the lowest levels of both staff and client injuries (see Figure 3–7, page 98).

**Figure 3–6:** *Sample Crisis Response Plan*

Immediate responsibilities of person(s) who finds the attempter
- check, call, care (follow first aid training)
- secure the area
- notify the crisis response team

Crisis response team responsibilities
- ensuring safety of clients
  - identification of clients at increased risk
  - prevention of contagion
  - assessment of program stability and needs
  - attending to needs of attempter
- communications (family, staff, clients, media, community)
- support of staff, family of the attempter/completer, other clients and their families
- reporting requirements
  - mortality committee
  - sentinel event report: central administration and regional administration
  - police
  - client's agency
- Provision of opportunities for closure and of ongoing support

Back-up plan (alternate crisis response team members)

*Source:* The Devereux Foundation, Villanova, PA. Used with permission.

The Devereux CPI program, developed in the mid-1990s, is being implemented in many, but not all, of Devereux's treatment centers. This fact reflects Devereux's current policy of allowing treatment center directors to select their own crisis prevention and intervention curricula and the existence of state laws in a small number of states, including New York, which mandate use of an approved, state-selected curriculum.

Because of the numerous CPI curricula in use and the data providing evidence of differing levels of injuries based on CPI curricula, in mid-1998, Devereux established a physical interventions task force to
- ascertain the best practices for crisis prevention and intervention for each age and disability group served by the organization; and
- make recommendations for the use of this method(s) across all centers, thereby decreasing the risk to clients and employees associated with implementation of both preventive and intervention techniques.

Helene Boinski-Bartlett, Devereux's southern/western operating group QI coordinator, chairs the task force which includes representatives from the corporate legal, human resources, clinical affairs, and training staff.

The task force is reviewing the current Devereux CPI program with an external CPI expert. It also is reviewing the statutes of the states in which Devereux operates to ensure the organization's compliance with requirements for each age group and population served. Based on a review of the research literature, the task force is determining current best practices across all age and disability categories and assessing whether the Devereux CPI program is congruent with best practices and state and federal statutes. The task force is recommending changes to the Devereux CPI program, as necessary, and recommending adoption of the best practices for each age and disability group. Finally, the task force is developing the rollout of CPI training.

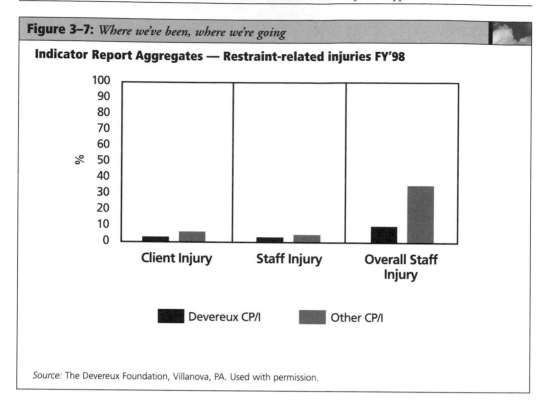

**Figure 3–7:** *Where we've been, where we're going*

Indicator Report Aggregates — Restraint-related injuries FY'98

Source: The Devereux Foundation, Villanova, PA. Used with permission.

Kiesling says, "Our expectation is that a further-improved curriculum will have a positive impact on reducing restraint use and restraint-related injuries." "We're using the indicator report to zero in on injuries and to study the occurrence of that type of risk event. Armed with the data, we're able to develop some ideas about causation and set in motion processes to reduce or eliminate future risk events," describes Savin.

## The Outcomes Management Initiative: Phase 2

In mid-1998, Devereux identified and began to address the need for clinical outcomes information to be used not only for internal and external benchmarking but also for the marketing of Devereux's programs and services. Tom Shurer, a member of the information resources staff, describes the need: "Our indicator report lets us look at aggregated data, but we are not able to break such data down by program, service, or client type. We also are limited by the amount of technology and expertise available at the center level for collection of data. In addition, although looking at process indicators is helpful, we want to introduce some true clinical measures that would let us benchmark and respond to payer performance contract requirements."

As a first step, the Institute of Clinical Training and Research organized and hosted a national outcomes conference for Devereux staff nationwide. During the conference, a team from the University of Southern Florida presented a logic model which suggests to organizations trying to initiate an outcomes process that they look at the services they provide and the individuals they serve to identify those clinical indicators most meaningful to their constituencies and use such indicators to drive what's measured.

Center staff participated in an exercise aimed at identifying the outcomes that would indicate high-quality performance by their program. Outcomes, including such measures as decreased maladaptive behavior, positive family involvement, increased communication, and a safe environment, were compared across Devereux's four affinity groups (children and adolescents with emotional/behavioral disorders, adults with mental retardation/developmental disabilities, and so forth).[8] A data collection tool based on these measures was evaluated for its ability to collect detailed client- and center-based data that could be disaggregated by diagnosis, presenting problems, and so forth.

Following the conference, Devereux established a national outcomes initiative to "strengthen outcomes-based management as a corporate value and position Devereux to capture and organize clinical outcomes information." This database-driven initiative will provide a data collection instrument that standardizes Devereux's discharge follow-up process and can be used by all centers. It also will provide simple tools to aid in the analysis of the outcomes data required to support internal and external demands, including outcomes-related performance contract requirements, the Joint Commission's ORYX initiative, and potential National Committee for Quality Assurance (NCQA) requirements. Writes Savin in an internal memo outlining the initiative's objectives, "Tightly integrated with the existing quality improvement process, this initiative will help Devereux identify and standardize our best practices, which, when marketed appropriately to our payers and the behavioral health care community, will enhance our leadership position."

# PROGRAM PROFILE

## *Reducing Restraint Use Through Systems Redesign*

### Foundations Behavioral Health

## About the Organization

Foundations Behavioral Health ("Foundations") is a freestanding nonprofit psychiatric hospital providing inpatient, residential, partial hospitalization, in-home, community-based "wrap-around," and outpatient behavioral health care services to adolescents, ages 12 through 18. Located in Doylestown, Pennsylvania, which is the seat of Bucks County and has a population approaching 600,000, Foundations draws its client base from both the county and Philadelphia, which is located approximately 15 miles to the south. With 150 employees, five privileged psychiatrists, and one privileged internist, Foundations is licensed to serve 70 clients and averages 30 admissions per month. The average length of stay for its 50 inpatient beds is four to five months and 12 to 15 months for its 20 residential beds.

Treatment is provided in seven cottages offering a homelike environment for troubled teenagers who need a structured, supervised program. Each cottage is home for ten to twelve adolescents who progress through different levels of care and treatment based on individualized treatment plans. The cottages function as independent households: patients and staff prepare meals and take care of the cottages together.

The goal for each adolescent is to encourage positive behavior, improve social and daily living skills, and help resolve personal and family issues. Programs emphasize individual responsibility; peer involvement; behavioral self-control; and emotional growth through individual psychotherapy, community meetings, and group and family therapy. Education is part of the daily treatment program. Certified teachers teach in on-campus classrooms. Community service and supervised off-ground activities are also integral to the treatment program.

Many of Foundations' patients arrive at the organization after having failed multiple treatment programs offered through the Philadelphia-based Department of Human Services. "They are the tough of the tough kids," describes Joyce Winters, MSN, director of clinical services. "Moreover, our patient population is getting even tougher as federal programs are cut back, and hence, the kids arrive here having received fewer preliminary services."

## Need for the Initiative

In early 1996, Foundations Behavioral Health was a much different place than it is today. The organization was experiencing significant challenges that adversely impacted all functional areas. Perhaps the most visible evidence of its challenges appeared when entering any one of the seven cottages. Winters describes: "It was not uncommon to see a restraint jacket on a child. The jacket had a neck on top and sometimes the jacket, neck, and four-point restraint were all used at the same time. Frequently, an adolescent might be seen sitting in the middle of a group therapy session restrained on a chair."

The use of restraint was common and accepted. Although the organization had a well-written policy and procedure on restraint use, "It was simply on paper. No one knew about it in practice," mentions Winters. The cottages operated independently. Each cottage had a different structure, different programs, and different philosophies. This resulted in a wide variation in the level of care provided. "Going from one cottage to another felt like going from a hospital at one end of town to another," says Winters.

A multidisciplinary performance improvement team, which started to analyze the organization environment in early 1997, cited numerous problems in each functional area, each contributing to the high rates of restraint use. In the area of *leadership*, the team indicated that leaders had not established an organizationwide philosophy on the use of restraint, or a process for education and training regarding restraint and alternatives to restraint. Policies and procedures did not adequately describe protocols for restraint use. Expectations for ongoing measurement of episodes of restraint had not been established. As a result, staff members used their "own techniques." Across the staff and cottages, there were often four or five different ways of dealing with one situation, including restraint procedures. In addition, there was no organizationwide mechanism or process to identify areas requiring performance improvement.

Statistics were maintained, but performance improvement initiatives were not identified or undertaken based on the data and information. Treatment expectations for the type of patients being treated had not been formulated.

In the *assessment* area, the team indicated that patients who had potential for violence or restraint and patients receiving PRN medications were inadequately assessed. In addition, reassessments were not performed frequently enough to facilitate early release of patients from restraint. Reassessments generally were performed every two or four hours, and patients generally were observed every 15 minutes; however, they were observed for safety only rather than based on criteria that would allow their release from restraint. The treatment plan did not adequately address alternative measures to restraint. "Alternatives to control patients were considered, rather than alternatives that would enhance the kids' behavior management learning skills," describes Winters. Finally, tools to facilitate accurate documentation of assessments and reassessments were lacking.

In the area of *human resources*, staff had not been trained in de-escalation techniques and the management of aggression. Hence, their ability to diffuse an explosive situation was limited to nonexistent. "A child's anxiety could be building up over a long period of time, and no interventions would occur until the child reached the peak of his or her episode and was 'taken down' and restrained," says Winters. Staff techniques in the use of restraint were inconsistent with written policies and procedures, and there was no system to evaluate staff competency in the use of restraint. Staff injuries were frequent and turnover was high.

Numerous problems also existed in the area of *rights and ethics*. The staff did not consider restraint use a measure of last resort or a "special procedure" requiring clinical criteria for use. The organization's climate emphasized control of patients; hence, the use of restraint through jackets and leather were well accepted.

In the area of *care of the individual*, again, the treatment philosophy was also focused on controlling the patient. More emphasis was placed on patient compliance than on the teaching of social skills to correct maladaptive skills and behavior. In addition, little emphasis was placed on active treatment, especially achievement of goals and objectives of the treatment plan. Staff communication with patients was frequently confusing for the patient because many staff members communicated simultaneously. At the early sign of a crisis, the crisis button was pushed and the staff members who responded would "take the patient down" without leader direction. Restraint was carried out for the entire duration of the order. After the use of restraint, staff did not perform postvention sessions with the patients to facilitate learning of new skills. The treatment team was not multidisciplinary and did not communicate adequately across shifts.

In the area of *environment of care*, the organization's environment, space, and staff structure were not conducive to efficient teamwork or safety. All but one of the cottages lacked separate rooms for use of restraint or seclusion and designated nurses' stations. Cottages with damaged property were left unrepaired for long periods of time and the cost of repairs was high. In short, Foundations Behavioral Health was in great need of organizationwide change and improvement. Establishment of the roots of that change began in July 1996 when a whole new management team, including a new president and chief financial officer, arrived. Winters joined the staff in November and was given carte blanche, through the support of the management team and medical staff, to determine what needed to be done to improve the organization and to implement the necessary changes.

## *The Restraint Reduction Initiative*

Winters' first step was to establish a multidisciplinary team to tackle a performance improvement initiative aimed at reducing the use of restraint organizationwide. The team, formed in February 1997, included therapists, program directors, nursing staff, and mental health clinicians.

Data on restraint use provided an initial impetus. In January 1997, 111 separate episodes of restraint use occurred organizationwide, reflecting a 40% increase from December 1996.

During a two-week period in February, the team distributed and discussed existing restraint policies and procedures and reviewed every episode of patient restraint and staff or patient injury. After receiving training in interviewing techniques, team members interviewed staff on different shifts and in different cottages about their understanding of the use of restraint, policies and procedures, priorities to reduce restraint, de-escalation techniques, and alternatives to restraint. The team observed episodes of crisis development and any interventions used before to restrain. They analyzed available and needed resources for reducing restraint use and reviewed the documentation, tools, and criteria for authorization of restraint.

The team used the FOCUS-PDCA process (Find-Organize-Clarify-Understand-Select–Plan, Data-Check-Act) to guide the effort and divided the improvement effort into two phases, each using this process. Phase 1 occurred between March and June 1997, phase 2 between June 1997 and June 1998. The goal of the first phase was to reduce restraint episodes by 50% in three months. The second phase's goal was to reduce restraint episodes by another 30% by improving key clinical processes identified in the phase 2 priorities.

### Phase 1

Education provided the starting place. During the first phase, the team provided eight-hour mandatory organizationwide training on the management of aggression and the therapeutic use of restraint. Winters describes: "We took pieces of Milwaukee's Crisis Prevention Institute de-escalation techniques and wove them through a discussion of the culture of the organization. We spent a lot of time talking about current practice and culture, recognizing that our culture, clearly one of control, needed to change."

Staff members were trained to recognize early or dormant stages of anger and anxiety. "If you catch a child in the early stages of anxiety, you can use a variety of positive techniques to reduce that child's anxiety before it escalates. If a staff member misses those early signs because his or her skills are not sharp enough, there may be fewer choices remaining for how to handle the child," explains Winters.

Beginning in March 1997, similar training was provided to all new hires through orientation sessions that communicated the mission, vision, and values of the new management team. Management staff attended a two-day training session on performance improvement to enhance their understanding of the role of process and system management in care delivery. It became clear to the leadership, that the organization needed to improve clinical systems through cross-functional teams with clear measures for improvement.

A site visit by the Philadelphia-based Department of Human Services, with which Foundations has a major contract, confirmed the extent of change needed. "DHS expressed concern about the number of kids in restraints. They told us that the care provided at Foundations should not be custodial in nature and asked us what skills we were teaching our patients."

In the meantime, teams were already hard at work revising and developing organization policy and procedures on the use of restraint, seclusion, and management of patient aggression. Program schedules were revised to allow for at least five hours of active treatment per day. Critical incidents were reviewed with the department heads and staff involved. The team provided weekly graphs of restraint episodes to all units to allow staff to benchmark for the targeted performance improvement objective. "This was threatening for many because problem areas were clear," says Winters. "However, it helped to change behavior. Staff members were able to look at the techniques used by peers and study how peers with low restraint use rates solved problems without the use of restraint."

Debriefing, postvention, sessions were initiated following restraint episodes. Because behaviors causing restraint commonly are shared by other patients in the community, restraint use can serve as a teaching tool. "During postvention sessions, patients brainstormed about how Johnny could have done things differently and avoided the need for restraint," explains Winters. Data were collected on restraint episodes and on cancellation of group sessions and its relationship to episodes of restraint.

The early results were impressive. From March to June 1997, the number of restraint episodes dropped by 36%. All employees had completed training on aggression management, and the new policy and procedure on restraint had been approved by the medical staff, senior management, and the governing board. One cottage had been renovated to include a nurses' station and seclusion room, a therapist was added to each unit, group sessions were canceled less frequently, and postvention debriefing had increased significantly.

**Phase 2**

Rarely can cultures be changed and major organization change be implemented overnight. In June 1997, Foundations experienced a sentinel event when a patient died while in restraint. The findings of the root cause analysis performed following the event further validated the deficiencies of Foundations' systems and processes. Education, training, competence evaluation, assessment, care planning, care provision, and the environment of care each were in need of significant improvement.

Organization resistance provided a challenge. During the early portions of the second phase, the culture of control, compliance, and crisis containment had not yet been replaced by one of collaborative teaching and learning of new approaches and new skills for maladaptive behaviors. Programming helped entrench this culture. "Our goal for the second phase of the improvement initiative was to reduce restraint use by another 30%. However, we realized that we couldn't reduce the use of restraint further unless we improved key clinical processes and changed the treatment program itself," mentions Winters.

The clinical director appointed a cross-functional, interdisciplinary team to address priorities in clinical system improvement. The team included nurses, mental health technicians, managers, human resources staff, physicians, utilization review staff, and admissions staff. Project Renaissance, a complete overhaul of the organization's operations to improve key functions, was launched. Performance improvement priorities for fiscal year 1997-98 were established and approved. They were to

- implement an organization shift to performance improvement;
- improve human resources functions to meet training and competency needs of the clinical staff;
- establish multidisciplinary, cross-functional teams to evaluate and improve key clinical processes;
- evaluate and improve continuum of care functions to meet the needs of the managed care marketplace;
- clarify expectations for organizationwide committee structure/reporting mechanisms; and
- provide a safe environment by continuing to reduce the use of restraint.

A multidisciplinary team reviewed the programs of several hospitals. The team determined that a social learning model had to be integrated into a cognitive behavioral model. "The adolescents lacked social skills to deal with real world issues without getting angry," describes Winters. The team developed a new organizationwide philosophy for treatment. It was based on the premise that, for patients to make significant changes in maladaptive behaviors, they would need to have the knowledge and time to practice the new skills with ongoing feedback about "here and now" behaviors. Treatment programs should be a "microcosm" of the outside world so that maladaptive behaviors played out in the treatment environment can be changed through staff feedback and skills training.

The team continued to review episodes of restraint, observe group sessions and staff skills, and explore reasons why behavioral change in acquiring new skills were not occurring. The medical staff supported the reduction of restraint use throughout the initiative. Discussions with the medical staff provided insight into current concepts of programming and treatment. Staff received little training on key clinical issues or therapeutic programs. The current systems for documenting and communicating patient issues were reviewed. The forms used were not available in all the cottages or consistent from unit to unit. The level system and privileges were control based and not motivating to patients.

Through teamwork, the Foundations staff began to address each and every deficiency. Guidelines for treatment planning meetings were established and enforced. The team revised the then-current behavior modification system to incorporate the cognitive behavioral and social model into programming. The team developed forms, policies, and tools to enhance communication of treatment issues. For example, staff developed a multidisciplinary assessment form and clear routines for each shift with delineated roles and responsibilities for the staff by profession. A 30-day chart was developed to track each patient's behavior (see Figure 3–8, page 108). Staff also developed a new multidisciplinary progress form that was problem oriented and goal oriented (see Figure 3–9, pages 109 through 116, for the multidisciplinary treatment planning tools). Units or cottages were redesigned and reorganized to support and enhance work output. All medical record forms were standardized. Hot files were placed on walls for quick availability of key information.

Ongoing staff training and competence assessment were key factors in the initiative. Winters and her colleagues developed competence standards for registered nurses, mental health technicians, and therapists. To assess staff competence in the new restraint procedures and protocols, Winters developed written and oral tests and had the staff demonstrate competence during actual incidents. She used incident reports as an educational tool, asking staff members how they could have prevented restraint use from occurring in each episode. "We used data from ongoing monitoring and wove the data into competence monitoring. These were real events, so the staff could relate to the data," mentions Winters.

Winters further refined and defined the competence testing for registered nurses. She developed a three-tiered system. The first tier includes all nurses who work with patients. They receive management of aggression training and must be certified as competent through an assessment process. On the second tier are nurses who can take orders for restraint. On the third tier is a small number of nurses who can reorder restraint and extend restraint orders. "We wanted to intensify the approval process for extending restraint orders so that this would happen only in rare instances," says Winters. To identify nurses eligible for category 2 and 3 certification, Winters reviewed staff profiles that included data on the number of patient hours in restraint by nurse. Nurses with no episodes of restraint use were of interest as were those with low numbers of patient restraint hours. "Nurses with low numbers of restraint hours obviously were skilled in taking kids out of restraint within 20 minutes, for example," mentions Winters. "We put an end to kids being in restraint for eight hours. We don't think that a kid should need to be in restraint even for two hours."

If a child was placed in restraint, Winters trained the staff to evaluate, according to solid criteria, whether the individual was ready to come out of restraint. Observations focus not simply on whether the child is safe, but whether the child can be taken out of restraint. With each observation, staff members ask themselves the "COPING" questions:

- Is the individual in Control?
- Are the staff member and child Oriented to the circumstances around restraint use?
- Can the staff member and client identify a Pattern as to why and when the circumstances occurred?
- Having made a connection with the client, can staff Investigate alternatives?
- Will the individual Negotiate or do things differently so that this won't happen again?
- Can the staff member Give control back to the child?

"We're talking about whether there will be a change in the child. Change ultimately is what is going to make a difference in this child's life. The child will not be living in an institution his or her whole life. We have to be able to give control back to that child through teaching him or her alternative skills to those that landed him or her in restraint," says Winters.

## Program Results

Through its restraint reduction performance improvement initiative, Foundations Behavioral Health successfully reduced the use of restraint by 67% over five quarters. Staff reduced the duration of time per restraint episode by using time-limited orders that could be renewed only by registered nurses with special competencies, as well as by providing extensive education on observations to make quicker decisions on early release. Foundations eliminated the use of jackets and implemented protocols on the use of restraint and seclusion to encompass more stringent orders and guidelines.

Foundations' improvement efforts extended far beyond reducing the use of restraint. The efforts were systems based, changing every functional operation in the organization. In the area of *patient education*, the staff developed and implemented a teaching-learning model that enables patients to learn new skills in social and interpersonal arenas. In the area of *assessment*, all patients are now assessed for potential violence and reassessed throughout their stay. In the *human resources* area, performance improvement and aggression management training and competence assessment help ensure continued organization improvement and reduced need for restraint use. In the area of *leadership*, the leaders established organizationwide performance improvement processes, treatment objectives, and policies and procedures for education and training, restraint use, and performance measurement. Figure 3–10, pages 117 through 127, provides the organization's resultant restraints policy and procedure and monitoring tools. Staff orientation and education about policies and procedures on *rights and ethics* improved significantly. *Care of patient* processes underwent significant change and improvement. Treatment through interdisciplinary teams is now consistent across all of the cottages and focuses on the teaching of social skills to correct maladaptive behavior. In the area of the *environment of care*, cottages were modified to provide a safe and treatment-oriented space. In the area of *information management*, data were collected and analyzed to facilitate the provision of quality care.

Winters concludes, "Every policy and procedure existent in early 1996 was revised and rewritten." Can Foundations Behavioral Health relax a bit? "Never," says Winters, "We cannot afford to say that any system or process is 'done.' We must continue to oversee the processes on a daily basis and revise them as necessary over time."

**Figure 3–8:** *Behavior Chart*

Unit: _____

Patient Name: _____

| Month: | Date | 1 | 2 | 3 | 4 | 5 | 6 | 7 | 8 | 9 | 10 | 11 | 12 | 13 | 14 | 15 | 16 | 17 | 18 | 19 | 20 | 21 | 22 | 23 | 24 | 25 | 26 | 27 | 28 | 29 | 30 | 31 |
|---|---|---|---|---|---|---|---|---|---|---|---|---|---|---|---|---|---|---|---|---|---|---|---|---|---|---|---|---|---|---|---|---|
| | Level 4 | | | | | | | | | | | | | | | | | | | | | | | | | | | | | | | |
| | Level 3 | | | | | | | | | | | | | | | | | | | | | | | | | | | | | | | |
| | Level 2 | | | | | | | | | | | | | | | | | | | | | | | | | | | | | | | |
| | Level 1 | | | | | | | | | | | | | | | | | | | | | | | | | | | | | | | |
| | On Deck | | | | | | | | | | | | | | | | | | | | | | | | | | | | | | | |
| .7-3 | Restraint | | | | | | | | | | | | | | | | | | | | | | | | | | | | | | | |
| | Seclusion | | | | | | | | | | | | | | | | | | | | | | | | | | | | | | | |
| | Time Out | | | | | | | | | | | | | | | | | | | | | | | | | | | | | | | |
| | Physical Hold | | | | | | | | | | | | | | | | | | | | | | | | | | | | | | | |
| 3-11 | Restraint | | | | | | | | | | | | | | | | | | | | | | | | | | | | | | | |
| | Seclusion | | | | | | | | | | | | | | | | | | | | | | | | | | | | | | | |
| | Time Out | | | | | | | | | | | | | | | | | | | | | | | | | | | | | | | |
| | Physical Hold | | | | | | | | | | | | | | | | | | | | | | | | | | | | | | | |
| 11-7 | Restraint | | | | | | | | | | | | | | | | | | | | | | | | | | | | | | | |
| | Seclusion | | | | | | | | | | | | | | | | | | | | | | | | | | | | | | | |
| | Time Out | | | | | | | | | | | | | | | | | | | | | | | | | | | | | | | |
| | Physical Hold | | | | | | | | | | | | | | | | | | | | | | | | | | | | | | | |
| | Total for Day | | | | | | | | | | | | | | | | | | | | | | | | | | | | | | | |
| | Restraint | | | | | | | | | | | | | | | | | | | | | | | | | | | | | | | |
| | Seclusion | | | | | | | | | | | | | | | | | | | | | | | | | | | | | | | |
| | Time Out | | | | | | | | | | | | | | | | | | | | | | | | | | | | | | | |
| | Physical Hold | | | | | | | | | | | | | | | | | | | | | | | | | | | | | | | |
| | Staff Initial | | | | | | | | | | | | | | | | | | | | | | | | | | | | | | | |
| Staff Signature | | | | | | | | | | | | | | | | | | | | | | | | | | | | | | | | |
| | | | | | | | | | | | | | | | | | | | | | | | | | | | | | | | | |
| | | | | | | | | | | | | | | | | | | | | | | | | | | | | | | | | |
| Inpatient Treatment | | | | | | | | | | | | | | | | | | | | | | | | | | | | | | | | |

*Source:* Foundations Behavioral Health, Doylestown, PA. Used with permission.

**Figure 3–9:** *Foundations Behavioral Health – Forms*

**Multidisciplinary Treatment Plan**

*ISP / Discharge Plan*

Date plan prepared: _____ Unit: _____

Admission Date: _____ Birthdate: _____ Current Age: _____

❑ Voluntary    ❑ Involuntary Commitment    Status #: _____

Treatment Custody: _____ Placement Custody: _____

### Psychiatric Diagnosis

| | Code | Complete Diagnosis |
|---|---|---|
| AXIS I | | |
| AXIS II | | |
| AXIS III | | |
| AXIS IV | | |
| AXIS V | | Current GAF = |

Physician's Certificate of Need: *Justification for this level of care.*

_____

_____

_____

_____

Criteria for Discharge:

_____

_____

_____

_____

Anticipated Length of Stay:

_____

_____

_____

_____

*Source:* Foundations Behavioral Health, Doylestown, PA. Used with permission.

*(continued on next page)*

**Figure 3–9:** *Foundations Behavioral Health – Forms (continued)*

## Master Problem List

Problem numbers do NOT change over the course of treatment. When the problem is resolved, this is indicated below and in a Progress Note. NEW problems addressed are assigned NEW numbers.

| # | Problem List | A,B,C,D Code | Date Added | Date Resolved |
|---|---|---|---|---|
| 1 | | | | |
| 2 | | | | |
| 3 | | | | |
| 4 | | | | |
| 5 | | | | |
| 6 | | | | |
| 7 | | | | |
| 8 | | | | |
| 9 | | | | |
| 10 | | | | |
| 11 | | | | |
| 12 | | | | |
| 13 | | | | |
| 14 | | | | |
| 15 | | | | |
| 16 | | | | |
| 17 | | | | |
| 18 | | | | |
| 19 | | | | |
| 20 | | | | |
| 21 | | | | |
| 22 | | | | |
| 23 | | | | |

Code: A=Active
B=Deferred for further attention
C=Referred by another provider
D=Resolved

*(continued on next page)*

**Figure 3–9:** *Foundations Behavioral Health – Forms (continued)*

## Multidisciplinary Treatment Plan

Name: _____

Med Rec#: _____

A.   Problem #: Medical/Nursing _____

A1. _____   Goal: _____

A2. _____   Goal: _____

A3. _____   Goal: _____

As manifested by:

A1. _____

A2. _____

A3. _____

| Objective | Date Ident. | Interventions | Discip. | Target Date | Resolved Date |
|-----------|-------------|---------------|---------|-------------|---------------|
| A1 |  |  |  |  |  |
| A2 |  |  |  |  |  |
| A3 |  |  |  |  |  |

(continued on next page)

**Figure 3–9:** *Foundations Behavioral Health – Forms (continued)*

**Multidisciplinary Treatment Plan**

Name: _____
Med Rec#: _____

B.  Problem #: Psychiatric _____

B1. _____ Goal: _____
B2. _____ Goal: _____
B3. _____ Goal: _____

As manifested by:

B1. _____
B2. _____
B3. _____

| | Objective | Date Ident. | Interventions | Discip. | Target Date | Resolved Date |
|---|---|---|---|---|---|---|
| B1 | | | | | | |
| B2 | | | | | | |
| B3 | | | | | | |

*(continued on next page)*

**Figure 3–9:** *Foundations Behavioral Health – Forms (continued)*

**Multidisciplinary Treatment Plan**

Name: _____
Med Rec#: _____

C. Problem #: Functional/Social Interpersonal

C1. _____ Goal: _____
C2. _____ Goal: _____
C3. _____ Goal: _____

As manifested by:

C1. _____
C2. _____
C3. _____

| Objective | Date Ident. | Interventions | Discip. | Target Date | Resolved Date |
|-----------|-------------|---------------|---------|-------------|---------------|
| C1 | | | | | |
| C2 | | | | | |
| C3 | | | | | |

(continued on next page)

**Figure 3-9:** *Foundations Behavioral Health – Forms (continued)*

## Multidisciplinary Treatment Plan

Name: _____

Med Rec#: _____

D.  Problem #: ☐ Academics  ☐ Others

D1. _____    Goal: _____

D2. _____    Goal: _____

D3. _____    Goal: _____

As manifested by:

D1. _____

D2. _____

D3. _____

| Objective | Date Ident. | Interventions | Discip. | Target Date | Resolved Date |
|-----------|-------------|---------------|---------|-------------|---------------|
| D1 | | | | | |
| D2 | | | | | |
| D3 | | | | | |

*(continued on next page)*

**Figure 3–9:** *Foundations Behavioral Health – Forms (continued)*

**Multidisciplinary Treatment Plan**

Name: _____

Med Rec#: _____

*Discharge Planning*

Summary of Strengths In:

A. Community:_____

_____

_____

_____

_____

B. Home:_____

_____

_____

_____

_____

C. School: _____

_____

_____

_____

_____

*Discharge Plan*

I.  ❑ Home        Name: _____        Relationship:_____

              _____                    _____

II. ❑ Residential          _____FBH              _____Non-FBH
    ❑ Group Home: _____
    ❑ Therapeutic Foster Home: _____

III. ❑ Partial             _____FBH              _____Non-FBH
     ❑ Wrap Around         _____FBH              _____Non-FBH
     ❑ Outpatient: _____
     ❑ Others: _____

IV. ❑ Support Groups: _____
    ❑ Case Management: _____
    ❑ Financial Management: _____
    ❑ Vocational Services: _____
    ❑ Education: _____

*(continued on next page)*

**Figure 3–9:** *Foundations Behavioral Health – Forms (continued)*

**Multidisciplinary Treatment Plan (MTP)**
Patient/Resident Name:
Medical Record Number:

| *MTP Signatures* |
| --- |

Psychiatrist                                        Therapist

Registered Nurse                              Patient/Resident

Parent/Guardian                              Parent/Guardian

Patient's/Resident's Comments:

If patient/resident is a minor under 14 or has been adjudicated legally incompetent, the parent or guardian must sign this MTP.

Parent/Guardian                              Date

If a parent or guardian's signature is required and the parent or guardian is unable to be present at the MTP Session,
a verbal approval of this MTP may be obtained by phone with two witnesses.

Verbal approval of this MTP was given by

Parent or Guardian                              Date

Witness                              Date                    Witness                              Date

**Figure 3–10:** *Foundations Behavioral Health Nursing Department Policy and Procedure—Restraint*

| Foundations Behavioral Health | | | | | | Page 1 of 7 | |
|---|---|---|---|---|---|---|---|
| Department: Nursing | | | | | | Policy Number | NSG- |
| Also applies to the following Policies and Procedures: | | | | | | Effective Date: | |
| IP | RES | PH | OP | Wrap | | Revised and/or Reviewed | |
| | | | | | | | |
| References: *CAMBHC* | | | | | | | |
| | | | | | | | |

### Definitions

**Restraint:** Any method of applying *involuntary* restriction on a patient's bodily movement or access to his or her body areas.

### Policy

The uses of mechanical restraint and seclusion are limited to psychiatric crisis/emergencies when other treatment interventions have clearly failed to address the patient's presenting clinical needs, and the patient presents a danger to self and/or others and is a significant danger and disruption to the milieu.

### Purpose and Use

Restraint is a high-risk procedure that is intended to be used only when less restrictive methods have not succeeded or clearly are not likely to succeed in preventing injury to a patient or others. Any application of restraint must involve consideration of the degree and likelihood of the harm that may be *prevented* by the restraint compared to the degree and likelihood of the harm that may be *produced* by the restraint. Restraint is to be applied for no longer than it is clearly needed, and any doubts about the need for restraint should be resolved in favor of using an alternative to restraint.

### Restraint Reduction Program

Reducing the frequency of restraint use in this organization is a high priority. All appropriate staff members will receive a review of the available means of avoiding restraint use as part of their initial orientation and annual in-service training. Statistics regarding the frequency of restraint use and correlations between frequency and other variables will be collected and assessed at least monthly. And the information obtained from statistical reviews will be used to determine what measures are likely to be effective in reducing restraint use.

### Undesirable Effects on Restraint

Restraint has been demonstrated to produce serious negative physical, psychological, and social effects, including skin lesions, overheating and dehydration, temporary or permanent incontinence, feelings of demoralization and humiliation, and temporary or permanent disruption of adult identity. In evaluating the applicability of restraint to any clinical situation, the patient's susceptibility to these effects must be taken into account. And when a patient is restrained, periodic observation of the patient's condition should include consideration of whether any of these undesirable effects is developing.

*Source:* Foundations Behavioral Health. Used with permission.

*(continued on next page)*

**Figure 3–10:** *Foundations Behavioral Health Nursing Department Policy and Procedure—Restraint (continued)*

### Alternatives

The policy of this organization is to reduce the frequency of restraint use to the greatest extent possible. Before every application of restraint, consideration must be given to the possibility of using an alternative method that is less dangerous and less restrictive than restraint. Alternatives include the following:

a) Using PRN medications at early signs of anxiety.

b) Being consistent in the enforcement of the behavior management principles.

c) Using time-out.

d) Encouraging patients to focus on their "target behaviors" and the goals and means of acquiring the knowledge and skills to practice control over anger and violence as it relates to the social model.

e) Collaborating with patient and participating in processing restraint episodes to learn alternative behaviors.

f) Paying increased attention to orienting new patients.

g) Educating patients who are at risk for restraint regarding behavior that might trigger restraint use, available restraint alternatives to use if the patient is in difficulty, and behavior that might lead to release from restraint if restraint becomes necessary.

h) Unobtrusively identifying patients who are at high risk for restraint so that nursing staff can increase observation and preventive efforts.

i) Carefully observing patient groups in psychiatric units to detect early stages of aggression and intervening before the aggression leads to physical conflict.

j) Increasing emphasis on patient-staff interaction, such as encouraging staff to do paper work in areas in which they can observe and interact with patients.

### Staff Training

Only staff who are trained in applying restraint, monitoring restrained patients, and releasing patients from restraint will be involved in restraint-related activities. Training for these roles will be provided to all nursing staff members as part of their initial orientation and annual in-service training. At least 50% of each training session will be devoted to the practical application of principles and the use of various restraint devices to minimize danger to patients and staff. Staff who attend such training sessions will be required to complete a brief pencil-and-paper test to demonstrate that they understand the principles presented. Ongoing competency evaluations will be made by random observations, through the analysis of monthly statistics on risk management and interviews with patients who have been restrained. Staff members are not to participate in the application, monitoring or removal of restraint until they demonstrate competence in related decisions and tasks. Staff will be required to periodically demonstrate competence through testing at the completion of orientation and in-service training. Individual staff members may also be asked to take additional training or undergo testing if observations by supervisors or the occurrence of work-related incidents with patients suggest a need to do so.

### Protection of Patient's Rights, Dignity, and Well-being

Because restraint use presents a danger to a patient's rights, dignity, and well-being, specific efforts must be taken to protect these values. Patient rights must be protected by obtaining the consent of a patient or guardian before implementing restraint procedures whenever possible. Restraint must be applied humanely and as briefly as possible, and staff must keep in mind the danger restraint presents to a patient's self-esteem, feelings of independence, and pride. Staff must also exercise special care to avoid the negative physical and psychological effects of restraint and must meet all of a patient's essential needs during a restraint episode, including food, liquids, access to the toilet, exercise, and protection of skin.

*(continued on next page)*

**Figure 3–10:** *Foundations Behavioral Health Nursing Department Policy and Procedure—Restraint (continued)*

### Assessment of Patient's at Risk for Restraint

Low risk: if a patient can communicate, listen, problem solve and follow simple instructions. High risk: if a patient is not able to listen or communicate, has increased motor agitation, history of violent episodes, translates aggression in behavior, and has lost rationality.

Indications that patients are at risk for restraint:
a) Agitation with clinical indications of acting out behavior.
b) Escalating behaviors not responding to verbal interventions, including threatening verbal statements, aimless and wandering, confusion and disorientation, pacing, striking out at objects, clenched fists.
c) Challenging and testing behaviors.
d) Any behaviors indicative of hurting self or others.
e) Poor social, functional, and interpersonal skills.

Items to ask about at time of admission:
1. Has the patient had a history of anger and loss control?
2. What are the patient's thoughts about being angry and getting physically violent?
3. What does the patient do with angry feelings?
4. What was the greatest level of anger ever experienced by the patient, and what did the patient do as a result?
5. What made the anger go away?

Items to ask about if the patient has a history of aggressive behavior:
1. History of confusion.
2. Drug and alcohol consumption.
3. History of brain damage.
4. Past history of being restrained during psychiatric hospitalizations.

### Types of Restraint

a) Team control—The patient is restrained by having two staff members secure the patient's extremities so the patient cannot move. This type of restraint is team control.
b) Therapeutic hold—When a patient is extremely out of control and the "team control" technique is not an adequate amount of control, the patient can be gently and safely taken down to the floor.
c) Mechanical restraint is defined as the use of leather cuffs applied to fists and ankles and used in conjunction with straps to a bed to restrict the movement of a patient's extremities.

### Authorization

a) Only physicians who have received training and have been granted the privilege to order restraint can initiate the order.
b) A registered nurse may authorize the use of restraint in an emergency for "1 hour" to obtain a physician's order. The order has to be written by a qualified RN and has to be confirmed by the physician within one hour, by telephone or person, and countersigned by the physician after he has personally examined the patient, within 24 hours.
c) The physician's orders must
   - be time limited;
   - have a definite start and end time (9:15–11:15);
   - not exceed 2 hours for adolescents (9 to 17 years of age);
   - not exceed 1 hour for children (under 9);
   - be dated, with time and signature;
   - indicate the type of restraint method used;

*(continued on next page)*

**Figure 3–10:** *Foundations Behavioral Health Nursing Department Policy and Procedure—Restraint (continued)*

- state that no known medical contraindications exist;
- state name of the individuals who accepted the order and carried it out.
- present clinical justification (describe the behaviors that indicate that the patient presents a danger to self or others or serious milieu disruption);
- list the less restrictive alternatives that were used and failed;
- state the criteria for discontinuation and early release if indicated;
- state that PRN orders for restraint are not accepted; and
- grant permission to continue the original order at increments of 2 hours up to 8 hours by a licensed RN.

### Definition of Staff Competency

*I. Qualified, licensed RN*

There are RNs who are authorized to take restraint orders. The RNs must complete the eight-hour hospital sponsored training program on management of aggression and pass the examination on use of restraint procedures. The names of qualified staff will be approved by the medical staff and posted on the unit.
   a) The authorization will need to be recertified annually with a review and written test.
   b) The personnel files must contain evidence of such.

*II. Competently trained staff*

Those who are authorized to apply restraint and monitor and release restrained patients, including patient care staff, mental health technicians and therapists who complete the eight-hour hospital sponsored training program and pass the examination on use of restraint procedures.
   - These staff must pass both the written and practical examination on how to apply restraint, release patients from restraint, and monitor restrained patients.
   - Their personnel files must contain evidence of such.
   - They must also be recertified annually.

*III. Licensed, qualified, and authorized staff*

a) RNs who are authorized to reassess restrained patients and continue restraint orders up to eight hours.
b) These staff must
   - have completed eight hours of hospital sponsored training on management of aggression;
   - have completed probationary period;
   - have passed both written and practical examination on how to apply restraint, release from restraint, and monitor restrained patients;
   - demonstrate their competency in concurrent audits of restraint; and
   - demonstrate their competency in random interviews on policy and procedure.

### Care of Patients in Restraint

a) The patient is walked by using the "team transport" techniques used in CPI.
b) All four limbs should be held down until full leather restraint is applied.
c) The hold should be above and below the joints to maximize immobilization of
   - wrist and elbow for hands
   - knee and ankle for legs
   - both shoulders
d) Restrain arms, one up and one down, parallel to legs.
e) Restrain legs parallel with the aid of a short leather band between the legs, especially for females.
f) Leader continues to communicate as limbs are being secured to bed.

*(continued on next page)*

**Figure 3–10:** *Foundations Behavioral Health Nursing Department Policy and Procedure—Restraint (continued)*

g) When all four limbs are secured, the leader will ask the team to release hold on limbs, one at a time, to check freedom of movement.

h) Full leather restraint should be only done in a hospital bed.

i) Clothing may remain on. However, any restricting items such as shoes, socks, eyeglasses, and belts must be removed. If the clothing has pockets, the pockets must be checked and items removed.

j) The patient is to be restrained only in the safe room.

k) When in a crisis and if the restraining was done in a double occupancy room, the patient should be transferred to the seclusion room as soon as possible, or the roommate transferred out.

l) The patient is never to be restrained on just one side.

m) Prevent restraints from constricting circulation or injuring the skin:
1. Check circulation of restrained area <u>every two hours</u>.
2. Remove restraint (one restraint at a time) <u>every two hours</u> and give skin care.
3. Pad areas to which restraint is applied, if necessary.
4. The patient should be offered a urinal/bedpan <u>every two hours</u> or taken to the bathroom <u>every four hours</u>.
5. The patient's rights, dignity, and well-being are protected during the use of restraint.

n) Meals to be offered during meal times. Meals will be fed to the patient, if necessary. Offer fluids to the patient at least every hour.

o) The patient is to be observed every 15 minutes.

p) The patient is to be placed on close observation for the first <u>24 hours</u> after discontinuation of leather restraint.

q) The patient shall be talked to in a manner that is respectful.

r) The restraint must be from a bag that has been cleaned.

s) The patient shall have clean linen.

t) The patient's privacy shall be maintained at all times.

u) The patient's blood pressure should be taken <u>every two hours</u>.

### Assessment

a) The qualified RN must assess the patient every hour for
1. completion of the flow sheet that monitors the major needs of patients;
2. mental status, physical status, and skin integrity;
3. effect of PRN medications on target symptoms;
4. blood pressure (every two hours); and
5. orientation to surroundings.

b) The following parameters are to be considered in making an assessment for discontinuing restraint. The acronym for COPING outlined here is to be used:

C = Control—Client and staff must be under emotional and physical control.

O = Orient—Find out the facts that occurred. Don't be judgmental during this time. Listen to the client's perspective.

P = Pattern—Determine whether a pattern of past behavior is evident.

I = Investigate—Find an alternative to behavior that is inappropriate.

N = Negotiate—Agree to a verbal contract that the client will understand. Make sure that they know what they can do instead of having inappropriate behavior.

G = Give—Give control back to the client. Clients must realize that they have the responsibility to control their own behavior.

c) Criteria to discontinue should be assessed on an ongoing basis no less than every 15 minutes.

d) The decision to release restraint can be made by a "qualified, licensed RN."

*(continued on next page)*

**Figure 3–10:** *Foundations Behavioral Health Nursing Department Policy and Procedure—Restraint (continued)*

### Maintenance of Restraint Devices

A mechanical restraint bag will be kept that contains four leather cuffs and four leather straps and a set of keys for the keylock buckle. A check of the mechanical restraint bag on the unit will occur at the start of every shift to ensure that a complete, clean set of restraint devices is available in each bag. Documentation of the integrity of all sets (bags) will be documented on the mechanical restraint audit form. The form is to be kept on file at the end of month. A supervisor will collect the form. Any missing or soiled restraint devices are to be reported to the supervisor, who will assist in correcting the problem.

Straps are washed as needed if not soiled with body fluids. All leather cuffs and straps that are soiled with blood or body fluids are to be treated as infectious waste and disposed of per infectious waste policy. A supervisor must be notified before any restraint devices are disposed of. Replacement for discarded restraints must be made at time of disposal.

### Documentation

Physician
1) A physician must complete a physician's order (physician's order form).
2) A physician must perform a face-to-face evaluation in 24 hours and write a progress note that
   - justifies restraint, and
   - describes the patient's response
3) If the patient has more than three episodes in a week, the psychiatrist has to be involved in a treatment team meeting to identify ways of reducing episodes.

RN
1) Ensure that the physician's order meets the criteria for restraint use and is complete.
2) Write nurse a note that:
   - Describes the patient's behavior before restraint and levels of intervention attempted;
   - Includes evidence of clinical criteria for the use of restraint;
   - Describes the correct use of procedure for placing the patient in restraint;
   - Every hour, DAP, reflecting need to continue or discontinue restraint;
   - Documents (in a flowsheet) monitoring of the patient and attention to the patient's needs;
   - Summarizes the outcome of "coping" when the patient meets the criteria for release;
   - Summarizes the outcome of "coping" if the patient does not meet the criteria for release and includes clinical justification to continue (in such case the protocols for renewing the order must be followed);
   - Documents the exact time of early release (if early release was done);
   - Has all columns in the restraint log completed; and
   - Documents injuries (whether present or absent).
3) Notify the house supervisor who will complete concurrent audit form.

### Post-restraint Care

Continue to work with the patient on completing and processing events leading up to restraint and plan for the next 24 hours. The patient is to be placed on close observation for 24 hours.

*(continued on next page)*

**Figure 3–10:** *Foundations Behavioral Health Nursing Department Policy and Procedure—Restraint (continued)*

## Audit of Patients In Restraint/Seclusion

MR#: _____    Name of RN Initiating: _____

Date: _____    Name of RN Discontinuing: _____

Reviewer: _____    Total Hours: _____

Length of Stay of Patient: _____

|  | YES | NO |
|---|---|---|
| *Physician's Orders* | | |
| - Restraint Order Sheet Complete. There is clinical justification. | ❏ | ❏ |
| - Timed, dated, signed. | ❏ | ❏ |
| *RN or LPN Documentation* | | |
| - Evidence of lesser restrictive levels of intervention attempted. | ❏ | ❏ |
| - Clinical justification for restraints/seclusion. | ❏ | ❏ |
| - One hour assessment in DAP to justify continuation or discontinuation. | ❏ | ❏ |
| - Flow sheet completed for all elements. | ❏ | ❏ |
| - Flow sheet signed and dated. | ❏ | ❏ |
| - Documentation for criteria for release or early release. | ❏ | ❏ |
| - Effect of PRN on regular medications on <u>target</u> symptoms. | ❏ | ❏ |
| - Documentation that patient's needs were met. | ❏ | ❏ |
| - Documentation if patient has sustained injuries/rug burns, etc. | ❏ | ❏ |
| - If order has been extended for additional time, then: | ❏ | ❏ |
|    - It is at age-specific increments (one hour for children, two hours for adolescents). | ❏ | ❏ |
|    - Approved and ordered by authorized RN. | ❏ | ❏ |
|    - Physician's Order Sheet completed. | ❏ | ❏ |
| - Treatment Plan "Restraint Sheet" is congruent. | ❏ | ❏ |
| - Patient has no injuries. | ❏ | ❏ |
| *Evidence of Techniques Used* | | |
| - Team control | ❏ | ❏ |
| - Team transport | ❏ | ❏ |
| - Therapeutic hold | ❏ | ❏ |

*Conclusions*

System Problems




Training Problems




Performance Problems




*(continued on next page)*

**Figure 3–10:** *Foundations Behavioral Health Nursing Department Policy and Procedure—Restraint (continued)*

## Patient Questionnaire

(To be completed by the Director of Clinical Services)

Within 24 hours after a patient has been secluded or restrained, the therapeutic values of the intervention will be measured.

1. Do you know why you were secluded/restrained?

   *Yes    No*

2. Did being secluded/restrained help you gain control of yourseif?

   *Yes    No*

3. What do you think was the reason you were secluded/restrained?

   _____
   _____
   _____

4. Did you feel safe while you were secluded/restrained?

   *Very Safe    Safe    Somewhat Safe    Not Safe*

5. Were you given a chance to gain control of yourself before you were secluded/restrained ?

   *Yes    No*

   Were you:

   | *Talked to* | *Reasoned With* | *Given Time Out With Staff* | *Given Room Time* | *CPI Team Control* |

6. Were you offered a PRN medication?

   *Yes    No*

7. During the seclusion/restraint process, when were you offered a PRN medication?

   *Before    During    After*

8. Do you know what skills you have to learn to prevent going into seclusion or restraint?
   *List:* _____
   _____
   _____

9. Were there any differences between this incident and the last incident when you were secluded/restrained?

   *Yes    No*

10. Do you have any suggestions to prevent your being secluded/restrained?

    *Yes    No*

11. Do you know what your goals are today?

    *Yes    No*

*(continued on next page)*

**Figure 3–10:** *Foundations Behavioral Health Nursing Department Policy and Procedure—Restraint (continued)*

(continued on next page)

**Restraint Bag Audit**

Month: _____

| Day | 1 | 2 | 3 | 4 | 5 | 6 | 7 | 8 | 9 | 10 | 11 | 12 | 13 | 14 | 15 | 16 | 17 | 18 | 19 | 20 | 21 | 22 | 23 | 24 | 25 | 26 | 27 | 28 | 29 | 30 | 31 |
|---|---|---|---|---|---|---|---|---|---|---|---|---|---|---|---|---|---|---|---|---|---|---|---|---|---|---|---|---|---|---|---|
| Restraint Bag Complete — Yes / No | | | | | | | | | | | | | | | | | | | | | | | | | | | | | | | |
| 7 AM – 3 PM | | | | | | | | | | | | | | | | | | | | | | | | | | | | | | | |
| 4 Straps | | | | | | | | | | | | | | | | | | | | | | | | | | | | | | | |
| 4 Cuffs | | | | | | | | | | | | | | | | | | | | | | | | | | | | | | | |
| Key | | | | | | | | | | | | | | | | | | | | | | | | | | | | | | | |
| Signature: _____ | | | | | | | | | | | | | | | | | | | | | | | | | | | | | | | |
| Restraint Bag Complete — Yes / No | | | | | | | | | | | | | | | | | | | | | | | | | | | | | | | |
| 3 PM – 11 PM | | | | | | | | | | | | | | | | | | | | | | | | | | | | | | | |
| 4 Straps | | | | | | | | | | | | | | | | | | | | | | | | | | | | | | | |
| 4 Cuffs | | | | | | | | | | | | | | | | | | | | | | | | | | | | | | | |
| Key | | | | | | | | | | | | | | | | | | | | | | | | | | | | | | | |
| Signature: _____ | | | | | | | | | | | | | | | | | | | | | | | | | | | | | | | |
| Restraint Bag Complete — Yes / No | | | | | | | | | | | | | | | | | | | | | | | | | | | | | | | |
| 11 PM – 7 AM | | | | | | | | | | | | | | | | | | | | | | | | | | | | | | | |
| 4 Straps | | | | | | | | | | | | | | | | | | | | | | | | | | | | | | | |
| 4 Cuffs | | | | | | | | | | | | | | | | | | | | | | | | | | | | | | | |
| Key | | | | | | | | | | | | | | | | | | | | | | | | | | | | | | | |
| Signature: _____ | | | | | | | | | | | | | | | | | | | | | | | | | | | | | | | |

**Figure 3–10:** *Foundations Behavioral Health Nursing Department Policy and Procedure—Restraints (continued)*

**Foundations Behavioral Health**

**Observation Record for Seclusion/Restraint**

Patient Name: _____

Medical record #: _____

| Date: _____ | Early Release: | Yes | No |
| Time In: _____ | Order Continued: | Yes | No |

| | Time | Sleeping | Awake | Clothing Checked | Assess to Discontinue | Meets Criteria to Continue | Medication Given | Nourishment & Fluids (q1hr) | Toileting Offered (q2hr) | Skin Care (q2hr) | Circulation Checks (q1hr) | Repositioned & ROM (q2hr) | BP (q2hr) | Assess by RN (q1hr) | MHT Initials | RN/LPN Initials |
|---|---|---|---|---|---|---|---|---|---|---|---|---|---|---|---|---|
| Start | :15 | | | | | | | | | | | | | | | |
| | :30 | | | | | | | | | | | | | | | |
| | :45 | | | | | | | | | | | | | | | |
| **HR1** | :00 | | | | | | | | | | | | | | | |
| | :15 | | | | | | | | | | | | | | | |
| | :30 | | | | | | | | | | | | | | | |
| | :45 | | | | | | | | | | | | | | | |
| **HR2** | :00 | | | | | | | | | | | | | | | |
| | :15 | | | | | | | | | | | | | | | |
| | :30 | | | | | | | | | | | | | | | |
| | :45 | | | | | | | | | | | | | | | |
| **HR3** | :00 | | | | | | | | | | | | | | | |
| | :15 | | | | | | | | | | | | | | | |
| | :30 | | | | | | | | | | | | | | | |
| | :45 | | | | | | | | | | | | | | | |
| **HR4** | :00 | | | | | | | | | | | | | | | |

**Checkmark = Presented/Implemented/Offered**

R = Refused

| Staff Signature | Staff Signature | Staff Signature |
| 7 am – 3 pm | 3 pm – 11 pm | 11 pm – 7 am |

*(continued on next page)*

**Figure 3–10:** *Foundations Behavioral Health Nursing Department Policy and Procedure—Restraint (continued)*

**Doctor's Order Sheet**

*Restraint/Seclusion Orders*

Patient Name:_____

Med Rec#: _____

1. Restrain patient with
   leather (hard) restraint devices
   ❑ Left arm    ❑ Right arm    ❑ Left leg    ❑ Right leg

   Less restrictive measures tried: ❑ Talked to    ❑ Limit setting
   ❑ Given          ❑ Room          ❑ Medication  ❑ Physical hold
      time-out         restriction                      (less than 15 minutes)

2. Purpose of restraints:
   ❑ High risk of injury to self:_____
   ❑ High risk of injury to others: _____
   ❑ Other:_____

3. Patient to be restrained for_____hours, from _____to _____.

4. Seclude patient for_____hours, from _____to _____.

5. No known contraindications.  ❑ Yes  ❑ No

6. Purpose for seclusion:
   ❑ High risk of injury to self.  ❑ High risk of injury to others.
   ❑ High risk for causing substantial property damage.
   ❑ High risk for causing significant disruption of treatment environment.
   ❑ Qualified RN may reorder q2 hours X 3 after reassessment.

Restraint and seclusion may not be ordered on PRN basis. Maximum time length is eight hours after which restraint must be reordered.

Date ordered:_____    Time: _____

RN Signature (needed for telephone or verbal orders):
_____

Physician Signature: _____

Reorders: If continuation is required, please date, sign and indicate the type of restraint and reason as above. (Note: If there are more than three episodes of restraint in seven days or if there is a need for 24 continuous hours of restraint, the physician or care team should review the plan of care.)

| Date | Physician Signature | Type/Restraint | Reason/Restraint | # Hours | RN Signature |
|------|---------------------|----------------|------------------|---------|--------------|
|      |                     |                |                  |         |              |
|      |                     |                |                  |         |              |
|      |                     |                |                  |         |              |
|      |                     |                |                  |         |              |
|      |                     |                |                  |         |              |

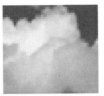

*Chapter Four*
# Responding to an Adverse or Sentinel Event: Initial Strategies

*Chapter Four*

# Responding to an Adverse or Sentinel Event: Initial Strategies

**Y**our organization just had a client die while in restraint. What should you do? What steps should be taken to manage the clinical consequences? Who needs to be notified? Who should do the notifying? What does the Joint Commission require? What do other agencies require? What are the legal and ethical considerations of disclosure to other clients? Some of these questions are beyond the scope of this book; the answer to others really is It depends. Although no hard-and-fast rules exist, some general guidelines can be useful. This chapter provides such guidelines while urging readers to consult additional sources of information.

## Immediate Strategies

Following the occurrence of a sentinel event, organizations need to simultaneously take a number of actions. These include providing prompt and appropriate care for the affected client, containing the risk of an immediate recurrence of the event, and preserving the evidence.

## Appropriate Care

The prompt and proper care of a client who has been affected by an adverse or sentinel event should be providers' and organization staff members' first concern following the event. Care could involve stabilizing the individual, arranging for the individual's transportation to a health care facility for surgery or testing, providing medications, taking actions to prevent further harm, and/or reversing the harm that has occurred, if possible. Communication with the family is absolutely vital during the time period immediately following the event. Patrice Spath writes: "When a serious adverse event occurs, sincere sympathy and compassion expressed to the patient and family is often the most important response to help defuse a potentially volatile situation."[1] Communication needs and strategies are discussed fully later in this chapter. When appropriate, physicians should obtain medical consultation related to the adverse event and arrange to receive necessary follow-up information from the consultants.

## Risk Containment

A sentinel event has just occurred; the event involves a drowning, a suicide, a restraint-related injury, or a number of alternatives. The organization must respond by containing the risk of immediate recurrence of the event. If a client drowned in the facility's pool, are other clients at risk? If a client jumped from an unsecured fourth-story window, is that window still open and unsecured? If a client was strangled by slipping through sidebars while restrained with a jacket, are other clients at risk for similar injuries? If so, the organization must take immediate action to safeguard such clients from a repetition of the unwanted occurrence. Actions may involve closing a pool, securing windows, and so forth. Additional staff may be necessary to alleviate the potential of other clients committing suicide in a copycat fashion. Risk-management texts, articles appearing in the literature, and associations such as the American Society for Healthcare Risk Management* can provide detailed guidance.

## Preservation of Evidence

To learn from an error and understand *why* it occurred, it is critical to know exactly *what* occurred. Preserving the evidence is key to this process. Immediate steps should be taken to secure any biological specimens, medications, equipment, medical or other records, and any other material that might be relevant to investigating the error.[2] In medication-related events, syringes of recently used medications and bottles of medications should be preserved and sequestered. Because such evidence may be discarded as a part of routine operations, for example when empty vials are thrown in trash cans, it is critical to obtain and preserve the evidence promptly. Protocols established by the health care organization should specify the steps to be taken to preserve relevant evidence following a sentinel event.

# Notification of Appropriate Parties

When a sentinel event occurs, personnel involved in the incident should promptly notify those in charge of error reporting and investigation within the organization, as well as supervisors, quality and risk-management professionals, and administrators. These individuals can determine how to best notify other parties, including the press and external agencies. Legal counsel should be sought early in the process. Counsel can provide guidance in how to discuss the situation with the family, how to prevent disclosure of potentially libelous information, and how to handle media relations.[3]

Spath recommends that organizations maintain two lists of key people to contact following a sentinel or adverse event: one list of the key individuals *within* the organization and the other of individuals *outside* the organization.[4] Both lists should be kept up to date with current telephone numbers and should be accessible to managers, supervisors, and members of a crisis management team. A sample sentinel event notification checklist appears as Figure 4-1, page 133.

Responding to media queries via organization protocols will help to avert complications related to patient or client confidentiality, legal discovery, and heat-of-the-moment coverage.[5] Notification requirements should be reflected

* 312/422-3980

**Figure 4–1:** *Sentinel Event Notification Checklist*

This checklist can be used as a guide to properly notify the relevant hospital officials following the occurrence of a sentinel event and to document their responses. Fill in the appropriate names/phone numbers and keep this checklist in a location readily accessible to managers/supervisors. Periodically review the accuracy of the names and contact numbers listed on the checklist.

❏ **Chief Executive Officer**
Name: _____
Phone number during regular working hours:_____
After-hours phone number: _____
Name/phone of designated backup: _____
Notified by: _____Date/Time: _____
Results of contact:_____
_____

❏ **Chief Nursing Officer**
Name: _____
Phone number during regular working hours:_____
After-hours phone number: _____
Notified by: _____Date/Time: _____
Results of contact:_____
_____

❏ **Medical Staff President**
Name: _____
Phone number during regular working hours:_____
After-hours phone number: _____
Name/phone of designated backup: _____
Notified by: _____Date/Time: _____
Results of contact:_____
_____

❏ **Risk Manager**
Name: _____
Phone number during regular working hours:_____
After-hours phone number: _____
Name/phone of designated backup: _____
Notified by: _____Date/Time: _____
Results of contact:_____
_____

❏ **Legal Counsel**
Name of firm: _____
Phone number during regular working hours:_____
After-hours phone number: _____
Notified by: _____Date/Time: _____
Results of contact:_____
_____

❏ **Chair, Board of Directors**
Name: _____
Phone number during regular working hours:_____
Notified by: _____Date/Time: _____
Results of contact:_____
_____

❏ **Director of Public Relations**
Name: _____
Phone number during regular working hours:_____
After-hours phone number: _____
Notified by: _____Date/Time: _____
Results of contact:_____
_____

*Source:* Brown-Spath Associates, Forest Grove, OR.

in organization policies and procedures. These should include policies for communication with the client and family, described further in the next subsection.

## Communication and Disclosure by the Health Care Provider

Communication and disclosure by the provider with relevant parties following the occurrence of a sentinel or adverse event that led or could have led to client injury is critical. Relevant parties include

- clients and their families affected by the event;
- colleagues who could provide clarification, support, and an opportunity to learn from the error;
- the health care organization's and individual provider's liability insurers;
- appropriate organization staff, including risk managers or quality assurance representatives; and
- others who could provide emotional support or problem-solving help for the individual who made the error.

Conferring with other members of the care team following an adverse event enables the provider to clarify factual details and the sequence of what occurred. It also can help identify what needs to be done in response to the event.

Good provider-client communication is instrumental in achieving positive care outcomes. Yet health care professionals often do not tell clients or families about their mistakes. As reported earlier, only 24% of house officers anonymously surveyed by Albert Wu and his colleagues told the patient or family of their errors in diagnosis, prescription, evaluation, communication, and procedural complications that led to serious outcomes in 90% of the cases, including death in 31% of the cases.[6] Fear of malpractice litigation and the myth of perfect performance, which is discussed in Chapter 2, reinforce poor provider communication of errors to patients and consumers. There is little doubt that the current malpractice crisis is a deterrent to the openness required for quality improvement.[7] However, errors not communicated to clients, families, fellow staff members, and organizations are errors that do not contribute to system improvement.

Disclosing mistakes to clients and their families is difficult, at best. Yet legal and ethical experts generally advise practitioners to disclose mistakes to clients and their families in as open, honest, and forthright a manner as possible. Wu suggests that physicians have an ethical obligation to tell patients about significant medical errors when such disclosure

- would benefit the health of the patient,
- would show respect for the patient's autonomy, or
- would be called for by principles of justice.[8]

He also suggests that disclosure of a mistake may foster learning by compelling the physician to acknowledge it truthfully and that the physician-patient relationship can be enhanced by honesty.[9] Disclosing a mistake might possibly *reduce* the risk of litigation, in fact, if the patient appreciates the physician's honesty and fallibility as a fellow human being. A.B. Witman and S. Hardin report that the risk of litigation nearly doubled when physicians did not inform their patients of moderate mistakes.[10] S.J. McPhee and colleagues[11] offer physicians guidelines in disclosing medical mistakes to patients. Sidebar 4–1 (pages 136-137) outlines practical issues a physician may encounter in disclosing an error to patients or their families.

M.D. Feldman and J.F. Christensen[12] provide a graphic representation of the process involved in mistake disclosure (see Figure 4–2, page 138). The end results of mistake recognition and disclosure should be changes in practice by the physician and system changes by the organization, both to prevent recurrence.

What are the ethical requirements for disclosure as stated by some of the major associations of health care practitioners? The following paragraphs present guidelines from selected physician organizations, a major psychologist organization, a major nursing organization, and pharmacist organizations.

## Ethical Requirements for Disclosure of Errors by Physicians

The American Medical Association's *Code of Medical Ethics: Current Opinions with Annotations (1996–1997 Edition)* states: "Situations occasionally occur in which a patient suffers significant medical complications that may have resulted from the physician's mistake or judgment. In these situations, the physician is ethically required to inform the patient of all the facts necessary to ensure understanding of what has occurred. Only through full disclosure is a patient able to make informed decisions regarding future medical care…Concern regarding legal liability which might result following truthful disclosure should not affect the physician's honesty with a patient."[13]

The American Psychiatric Association advises psychiatrists to be familiar and practice in accordance with the American Medical Association's (AMA) ethical guidelines. In its publication, *The Principles of Medical Ethics: With Annotations Especially Applicable to Psychiatry,* the association writes, "While psychiatrists have the same goals as all physicians, there are special ethical problems in psychiatric practice that differ in coloring and degree from ethical problems in other branches of medical practices, even though the basic principles are the same."[14] The publication provides annotated guidelines for each AMA principle.

The *American College of Physicians' Ethics Manual, 3rd Edition* (1992) states: "Physicians should disclose to patients information about procedural and judgment errors made in the course of care, if such information significantly affects the care of the patient. Errors do not necessarily constitute improper, negligent, or unethical behavior. Information should be given in terms the patient can understand. The physician should be sensitive to the patient's response in setting the pace of disclosure…Disclosure should never be a mechanical or perfunctory process."[15]

## Ethical Requirements for Disclosure of Errors by Psychologists

The American Psychological Association's *Ethical Principles of Psychologists and Code of Conduct* states: "Psychologists uphold professional standards of conduct, clarify their professional roles and obligations, accept appropriate responsibility for their behavior, and adapt their methods to the needs of different populations. Psychologists consult with, refer to, or cooperate with other professionals and institutions to the extent needed to serve the best interests of their patients, clients, or other recipients of their services. Psychologists' moral standards and conduct are

**Sidebar 4–1:** *Practical Issues for Physicians in Disclosing Medical Mistakes to Patients*

## Medical Mistakes Requiring Disclosure

A medical mistake is a commission or omission with potentially negative consequences for the patient that would have been judged wrong by skilled and knowledgeable peers at the time it occurred.

## Deciding Whether to Disclose a Mistake

In general, a physician has an obligation to disclose clear mistakes that cause significant harm that is remediable, mitigable, or compensable. In cases where disclosing a mistake seems controversial, the decision should not be left to the individual physician's judgment. It is important to obtain a second opinion to represent what a reasonable physician would do and be willing to defend in public. This second opinion is best obtained from an institution's ethics committee or quality review board rather than from informal consultation with peers.

## Timing of Disclosure

Disclosure should be made as soon as possible after the mistake occurred but at a time when the patient is physically and emotionally stable.

## Who Should Disclose the Mistake?

When a mistake is made by a physician in training, responsibility is shared with the attending physician. It may be most appropriate for the attending and house officer to disclose the mistake to the patient together. When a mistake is made by a practicing physician, that physician should disclose the mistake to the patient. When the mistake results from the *system* of medical care delivery, it may be appropriate to involve an institutional representative, such as administrator, risk manager, or quality assurance representative, in the disclosure.

## What to Say?

Disclosure is often difficult for technical as well as emotional reasons. The facts of the case may be too complicated to be explained easily and may not be known precisely. The physician may be tempted to frame the disclosure in a way which obscures that a mistake was made. In telling the patient about an error, physicians should do the following:

- Treat it as an instance of "breaking bad news" to the patient;
- Begin by stating simply that they regret the mistake or error;
- Describe the decisions that were made, including those in which the patient participated;
- Describe the course of events in nontechnical language;
- State the nature of the mistake, consequences, and corrective action taken or to be undertaken;
- Express personal regret and apologize for the mistake;
- Elicit questions or concerns from the patient and address them; and
- Ask whether there is anyone else in the family to whom they should speak.

## Consequences of Disclosure

Physicians are often most concerned about the potentially harmful consequences that they themselves will incur by disclosing a mistake, particularly the possible risk of a lawsuit. Serious mistakes may come to light, even if the physician does not disclose them. Any perception that the physician tried to cover up a mistake might make patients angry and more litigious. The risks inherent in disclosing a mistake may be minimized if

- patients appreciate the physician's honesty;
- patients appreciate that physicians are fallible;

*Source:* McPhee SJ, et al: Practical issues in disclosing medical mistakes to patients. Presented at the Examining Errors in Health Care Conference, Rancho Mirage, CA: Oct 13–15, 1996.

*(continued on next page)*

**Sidebar 4–1:** *Practical Issues for Physicians in Disclosing Medical Mistakes to Patients (continued)*

- disclosure is prompt and open;
- disclosure is made in a manner that defuses patient anger;
- sincere apologies are made;
- charges for associated care are forgone; and
- a prompt and fair settlement is made out of court.

**Disclosure of Mistakes Made by Other Physicians**

Physicians may encounter situations where they recognize that a colleague physician has made a mistake. That colleague may choose to disclose the mistake or not. The physician recognizing the mistake has the following options:

- Wait for the other physician to disclose the mistake;
- Advise the other physician to disclose the mistake;
- Simultaneously advise quality assurance or risk management;
- Arrange a joint meeting to discuss the mistake; and
- Tell the patient of the error directly.

Physicians may be reluctant to disclose a colleague's error because of a lack of definitive information, fear of hurting the colleague's feelings, fear of straining a professional relationship, fear of a libel suit, the sense that they could easily have made the same error ("There but for the grace of God go I"), and social norms against "tattling" on peers.

personal matters to the same degree as is true for any other person, except as psychologists' conduct may compromise their professional responsibilities or reduce the public's trust in psychology and psychologists."[16]

On the topic of avoiding harm, the *Code* states: "Psychologists take reasonable steps to avoid harming their patients or clients, research participants, students, and others with whom they work, and to minimize harm where it is foreseeable and unavoidable." The *Code* does not contain formal guidelines for the disclosure of errors made by psychologists, but it does provide principles for seeking to contribute to the welfare of those with whom they interact professionally.

## Ethical Requirements for Disclosure of Errors by Nurses

The American Nurses Association *Code for Nurses with Interpretive Statements* states: "The nurse acts to safeguard the client and the public when health care and safety are affected by the incompetent, unethical, or illegal practice of any person. The nurse's primary commitment is to the health, welfare, and safety of the client. As an advocate for the client, the nurse must be alert to and take appropriate action regarding any instances of incompetent, unethical, or illegal practice by any member of the health care team or the health care system, or any action on the part of others that places the rights or best interests of the client in jeopardy."[17]

On the issue of accountability, the *Code* states: "The nurse assumes responsibility and accountability for individual nursing judgments and actions…Nurses are

**Figure 4–2:** *Evaluating Cause and Planning Improvement*

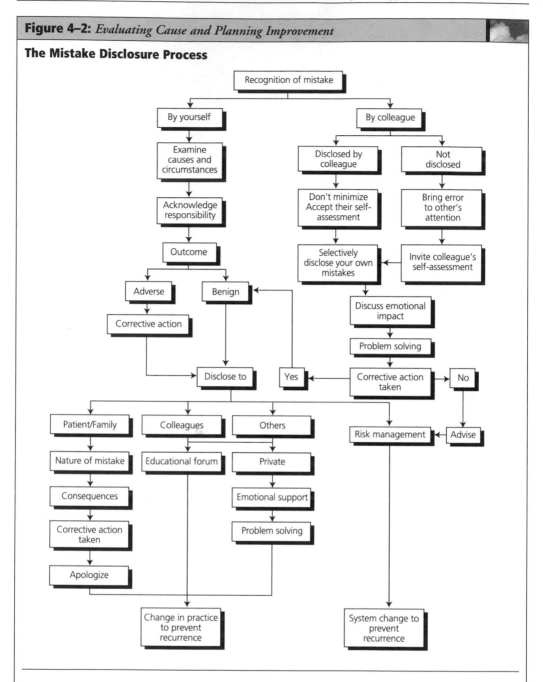

**The Mistake Disclosure Process**

This flowchart illustrates the steps to be taken in disclosing a mistake to patients and families, colleagues, and others from the time the error is identified to the time a change is made in individual practice or system process.

*Source:* Feldman MD, Christensen JF (eds): *Behavioral Medicine in Primary Care.* Stamford, CT: Appleton and Lange, 1997. Used with permission.

accountable for judgments made and actions taken in the course of nursing practice. Neither physician's orders nor the employing agency's policies relieve the nurse of accountability for actions taken and judgments made."

Although the *Code* does not contain formal guidelines for a nurse's disclosure to a patient or family member of an error made, it provides a framework for truthful disclosure of mistakes that jeopardize or could jeopardize the patient's well-being.

## Ethical Requirements for Disclosure of Errors by Pharmacists

The American Society of Health-Systems Pharmacists (ASHP) provides detailed guidelines on preventing medication errors in hospitals. Its *Guidelines on Preventing Medication Errors in Hospitals* recommends the following actions upon error detection:

- Provide any necessary corrective and supportive therapy to the patient.
- Document and report the error immediately after discovery, in accordance with written procedures. Provide an immediate oral notice to physicians, nurses, and pharmacy managers for clinically significant errors. A written medication error report should follow promptly.
- Initiate fact gathering and investigation for clinically significant errors, including appropriate product evidence (for example, packaging and labeling).
- Have appropriate supervisors and other organization personnel (that is, administration, risk management, legal counsel) review reports of clinically significant errors and the associated corrective activities.
- Confer on how the error occurred and how its recurrence can be prevented.
- Use information gained from medication error reports and other means that demonstrates continued failure of individual professionals to avoid preventable medication errors as a management and educational tool in staff development or, if necessary, modification of job functions or staff disciplinary action.
- Periodically review error reports and determine causes of errors and develop actions to prevent their recurrence (for example, conduct organization staff education, alter staff levels, revise policies and procedures, or change facilities, equipment, or supplies).
- Report medication errors to a national monitoring program to contribute to improved patient safety and to develop valuable educational services for the prevention of future errors.[18]

The American Pharmaceutical Association (APA) recommends that pharmacists report errors or sentinel events to the national reporting programs, such as the U.S. Pharmacopeia (USP), Food and Drug Administration (FDA), and Institute for Safe Medication Practices (ISMP).[19] If pharmacists work within organizations with internal error reporting systems, the APA recommends that they follow the organizations' reporting guidelines. The APA urges pharmacists to report errors so that system problems can be identified.

## Ethical Requirements for Disclosure of Errors by Social Workers

The National Association of Social Workers *Code of Ethics*[20] provides broad ethical principles that are based on social work's core values of service, social justice, the dignity and worth of the person, the importance of human relationships, integrity, and competence. Although the *Code* does not contain formal guidelines for a social worker's disclosure to a client or family member of an error made, it provides a framework for "ethical responsibilities flowing from all human relationships, from the personal and familial to the social and professional."

On the topic of integrity, the *Code* states that "social workers behave in a trust-worthy manner" and that "social workers act honestly and responsibly and promote ethical practices on the part of the organizations with which they are affiliated." On the topic of competence, the *Code* states that "social workers practice within their areas of competence." The *Code* makes it clear that social workers' primary responsibility is to promote the well-being of clients and that services should be provided to clients only in the context of a professional relationship based, when appropriate, on valid informed consent. Dishonesty, fraud, and deception are prohibited.

### Ethical Requirements for Disclosure of Errors by Certified Counselors

The *Code of Ethics* published by the National Board for Certified Counselors (NBCC)[21] provides a minimal standard for the professional behavior of all counselors certified by the NBCC. The *Code* provides an expectation of and assurance for the ethical practice for all who use the professional services of an NBCC certificate holder. The *Code* does not address the disclosure of errors specifically, but articulates a framework where "Ethical behavior among professional associates (both certified and noncertified counselors) must be expected at all times." Responsibility and accountability also are addressed. The *Code* states, "Certified counselors are accountable at all times for their behavior. They must be aware that all actions and behaviors of the counselor reflect on professional integrity and, when inappropriate, can damage the public trust in the counseling profession." According to the *Code*, "The primary obligation of certified counselors is to respect the integrity and promote the welfare of clients." Certified counselors have an obligation to withdraw from the practice of counseling if they violate the *Code of Ethics*.

## Documentation

Proper medical record documentation of errors or sentinel events is critical for continuity of care. Keyes offers the following tips regarding documentation:[22]

- Assign the most involved and knowledgeable member(s) of the health care team to record factual statements of the event in the patient's record;
- Record any medical follow-up completed, planned, or needed;
- Avoid writing information in the medical record that is unrelated to the care of the patient (such as "legal office notified");
- Avoid writing derisive comments about other providers. If you disagree with another clinician, document the basis for your treatment recommendations only; and
- If you add information to the patient's record after an adverse event has occurred, mark your entry with the actual date it is written, do not "backdate" any entries, and beware of creating entries that appear self-serving, especially explanations intended solely to justify your actions.

## Joint Commission Sentinel Event Policy and Requirements

In early 1996, the Joint Commission established a formal Sentinel Event Policy to provide consistent guidance on identifying, responding to, and reducing the risk of sentinel events in health care organizations. Through the policy, the Joint Commission aims to

- have a positive impact on improving patient care;
- focus the attention of an organization that has experienced a sentinel event on

understanding the causes that underlie that event and on making changes in the organization's systems and processes to reduce the probability of such an event in the future;

■ increase general knowledge about sentinel events, their causes, and strategies for prevention; and

■ maintain the public's confidence in the accreditation process.

The Joint Commission's Sentinel Event Policy is designed to encourage the self-reporting and analysis of sentinel events to learn about the relative frequencies and underlying causes, share "lessons learned" with other health care organizations, and thereby reduce the risk of future sentinel events. By addressing the issue of sentinel events, the Joint Commission seeks to strike a balance between the public's expectations of a credible accreditation process and the practical needs of health care organizations.

As previously described in Chapter 1, page 13, the Joint Commission currently defines a *sentinel event* as an unexpected occurrence involving death or serious physical or psychological injury or the risk thereof. Serious injury specifically includes loss of limb or function. The phrase "or the risk thereof" includes any process variation for which a recurrence would carry a significant chance of serious adverse outcome.

Accredited organizations are expected to identify and respond appropriately to *all* sentinel events occurring within their facilities or associated with services they provide. Appropriate response includes a thorough and credible root cause analysis (described in Chapter 5, pages 165 through 182) and action plan, implementation of improvements to reduce risk, and monitoring of the effectiveness of those improvements (described in Chapter 6, pages 211 through 213).

An organization's activities in response to sentinel events will be routinely assessed as part of triennial and random unannounced surveys. A description of the process and procedures involved in complying with the Sentinel Event Policy follows here. The flowchart (see Figure 4–3, page 142) provides a graphic representation of the process.

## New Sentinel Event Standards

Effective January 1, 1999, standards under the "Leadership" and "Improving Organization Performance" chapters relating specifically to the management of sentinel events have been added or revised. The standards appear as Sidebar 4–2, page 143-144.

### Survey Process

In conducting an accreditation survey, the Joint Commission will seek to evaluate the organization's compliance with the applicable standards and to score those standards based on performance throughout the organization over time (for example, the preceding 12 months for a triennial survey). For this reason, surveyors are instructed not to seek out specific sentinel events beyond those already known to the Joint Commission. The intent is to evaluate compliance with the applicable standards, that is, how the organization responds to sentinel events when they occur. During a full accreditation survey, the surveyor will assess the organization's compliance with these standards by

■ reviewing documents that describe the organization's process for responding to a sentinel event;

**Figure 4-3:** *Sentinel Event Process Flowchart*

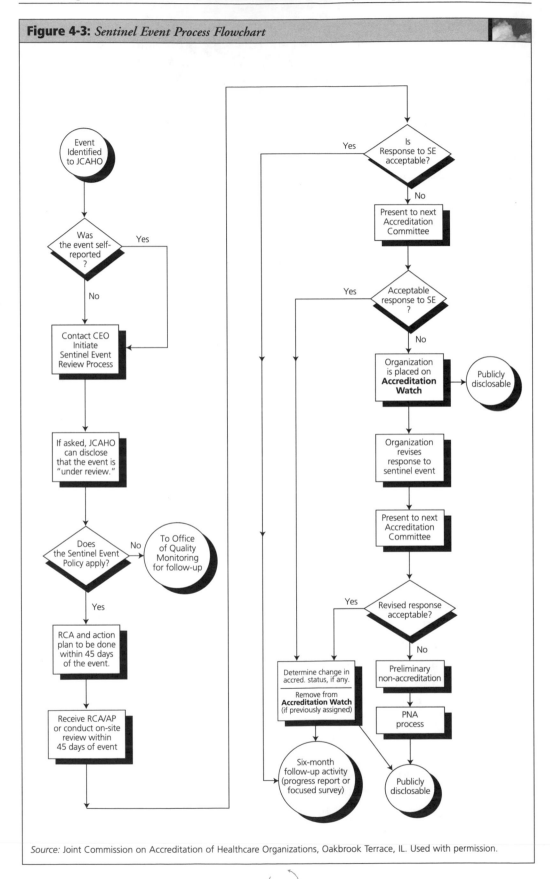

*Source:* Joint Commission on Accreditation of Healthcare Organizations, Oakbrook Terrace, IL. Used with permission.

142

**Sidebar 4–2:** Standards in the *1999–2000 Comprehensive Accreditation Manual for Behavioral Health Care* Relating to Sentinel Events

## Performance Improvement

**Standard PI.2** *New or modified processes are designed well.*

### Intent of PI.2

When processes, functions, or services are designed well, they draw on a variety of information sources. Good process design

a. is consistent with the organizations mission, vision, values, goals and objectives, and plans;

b. meets the needs of individuals served, staff, and others;

c. is clinically sound and current (for instance, use of practice guidelines, information from relevant literature, and clinical standards);

d. is consistent with sound business practices;

e. incorporates available information from other organizations about occurrence of sentinel events in order to reduce the risk of similar sentinel events; and

f. incorporates the results of performance improvement activities.

The organization incorporates information related to these elements, when available and relevant, in the design or redesign of processes, functions, or services.

**Standard PI.3.1.1** *The organization collects data to monitor the performance of processes that involve risks or may result in sentinel events.*

### Intent of PI.3.1.1

Organizations select processes which are known to be high-risk, high-volume, problem-prone areas related to the care and services provided. This information is correlated with the listing of frequently occurring sentinel events published by the Joint Commission, the organization's risk-management data, or information about problematic processes generated by field-specific or professional organizations.

Organizations select performance measures for processes known to jeopardize the safety of the individuals served or that are associated with sentinel events in similar health care organizations. At a minimum, the organization identifies performance measures related to the following processes as appropriate to the care and services provided:

- Medication use;
- Operative and other procedures that place individuals at risk;
- Use of blood and blood components;
- Restraint use;
- Seclusion; and
- Care or services provided to high-risk populations.

The detail and frequency of data collection have been determined and are appropriate for monitoring high-risk, problem-prone processes. Data are collected at the frequency and with the detail identified by the organization.

The performance measure data are used to evaluate outcomes or performance of problem-prone processes.

*Source:* Joint Commission on Accreditation of Healthcare Organizations, Oakbrook Terrace, IL. Used with permission.

*(continued on next page)*

**Sidebar 4–2:** Standards in the *1999–2000 Comprehensive Accreditation Manual for Behavioral Health Care* Relating to Sentinel Events *(continued)*

**Standard PI.4.3** *Undesirable patterns or trends in performance and sentinel events are intensively analyzed.*

**Intent of PI.4.3**

When the organization detects or suspects significant undesirable performance or variation, it initiates intense analysis to determine where best to focus changes for improvement. The organization initiates intense analysis when the comparisons show that

- important single events, levels of performance, patterns, or trends vary significantly and undesirably from those expected;
- performance varies significantly and undesirably from that of other organizations;
- performance varies significantly and undesirably from recognized standards; or
- when a sentinel event occurs.

When monitoring performance of specific clinical processes, certain events always elicit intense analysis. Based on the scope of care or services provided, intense analysis is performed for

- significant adverse drug reactions; and
- significant medication errors.

Intense analysis can also occur for those topics chosen by the leaders as performance improvement priorities or when undesirable variation occurs which changes the priorities. Of course, an organization may also initiate further analysis at any time to improve its current performance. Intense analysis involves studying a process to learn in greater detail about how it is performed or how it operates. A root cause analysis is performed for a sentinel event occurrence.

**Leadership**

**Standard LD.4.3.4** *Leaders ensure that the processes for identifying and managing sentinel events are defined and implemented.*

**Intent of LD.4.3.4**

When a sentinel event occurs in a health care organization, it is necessary that appropriate individuals within the organization be aware of the event, investigate and understand the causes that underlie the event, and make changes in the organization's systems and processes to reduce the probability of such an event in the future. The leaders are responsible for establishing processes for the identification, reporting, analysis, and prevention of sentinel events and for ensuring the consistent and effective implementation of mechanisms to accomplish these activities, including

- determination of a definition of sentinel event that is approved by the leaders and communicated throughout the organization;
- creation of a process for reporting of sentinel events through established channels within the organization and, as appropriate, to external agencies in accordance with law and regulation;
- creation of a process for conducting thorough and credible root cause analyses that focus on process and system factors; and
- determination of a risk-reduction strategy and action plan that includes measurement of the effectiveness of process and system improvements to reduce risk.

- interviewing organization leaders and staff about their expectations and responsibilities for identifying, reporting, and responding to sentinel events; and
- asking for an *example* of a sentinel event that has occurred in the past year to assess the adequacy of the organization's process for responding to a sentinel event.

Additional examples may be reviewed if needed to more fully assess the organization's understanding of, and ability to conduct, a root cause analysis. In selecting an example, the organization may choose a "closed case" or a "near miss" to demonstrate its process for responding to a sentinel event.

Surveyors will also review the effectiveness and sustainability of organization improvements in systems and processes in response to sentinel events previously evaluated under the Joint Commission's Sentinel Event Policy.

## Reviewable Sentinel Events

Only a subset of sentinel events is subject to review by the Joint Commission. This subset includes any occurrence that meets any of the following criteria:

- The event has resulted in an unanticipated death or major permanent loss of function, not related to the natural course of the patient's illness or underlying condition[π] or
- The event is one of the following (even if the outcome was not death or major permanent loss of function):
  - Suicide of a patient in a setting where the patient receives around-the-clock care (for example, hospital, residential treatment center, crisis stabilization center),[¶]
  - Infant abduction or discharge to the wrong family,
  - Rape,[§]
  - Hemolytic transfusion reaction involving administration of blood or blood products having major blood group incompatibilities, or
  - Surgery on the wrong patient or wrong body part.[£]

Specific examples of events that are and are not subject to review by the Joint Commission under the policy appear as Sidebars 4–3 and 4–4, pages 146 and 147. Figure 4–4, page 148, provides a graphic view of reportable and non-reportable events.

---

π  A distinction is made between an adverse outcome that is related to the natural course of the patient's illness or underlying condition (not reviewed under the Sentinel Event Policy) and a death or major permanent loss of function that is associated with the treatment, or lack of treatment, of that condition (reviewable).

*Major permanent loss of function* means sensory, motor, physiologic, or intellectual impairment not present on admission requiring continued treatment or lifestyle change. When major permanent loss of function cannot be immediately determined, applicability of the policy is not established until either the patient is discharged with continued major loss of function, or two weeks have elapsed with persistent major loss of function, whichever occurs first.

¶  This is an exception to the "not related to the natural course of the patient's illness or underlying condition" exemption in the first criterion.

§  The determination of *rape* is to be based on the health care organization's definition, consistent with applicable law and regulation. An allegation of rape is not reviewable under the policy. Applicability of the policy is established when a determination is made that a rape has occurred.

£  All events of surgery on the wrong patient or wrong body part are reviewable under the policy, regardless of the magnitude of the procedure.

---

**Sidebar 4–3:** *Examples of Voluntarily Reportable Sentinel Events Under the Joint Commission's Sentinel Event Policy*

The following are examples of sentinel events that are *voluntarily reportable*:

- A patient death, paralysis, coma, or other major permanent loss of function associated with a medication error;

- A suicide of a patient in a setting where the patient is housed around the clock, including suicides following elopement from such a setting;

- An elopement, such as an unauthorized departure of a patient from an around-the-clock care setting resulting in a temporally related death (suicide or homicide) or major permanent loss of function;

- A procedure on the wrong patient, wrong side of the body, or wrong organ;

- An intrapartum (related to the birth process) maternal death;

- A perinatal death, unrelated to a congenital condition, in an infant having a birth weight greater than 2,500 grams;

- An assault, homicide, or other crime resulting in patient death or major permanent loss of function;

- A patient fall that results in death or major permanent loss of function as a direct result of the injuries sustained in the fall; and

- A hemolytic transfusion reaction involving major blood group incompatibilities.

**Note:** *An adverse outcome that is directly related to the natural course of the patient's illness or underlying condition (for example, terminal illness present at the time of presentation), is not reportable except for suicide in or following elopement from a 24-hour care setting.*

---

## How the Joint Commission Becomes Aware of a Sentinel Event

Each health care organization is encouraged, but not required, to report to the Joint Commission any sentinel event meeting the aforementioned criteria for reviewable sentinel events. Alternatively, the Joint Commission may become aware of a sentinel event by some other means, such as communication from a patient, family member, or employee of the organization, or through the media.

If the Joint Commission becomes aware (either through voluntary self-reporting or otherwise) of a sentinel event meeting the aforementioned criteria that has occurred in an accredited organization, the organization is expected to

- prepare a thorough and credible root cause analysis and action plan within 45 calendar days of the event or of becoming aware of the event, and

- submit to the Joint Commission its root cause analysis and action plan, or otherwise provide for Joint Commission evaluation of its response to the sentinel event under an approved protocol, within 45 calendar days of when the occurrence of the event became known.

The Joint Commission will then determine whether the root cause analysis and action plan are acceptable. If the root cause analysis or action plan are not acceptable, the organization is at risk for being placed on Accreditation Watch by the Accreditation Committee (see page 152).

An organization which experiences a sentinel event that does not meet the criteria for review under the Sentinel Event Policy is expected to complete a root cause analysis. However, the root cause analysis need not be made available to the Joint Commission.

## Reasons for Reporting a Sentinel Event to the Joint Commission

Although self-reporting of a sentinel event is not required, there are several advantages to the organization that reports a sentinel event, including the following:

- Reporting the event enables the addition of the "lessons learned" from the event to be added to the Joint Commission's Sentinel Event Database, thereby contributing to the general knowledge about sentinel events and to the reduction of risk for such events in many other organizations;

- Early reporting provides an opportunity for consultation with Joint Commission staff during the development of the root cause analysis and action plan; and

- The organization's message to the public that it is doing everything possible to ensure that such an event will not happen again is strengthened by its acknowledged collaboration with the Joint Commission to understand how the event happened and what can be done to reduce the risk of such an event in the future.

The Joint Commission will consider all root cause analyses and action plans confidential and will treat them as such.

## Voluntary Reporting of Sentinel Events to the Joint Commission

If an organization wishes to report an occurrence in the subset of sentinel events that are subject to review by the Joint Commission, the organization will be asked to complete a sentinel event reporting form (see Figure 4–5, page 149). The organization sends this form to the Joint Commission's Office of Quality Monitoring by mail

---

**Sidebar 4–4:** *Examples of Nonreportable Sentinel Events Under the Joint Commission's Sentinel Event Policy*

The following are examples of events that are *not* reportable to the Joint Commission under the Sentinel Event Policy:

- A "near miss";

- Full return of limb or bodily function to the same level as before the adverse event by discharge or within two weeks of the initial loss of said function;

- A sentinel event that has not affected a recipient of care (patient, client, resident);

- Medication errors that do not result in death or major permanent loss of function;

- A suicide other than in an around-the-clock care setting or following elopement from such a setting;

- A death or loss of function following a discharge "against medical advice";

- Unsuccessful suicide attempts;

- An unintentionally retained foreign body without major permanent loss of function; and

- Minor degrees of hemolysis with no clinical sequelae.

**Figure 4–4:** *Sentinel Event Pyramid*

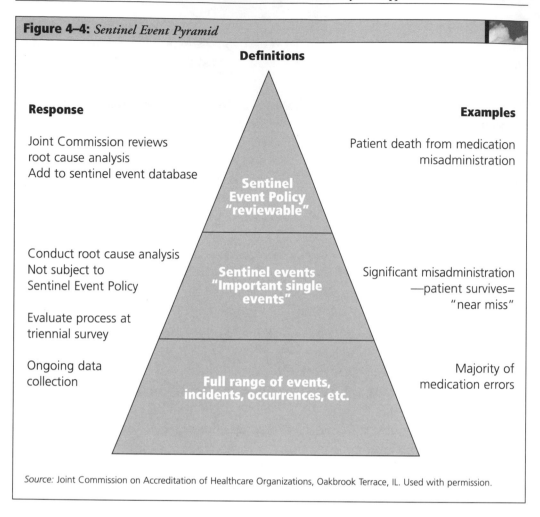

**Definitions**

**Response**

Joint Commission reviews
root cause analysis
Add to sentinel event database

Conduct root cause analysis
Not subject to
Sentinel Event Policy

Evaluate process at
triennial survey

Ongoing data
collection

**Examples**

Patient death from medication
misadministration

Significant misadministration
—patient survives=
"near miss"

Majority of
medication errors

Sentinel
Event Policy
"reviewable"

Sentinel events
"Important single
events"

Full range of events,
incidents, occurrences, etc.

*Source:* Joint Commission on Accreditation of Healthcare Organizations, Oakbrook Terrace, IL. Used with permission.

or by facsimile transmission at 630/792-5636. Copies of the sentinel event reporting form may be obtained by calling the Sentinel Event Hotline at 630/792-3700 or the Office of Quality Monitoring at 630/792-5642.

## Sentinel Events That Are Not Reported by the Organization

If the Joint Commission becomes aware of a sentinel event subject to review under the Sentinel Event Policy that was not reported to the Joint Commission by the organization, the chief executive officer of the organization is contacted and a preliminary assessment of the sentinel event is made.

## Initial On-site Review of a Sentinel Event

An initial on-site review of a sentinel event will usually not be conducted unless a potential ongoing threat to patient health or safety or potentially significant noncompliance with major Joint Commission standards is determined. If an on-site ("for-cause") review is conducted, the organization will be billed an appropriate amount to cover the costs of conducting such a survey.

## Disclosable Information

If, during the 45-day analysis period, the Joint Commission receives an inquiry about the accreditation status of an organization that has experienced a *reviewable*

**Figure 4–5:** *Sentinel Event Report Form*

### Joint Commission
#### on Accreditation of Healthcare Organizations

**Accredited Organization
Self-Reported Sentinel Event**

---

Full Name of Accredited Organization

---

Street Address        City        State    Zip Code

Date of Incident:_____

**Summary of Incident:** (Please describe the event but do **not** include names of patient(s), care-giver(s), or other individual(s) involved in the event. Another page may be added if necessary.)

_____

_____

_____

_____

_____

_____

_____

_____

Has Root Cause Analysis been started? _____Yes   _____No

---

Sentinel Event Contact (must be officer of organization) (please print full name)    Title

---

Signature        Date     Phone#

Please mail this completed form to the Joint Commission's Office of Quality Monitoring at the address below, or submit via facsimile to: Joint Commission, Office of Quality Monitoring, 630/792-5636. Direct questions about completing this form to 630/792-5642. Direct questions about your sentinel event as it relates to the Sentinel Event Policy to 630/792-3700, option 2, then option 3. You will be contacted to discuss any additional requirements including, as appropriate, completion of a root cause analysis.

*Source:* Joint Commission on Accreditation of Healthcare Organizations, Oakbrook Terrace, IL. Used with permission.

sentinel event, the organization's accreditation status will be reported in the usual manner without reference to the sentinel event.

If the inquirer specifically references the sentinel event, the Joint Commission will acknowledge that it is aware of the event and is working with the organization through the sentinel event review process.

## Legal Concerns Over Confidentiality

The basic "requirements" of the Sentinel Event Policy are to

■ perform a root cause analysis in response to a sentinel event, and
■ share relevant root cause analysis information with the Joint Commission.

Almost all organizations experiencing sentinel events appear to be moving quickly to address the first requirement. However, serious concerns regarding the potential discoverability of sentinel event-related information shared with the Joint Commission have created a significant barrier for organizations in many states in meeting the second requirement.

In response to these concerns, the Joint Commission has identified four alternatives for a health care organization to report, and the Joint Commission to review, information regarding the organization's response to a sentinel event. These alternatives are outlined on pages 151-152. The alternatives are intended to reduce the exposure of sensitive sentinel event–related information to discovery while preserving an environment that encourages the candid and thorough assessment of the root causes of sentinel events. The Joint Commission believes that the confidentiality protection needs of accredited organizations can be well met by one or more of these alternatives. Absent new state or federal legislative protections, however, there are no absolute guarantees that these alternatives will *ensure* the confidentiality of sentinel event-related information shared with the Joint Commission.

The Joint Commission also identified two contractual arrangements that should substantively address the legal concerns regarding potential waiver of confidentiality protections in certain states. These arrangements involve having the health care organization either

■ identify, through written agreement, the Joint Commission as a participating entity in the organization's peer review or quality improvement activities or
■ appoint the Joint Commission to the organization's peer review or quality improvement committee.

These arrangements clarify that the Joint Commission *is not* an external third party in the limited context of an intensive assessment of a sentinel event and, therefore, no waiver of confidentiality protections has occurred by sharing sentinel event–related information with the Joint Commission. These arrangements, especially the former, may permit an organization to readily comply with the Sentinel Event Policy (that is, submit its root cause analysis and action plan to the Joint Commission) or otherwise serve to enhance the protections afforded by the four alternatives.

The wording of two sample agreement options is shown in Sidebar 4–5, page 151. The Joint Commission's General Counsel is available to answer questions or to negotiate state-specific modifications to the agreements.

**Sidebar 4–5:** *Agreement Options*

**Sample ad hoc peer review committee member agreement**

The (name of health care organization) and the Joint Commission agree that the accreditation process involves working together to improve the quality of health care, and that in carrying out that function the Joint Commission will serve as an ad hoc committee member of the (name of health care organization) peer review committee for those aspects of the accreditation process involving quality improvement initiatives. Such appointment to the peer review committee shall be limited to the review of information generated for said committee directly related to the Joint Commission standards dealing with quality improvement and to the guidance furnished by the Joint Commission with respect to quality improvement initiatives.

**Sample consultant relationship agreement**

The (name of health care organization) and the Joint Commission agree that the accreditation process involves working together to improve the quality of health care, and that in carrying out that function the Joint Commission will serve as a consultant to the (name of health care organization) peer review committee for those aspects of the accreditation process involving quality improvement initiatives. Such consulting service to the peer review committee shall be limited to the review of information generated for said committee directly related to the Joint Commission standards dealing with quality improvement and to the guidance furnished by the Joint Commission with respect to quality improvement initiatives.

## Contact Information for Questions and Reporting of Sentinel Events

An organization that has any questions regarding sentinel events or intends to self-report a sentinel event should contact the Joint Commission's Sentinel Event Hotline at 630/792-3700.

## Submission of Root Cause Analysis and Action Plan

The organization that experiences a sentinel event subject to review under the Sentinel Event Policy is asked to submit two documents:

- The complete root cause analysis, including its findings, and
- The resulting action plan that describes the organization's risk reduction strategies and strategy for evaluating their effectiveness.

The "Framework for a Root Cause Analysis and Action Plan in Response to a Sentinel Event," (see pages 179-181), is available to organizations as an aid in organizing the steps in a root cause analysis and development of an action plan.

The root cause analysis and action plan are *not to include the patient's name or the names of caregivers involved in the sentinel event.*

Alternatively, if the organization has concerns about increased risk of legal exposure as a result of sending the root cause analysis documents to the Joint Commission, the following alternative approaches to review of the organization's response to the sentinel event are acceptable:

**Alternative 1:** Review of root cause analysis documents that are brought to Joint Commission headquarters by organization staff and taken back to the organization on the same day.

**Alternative 2:** An on-site visit by a specially trained surveyor to review the root cause analysis and action plan. The organization will be assessed a charge sufficient to cover the average direct costs of the visit.

**Alternative 3:** An on-site visit by a specially trained surveyor to review the root cause analysis and findings, without directly viewing the root cause analysis documents, through a series of interviews and review of relevant documentation. For purposes of this review activity, "relevant documentation" includes, at a minimum, any documentation relevant to the organization's *process* for responding to sentinel events and the action plan resulting from the analysis of the subject sentinel event. The latter serves as the basis for appropriate follow-up activity. The organization will be assessed a charge sufficient to cover the average direct costs of the visit.

**Alternative 4:** Where the organization affirms that it meets specified criteria respecting the risk of waiving legal protection for root cause analysis information shared with the Joint Commission, an on-site visit may be made by a surveyor specially trained to conduct interviews and review relevant documentation to obtain information about

- the *process* used by the organization in responding to sentinel events, and
- the relevant policies and procedures preceding and following the organization's review of the specific event, and the implementation thereof, sufficient to permit inferences about the adequacy of the organization's response to the sentinel event.

The organization will be assessed a charge sufficient to cover the average direct costs of the visit.

A request for review of an organization's response to a sentinel event using any of these *alternative* approaches must be received by the Joint Commission at least 15 days before the due date for the root cause analysis and action plan.

## Accreditation Watch Designation

*Accreditation Watch* is an attribute of an organization's Joint Commission accreditation status. A health care organization is placed on Accreditation Watch when a reviewable sentinel event has occurred and has come to the Joint Commission's attention and a thorough and credible root cause analysis of the sentinel event and action plan have *not* been completed within a specified time frame.

If an organization has experienced a *reviewable* sentinel event but fails to submit or otherwise make available an acceptable root cause analysis and action plan or otherwise provide for Joint Commission evaluation of its response to the sentinel event under an approved protocol within 45 days of the event or of its becoming aware of the event, a recommendation will be made to the Accreditation Committee to place the organization on Accreditation Watch. If the Accreditation Committee places the organization on Accreditation Watch, the organization will then be permitted an additional 15 days to submit an acceptable root cause analysis and action plan, or otherwise provide for Joint Commission evaluation of its response to the sentinel event under an approved protocol. The organization will be offered assistance in performing a root cause analysis of the event. The Accreditation Watch status is considered publicly disclosable information.

In all cases of an organization's refusal to permit review of information regarding a reviewable sentinel event in accordance with the Sentinel Event Policy and its approved protocols, the initial response by the Joint Commission is assignment of Accreditation Watch. Continued refusal may result in loss of accreditation.

## The Joint Commission's Response

Staff assesses the acceptability of the organization's response to the *reviewable* sentinel event, including the thoroughness and credibility of any root cause analysis information reviewed and the organization's action plan, and brings a recommendation to the Accreditation Committee at its next meeting following the due date for the organization's response.

If the response is *unacceptable*, the organization is required to address the inadequacies and submit, or make available for review, a new root cause analysis and action plan or otherwise provide for further Joint Commission evaluation of its response to the event. This must occur within 15 days of notification that the Accreditation Committee has found the response to be unacceptable.

Depending on the nature and extent of the inadequacies of the organization's initial response to the sentinel event, the Joint Commission will determine whether an on-site visit should be made to assist the organization in conducting an appropriate root cause analysis and developing an action plan.

If, on review, the organization's response is still not acceptable, or the organization fails to respond, staff will recommend to the Accreditation Committee that the organization be placed in Preliminary Nonaccreditation. If approved by the Accreditation Committee, this accreditation decision would be considered publicly disclosable information and the process for resolution of Preliminary Nonaccreditation would be initiated.

When the organization's response (initial or revised) is found to be *acceptable*, the Joint Commission issues an *Official Accreditation Decision Report* that

- reflects the Accreditation Committee's determination to (1) continue or modify the organization's current accreditation status and (2) terminate the Accreditation Watch, if previously assigned, and
- assigns an appropriate follow-up activity, typically a written progress report or follow-up visit to be conducted within six months.

## Follow-up Activities

The follow-up activity will assess, based on applicable standards, the implementation of system and process improvements identified in the action plan, the means by which the organization will continue to assess the effectiveness of those efforts, and the resolution of any type I recommendations. The follow-up activity will be conducted when the organization believes it can demonstrate effective implementation, but no later than six months following receipt of the *Official Accreditation Decision Report.*

A decision to maintain or change the organization's accreditation status as a result of the follow-up activity or assign additional follow-up requirements will be based on existing decision rules unless otherwise determined by the Accreditation Committee.

Each sentinel event evaluated under the Joint Commission's Sentinel Event Policy will be reviewed at the organization's next full accreditation survey.

This review will focus on implementation of risk-reduction strategies and the effectiveness of these actions.

## The Sentinel Event Database

To achieve the third goal of the Sentinel Event Policy, which is to increase the general knowledge about sentinel events, their causes, and strategies for prevention, the Joint Commission collects and analyzes data from the review of sentinel events, root cause analyses, action plans, and follow-up activities. These data and information form the content of the Joint Commission's Sentinel Event Database.

In response to concerns about potential increased legal exposure for accredited organizations through the sharing of such information with the Joint Commission, the Joint Commission has committed to the development and maintenance of this Sentinel Event Database in a fashion that will exclude organization identifiers. The three major categories of data elements include

- sentinel event data,
- root cause data, and
- risk-reduction data.

Aggregate data relating to root causes and risk reduction strategies for sentinel events that occur with significant frequency will form the basis for future error prevention advice to health care organizations through the Joint Commission's publication, *Sentinel Event Alert*, and other media.

## Handling Sentinel Event-Related Documents

Upon completing the review of any submitted root cause analysis and action plan and abstracting the required data elements for the Joint Commission's Sentinel Event Database, the original root cause analysis documents will be returned to the organization and any copies will be shredded. Handling of these sensitive documents is restricted to specially trained staff in accordance with procedures designed to protect the confidentiality of the documents.

The action plan resulting from the analysis of the sentinel event will initially be retained to serve as the basis for the follow-up activity. Once the action plan has been implemented to the satisfaction of the Joint Commission, as determined through follow-up activities, the Joint Commission will return the action plan to the organization.

# Requirements of Other Agencies

A detailed review of the sentinel event reporting requirements of state and federal agencies is beyond the scope of this book. Requirements vary by state and depend on the nature and outcome of the event. Readers are advised to obtain pertinent information from their state and federal agencies, including the Health Care Financing Administration, the Occupational Safety and Health Administration, the FDA, and others. The reporting requirements, both mandatory and voluntary, mentioned here are listed solely to give readers a feel for their range.

The FDA has regulatory purview over medical products including drugs, devices, and biologicals sold in the United States. Under the current Medical Device Reporting (MDR) requirements (21CFR803), both health care organizations and manufacturers must report certain types of clinical events involving medical

---

**Sidebar 4–6:** *The FDA and Physical Restraint*

The Food and Drug Administration (FDA) estimates that at least 100 deaths from improper use of restraint may occur annually and that many problems with restraint devices are never reported to the FDA. In July 1992, the agency issued an *FDA Backgrounder* report on the safe use of physical restraint devices.

In mid-1992, the FDA advised manufacturers that it considers patient restraint devices, such as safety vests and jackets, lap and wheelchair belts, and fabric body holders, to be prescription devices. As such, they must bear labeling stating that restraint devices can only be sold or used under the supervision of a licensed health care provider. The agency is working with industry to improve the labeling on restraint devices.

The agency may also consider reclassifying physical restraints to a more restrictive regulatory category, which would allow FDA to impose any "special controls" FDA deems necessary to ensure safer use.

In December 1991, the FDA informed health professionals of the potential hazards with restraint devices through its *FDA Medical Bulletin* (Vol. 21, No. 3). In addition, an FDA Safety Alert was sent to health professionals in all U.S. hospitals, nursing homes, and acute care facilities on July 15, 1991.

*Source:* Food and Drug Administration: Safe use of physical restraint devices. *FDA Backgrounder*, Jul 4 1992.

---

equipment directly to the FDA Office of Surveillance and Biometrics. Such events include those involving death or serious injury or illness, specifically those caused by user errors. Users are defined as either clinical or maintenance personnel. The objective of the requirements is not to establish responsibility for an adverse event but to obtain a comprehensive record of the use of medical devices in the clinical environment. For information on the FDA's position on physical restraint devices, see Sidebar 4–6, above.

The Safe Medical Devices Act of 1990 also requires all hospitals, nursing homes, and acute care facilities to report device-related adverse events to the FDA within ten working days of becoming aware of such situations. They must also report serious injuries or illnesses to the manufacturer within ten working days or to the FDA if the manufacturer is not known. Failure to report can result in civil monetary penalties or warning letters. A recent Government Accounting Office report found gross under-reporting by user facilities, in part because of lack of awareness of the reporting requirements and lack of feedback regarding outcomes when a report was filed.[23]

The FDA also has a national system called MedWatch for reporting medication-related events.[24] Reporting is voluntary for health care organizations but is mandatory for pharmaceutical manufacturers. The FDA receives only reports of serious adverse events defined as death, life-threatening, hospitalization (initial or prolonged), disability, congenital anomaly, and intervention to prevent permanent impairment or damage. All product problems may be reported anonymously to MedWatch via a toll-free number.* The confidentiality of those who report

---

* 1-800-FDA-1088.

the event and patients involved is strictly maintained. In 1994, the FDA received 130,000 reports. More than three-quarters of the reports were from manufacturers; the remainder were from physicians, pharmacists, other health care professionals, and consumers.

The USP in Rockville, Maryland, runs a Medication Errors Reporting Program in cooperation with a number of partners, including the ISMP in Warminster, Pennsylvania. Callers phone a toll-free number** or send information about medication errors and other adverse drug events which is shared with the medical community along with prevention education recommendations through a publication, *ISMP Medication Safety Alert.*

Mandates for provider-reporting systems for occupational illness and injury have existed in several states for many years. Because of inconsistencies across states and insufficient resources to initiate interventions when problems are identified, the National Institute for Occupational Safety and Health (NIOSH) developed a standardized, comprehensive system for reporting and follow-up called the Sentinel Event Notification System for Occupational Risks (SENSOR). SENSOR is a cooperative state-federal effort designed to develop local capability for preventing selected occupational disorders. The SENSOR system remains decentralized because reports are made to the health departments of the ten states participating in the program.

## References

1.  Spath P: Avoid panic by planning for sentinel events. *Hosp Peer Rev* June 1998, p 112-117.

2.  Perper JA: Life-threatening and fatal therapeutic misadventures. In Bogner MS (ed): *Human Error in Medicine.* Hillsdale, NJ: Lawrence Erlbaum Associates, 1994, p 33.

3.  Spath, p 117.

4.  Spath, p 117.

5.  Keyes C: Responding to an adverse event. *Forum,* Apr 1997, pp 2-3.

6.  Wu AW, et al: Do house officers learn from their mistakes? *JAMA* 265(16):2089-2094, 1991.

7.  Blumenthal D: Making medical errors into medical treasures. *JAMA* 272(23):1851-1857, 1994.

8.  Wu AW, et al: To tell the truth: Ethical and practical issues in disclosing medical mistakes to patients. *Gen Intern Med* 12(12)770-775, Dec 1997.

9.  Wu AW, McPhee SJ: Education and training: Needs and approaches handling mistakes in medical training. Presented at the Examining Errors in Health Care Conference, Rancho Mirage, CA: Oct 13-15, 1996.

10. Witman AB, Hardin S: Patients' responses to physicians' mistakes. *Forum,* Apr 1997, pp 4-5.

11. McPhee SJ, et al: Practical issues in disclosing medical mistakes to patients. Presented at the Examining Errors in Health Care Conference, Rancho Mirage, CA: Oct 13-15, 1996.

12. Feldman MD, Christensen JF (eds): *Behavioral Medicine in Primary Care.* Stanford, CT: Appleton and Lange, 1997.

13. American Medical Association Council on Ethical and Judicial Affairs: *Code of Medical Ethics: Current Opinions with Annotations,* 1996-1997 Edition. Chicago: AMA, 1996.

---

** Reports of medication errors can be made by telephone to the United States Pharmacopeia (USP) Medication Errors Reporting Program (1-800-23ERROR). Reports can be submitted to USP on a confidential basis if the reporter so chooses.

14. American Psychiatric Association: *The Principles of Medical Ethics: With Annotations Especially Applicable to Psychiatry*, Washington, DC: APA, 1998.

15. American College of Physicians: American College of Physicians' Ethics Manual. *Ann Intern Med* 117(11):947-960, 1992.

16. American Psychological Association: Ethical principles of psychologists and code of conduct. *Amer Psych* 47(12):1597-1611, Dec 1992.

17. American Nurses Association: *Code for Nurses with Interpretive Statements*. Washington, DC: ANA, 1985.

18. American Society of Hospital Pharmacists: ASHP guidelines on preventing medication errors in hospitals. *Am J Hosp Pharm* 50(2):305–314, 1993.

19. Personal communication with Susan Winckler, Director of Policy and Legislation, American Pharmaceutical Association, May 1997.

20. National Association of Social Workers: *NASW Code of Ethics*. Washington, DC: NASW, 1997.

21. National Board for Certified Counselors: *NBCC Code of Ethics*. Greensboro, NC: NBCC, 1998.

22. Keyes, p 3.

23. U.S. General Accounting Office: Medical device reporting: Improvements needed in FDA's systems for monitoring problems with approved devices. GAO/HEHS-97-21. Washington, DC: U.S. General Accounting Office, 1997.

24. Kessler DA: Introducing MedWatch: A new approach to reporting medication and device adverse effects and product problems. *JAMA* 269(21):2765-2768, 1993.

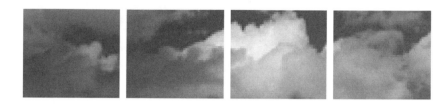

*Chapter Five*
**Conducting a Root
Cause Analysis, Part I—
Evaluating Causation**

*Chapter Five*

# Conducting a Root Cause Analysis, Part I— Evaluating Causation

To get rid of weeds, dig up the root;
to stop a pot from boiling, withdraw the fuel.

*Chinese Proverb*

This chapter provides practical information on how to conduct the first major portion of a root cause analysis in response to a sentinel event. This portion includes identifying proximate causes and underlying causes, designing and implementing interim changes, and identifying the root cause. In addition, tools and techniques that can aid the evaluation and measurement processes are briefly described along with their benefits.

## What Is Root Cause Analysis?

*Root cause analysis* is a process for identifying the basic or causal factors that underlie variation in performance, including the occurrence or possible occurrence of a sentinel event. A *root cause* is the most fundamental reason a problem—a situation where performance does not meet expectations—has occurred.

In common usage, the word *cause* suggests responsibility or a factor to blame for a problem. Our focus in this chapter and the next is elsewhere—on the positive, preventive approach to system change that can be implemented by using root cause analysis. Root cause analysis can do more than resolve that "A caused B." This process can also help an organization suggest productive solutions in the form of preventive system changes.

Hence, root cause analysis can be both reactive and proactive. Most frequently, the technique is used reactively—to probe the reason for problems that have already occurred. The process is then used to identify the most obvious opportunities for improvement that will prevent recurrence. The product of the root cause analysis is an action plan that identifies the strategies that the organization intends to implement to reduce the risk of similar events occurring in the future.

However, root cause analysis may also be used proactively to even greater organization benefit to study processes to prevent future problems from ever occurring. This approach, which is well known in the engineering world, focuses on the design of systems in which faults or problems are anticipated and, in effect, "designed out."

In the nuclear power and aerospace industries, sentinel events are rare because they have been anticipated. Systems, often with significant redundancies, have been built to protect against them. In contrast, sentinel events in the health care environment, involving death or serious injury or the risk thereof, occur relatively frequently and tend to be handled largely in a reactive way. Fundamentally, sentinel events in all environments provide two challenges:

- To understand how and why the event occurred; and
- To prevent the same or a similar event from occurring in the future.

To meet these challenges, organizations need to understand the *underlying causes* of the event (the causes that led to the proximate causes), not simply its superficial, obvious, or immediate causes (the *proximate causes*). Root cause analysis helps organizations look underneath the apparent or proximate causes to get at the root of an event (see Figure 5–1, below).

Root cause analysis has the following characteristics:

- It focuses primarily on systems and processes, not individual performance;
- It progresses from special causes in clinical processes to common causes in organization processes;
- It repeatedly digs deeper by asking Why? until no additional logical answer can be identified; and
- It identifies changes that could be made in systems and processes—through redesign or development of new systems or processes—that would improve the level of performance and reduce the risk of a particular serious sentinel event

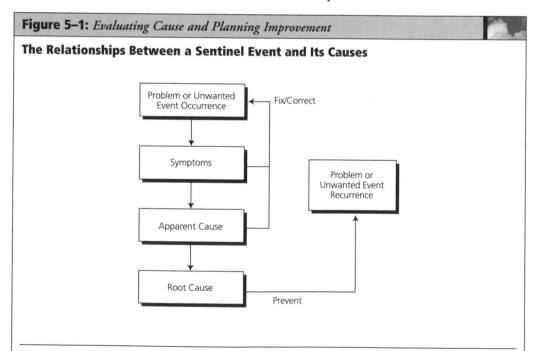

**Figure 5–1:** *Evaluating Cause and Planning Improvement*

**The Relationships Between a Sentinel Event and Its Causes**

Correcting problems, symptoms, and apparent causes will not prevent the recurrence of an unwanted event. Only finding and resolving the root cause of the event can do this.

*Source:* Wilson PF, Dell LD, Anderson GF: *Root Cause Analysis: A Tool for Total Quality Management.* Milwaukee: ASQC Quality Press, 1993, p.11. Used with permission.

occurring in the future. Or, it determines, after analysis, that no such improvement opportunities exist.

The first three characteristics are described later in this chapter, and the fourth is covered fully in Chapter 6, pages 203 through 221.

## Assessing the Performance of Systems, Not People

When health care outcomes are bad, when a client dies while in restraint, when machines fail, when a consumer commits suicide—in short, when sentinel events happen—blame and accusation emerge as the primary solution to the "problem." As described in Chapter 2, pages 35 through 38, all too frequently individuals are "rooted out" as the "bad apples" who created the problem. This approach is punitive in nature. The nurse who failed to observe the client according to the organization's protocols is reprimanded or suspended. The license of a physician who prescribed a lethal drug dosage is suspended, the physician's privileges are revoked, and a malpractice suit is filed. Punishment is exacted for "faulty" individual performance. Although this indeed can be the cause of some errors, it is not the cause of all, or even many.

Unfortunately, saying that we are looking for the "cause" of an outcome, often suggests that two conclusions will be reached:

- A determination of accountability; and
- An indication that, except for X, Y, or Z cause, the outcome would not have occurred.

When the outcome has been bad, such as a sentinel event, these conclusions can lead to an environment in which fear of blame and accusations of negligence serve as impediments to identification of systems and process flaws.

With root cause analysis, the focus is not punitive. Rather, it is on systems—on how to improve systems to prevent the occurrence of sentinel events. The approach involves digging into the organization's systems to find new ways to do things. It is focused on answering the question What should we *do* to prevent this in the future? instead of What should we *have done* to prevent this from having occurred? Pointing a finger at someone who can be blamed for a problem is not a part of this process. Rather, a problem is perceived as everyone's problem and everyone's challenge to fix or improve. The emphasis is on improving systems of which clinical processes and people are but a part.

For example, human error by a mental health worker in applying a therapeutic hold may be the proximate cause of a client's death. When staff members are trained in proper therapeutic holding techniques, they may be able to remember the techniques from year to year even if they don't have to use the techniques on a regular basis. However, errors in memory will and do occur even with the best-intentioned and most competent human beings.

Therapeutic holding and other aggression management techniques are likely to be improved only when they are seen as part of the larger education, training, and competence assessment system that involves all behavioral health care staff. Therefore, implementation of new continuing education and competence assessment programs geared to preventing a future error in therapeutic holding would be of benefit.

Success with root cause analysis is founded on the belief that although humans make mistakes and errors are inevitable, organization improvement is always possible and the ever-present goal. Root cause analysis has the highest potential for success in environments or organization cultures where individuals are not afraid to report errors. Punishment effectively alters or stifles the necessary climate. The organization's leaders need to be committed both to limiting individual blame and punishment and to the root cause analysis process as an effective way to identify improvement opportunities.

Focusing on improving systems rather than on individual performance will reduce the likelihood of future sentinel events. Errors by individual clinicians in the behavioral health care setting, for example, should generate an evaluation of the organizational systems that support their work. These include

- management of the environment in which care is provided, including equipment and activities;
- management of information, including lines of communication, accessibility of knowledge-based information, and linkage of information sources;
- measurement of performance with respect to both processes and outcomes;
- credentialing and privileging processes for physicians and psychologists, and the hiring and competency review processes for others; and
- initial orientation and training and continuing staff education.

An organization's management and clinical leaders are responsible for focusing attention on systems. Individuals have only limited control over their own ability to avoid certain kinds of human errors, such as errors in memory and attention. These errors can be prevented by designing tasks and processes that minimize dependency on such "weak" cognitive functions as short-term memory and attention.

## The Benefits of Perseverance

When an organization providing behavioral health services experiences a sentinel event, it should promptly initiate intensive assessment to reduce the variation and prevent the event from recurring in the future. This intensive assessment involves

- studying a process and learning its steps and decision points;
- identifying the various people, actions, and equipment required for the processes' outcomes;
- finding links between variables in performance; and
- ranking the frequency or importance of causes.

When this intensive assessment digs beyond the proximate cause—which is often a special cause, such as human error or equipment breakdown—it becomes root cause analysis.

Root cause analysis involves asking a series of questions, many of which may be difficult and uncomfortable to ask because of the fear of blame. It is possible that the answers that surface may be equally difficult to confront—perhaps there is something that the organization *should* have done differently. In addition, the answers may be difficult to act on inasmuch as change is often resisted or requires an up-front investment of money (even if the long-term benefits save money). Keep in mind, however, that effective, lasting change can only come about when the root cause of variation in performance is discovered and changed. There may, in fact, be more than one root cause underlying performance variation. Treating only the "symptoms," or the proximate special cause, may lead to some short-term improvements but will not prevent the variation from recurring.

Special causes of variation in processes (discussed in Chapter 1, pages 13 through 30) are usually apparent and, as the proximate causes, offer the most likely or obvious reasons for the variation. In the case of a sentinel event, the proximate cause is almost always a special-cause variation. Because drilling down to the root cause of performance variation can be difficult, the tendency is to mistake proximate special causes for the root cause. Another tendency is to stop searching for the root cause after taking corrective action on proximate special causes.

For example, organizations may assume that the problem is solved when the nurse who failed to observe a restrained client is fired or when a manager reissues a policy memo to remind others not to do what the nurse did. Organizations are strongly encouraged not to stop the process of assessment for the root cause prematurely. The long-term benefits of determining root causes and planning corresponding improvements far outweigh any short-term gains of premature closure in terms of consumer care, outcomes, and efficient use of human, material, and financial resources.

## Conducting a Root Cause Analysis

### Getting Organized

The first step involved in conducting a root cause analysis is to assign a team to assess the sentinel event. A team may need to be established on an ad hoc basis, or the core of an appropriate team may already exist in the form of a targeted performance improvement or some other team. The team should include staff at all levels closest to the issues involved, those with decision-making authority, and individuals critical to the implementation of potential recommended changes. The team should

- have its core members and leader/facilitator clearly identified;
- be empowered to do its assessment and make changes or recommendations for changes;
- be provided the resources, including time, to do its work; and
- have a defined structure and process for moving forward.

The team composition may need to change as the team moves in and out of areas within the organization that affect or are affected by the issues being analyzed. Organizations should allow for and expect this to happen. The core team members, however, should remain as stable as possible throughout the process, at least in terms of leadership and areas or functions represented on the team. For example, a core team investigating the root cause of a medication error should include representatives from nursing, medicine, administration, pharmacy or the pharmacy supplier, and information technology or management, as available. Core teams limited in size to fewer than ten individuals tend to perform with greater efficiency.

A team frequently can benefit from having a leader who serves more as a facilitator or resource person to provide help in applying the tools of root cause analysis. This person guides the team through the root cause analysis process while encouraging open communication and broad participation. The leader or facilitator might wish to consider various techniques for promoting high-quality group discussion, including

- using small groups to report on ideas;
- offering quiet time for thinking; and
- asking each person to offer an idea regarding causes or solutions in response to a why question before allowing evaluative comments or second turns at speaking.

It is best if the leader/facilitator is not a "stakeholder" in the processes and systems being evaluated.

At the beginning of the process, the team leader or facilitator should establish a way of communicating team progress and findings to senior leadership. Keeping senior leaders informed on a regular basis is critical to management support of the root cause analysis initiative and implementation of its recommendations. Although it is difficult to provide guidelines on what constitutes "on a regular basis," as this will vary widely depending on circumstances, communication with senior leaders should increase in frequency with

- serious adverse outcomes;
- repeated adverse events;
- events requiring solutions from multiple parts of the organization;
- possible solutions requiring the investment of sizable dollars; and
- the media's involvement in the case and its solutions.

Frequency of communication will also vary according to the actions required in the short term to prevent recurrence of the event. It should be weighed with the speed with which information emerges from the investigation. If information is emerging rapidly, the team leader should give thought to the most productive timing for communication.

The creation of a detailed work plan is also critical to the process and to securing management support. A plan outlining target dates for accomplishing specific objectives provides a tool against which to guide and measure the team's progress. A Gantt chart outlining key steps and time frames for a proximate cause improvement plan for an organization that experienced a suicide appears in Figure 5–2, page 167.

The full work plan should include target dates for major milestones and key activities in the root cause analysis process, including

- defining the event and identifying the proximate and underlying causes;
- collecting and assessing data about proximate and underlying causes;
- designing and implementing interim changes;
- identifying the root causes;
- planning improvement; and
- testing, implementing, and measuring the success of improvements.

## Defining the Event

The first key step taken by the root cause analysis team is to define the event—that is, to describe, as accurately as possible, what happened. In response to an event that has already occurred, the team might ask What actually happened? and What created the "red flag" warning of the occurrence of a sentinel event? Initially, the event can be defined simply, for example:

- Client committed suicide by hanging;
- Client died from overdose of drug;

**Figure 5–2:** *Conducting a Root Cause Analysis, Part 1—Evaluating Causation*

**Proximate Causes of Patient Suicide**

| Activity | 3rd Qtr 1996 | | | 4th Qtr 1996 | | | 1st Qtr 1997 | | | 2nd Qtr 1997 | | |
|---|---|---|---|---|---|---|---|---|---|---|---|---|
| | Jul | Aug | Sep | Oct | Nov | Dec | Jan | Feb | Mar | Apr | May | Jun |
| Establish review team | | | | | | | | | | | | |
| Begin process of root cause analysis | | | | | | | | | | | | |
| Expanded security rounds to include helipad | | | | | | | | | | | | |
| Revise Suicide Precaution Policy | | | | | | | | | | | | |
| Staff training: Suicide Precaution Policy | | | | | | | | | | | | |
| Staff training: assessment and interventions for patients with mental health needs | | | | | | | | | | | | |
| Staff training: patients leaving unit unattended | | | | | | | | | | | | |
| Team meetings to assess PDCA | | | | | | | | | | | | |
| Medical record review of all suicide precaution charts | | | | | | | | | | | | |
| Concurrent assessment of patients on suicide precautions | | | | | | | | | | | | |

This chart represents one organization's attempts to outline key steps and timeframes for a plan to eliminate proximate causes that led to a sentinel event (patient suicide). (PDCA, Plan-Do-Check-Act.)

*Source:* University Medical Center of Southern Nevada, Las Vegas. Used with permission.

- Fire killed individual in restraint; or
- Individual who was restrained died while trying to get out of bed.

Next, establishing a time line can be a key step in deciphering how the sequence of events unfolded and can become a vital, informative step in the root cause analysis. For example, asking probing questions such as When did the client receive a phone call? Who last saw the client? and What was the client's behavior? can become an important function in establishing the sequence of events. It is important to consider both the immediate cause (for example, the client committed suicide by hanging himself in the bathroom) as well as the antecedent events and processes that took place.

Part of this approach may include the "psychological autopsy" where staff try to put themselves in the mind of the client for the purpose of understanding what led to the adverse event that, at first, may seem random and idiosyncratic.

Using root cause analysis in a proactive way to prevent future problems from occurring, the team might ask What warnings might we hear, see, or experience that indicate that we might have a problem? What indicates or what might indicate a potential problem? or What could go wrong? The team should begin to consider performance measurement tools that might be helpful in responding to these questions.

Creating a more detailed definition of the event is the next part of this step. The description provides the when, where, and how details of the event. For example, with a sentinel event involving the death of a client in restraint, a more detailed definition of the event might state, "death of an 18-year-old male from burns and smoke inhalation following a fire started by the individual with matches in a room where the individual was restrained."

In addition, the team identifies the area or services affected by the event. For example, for the fire-related death of the client in restraint, the relevant areas might be nursing, security, and physical plant.

## Identifying the Proximate Causes

The next step taken by the team is to identify the proximate causes for the event. This generally can be gleaned by asking Why did the event happen? In most cases, identifying the proximate causes will be simple; in other cases, identifying the proximate causes might take some digging. As mentioned earlier, typically a proximate cause is a special-cause variation. In the health care environment, proximate causes tend to fall into a number of distinct categories, including

- human factors;
- process factors;
- equipment factors; and
- environmental factors, whether controllable or uncontrollable.

To identify the proximate cause of an event involving *human factors*, the team might ask What human factors were relevant to the outcome? To identify the proximate cause of an event involving *process factors*, the team might ask What are the steps in the process, as designed? and What steps were involved in and contributed to the event? To identify the proximate cause of an event involving *equipment factors*, the team might ask How did the equipment performance affect the outcome? To identify the proximate cause of an event involving *environmental factors*, the team might ask What factors directly affected the outcome? and Were such factors within or truly beyond the organization's control? Finally, the team might ask Are there any other factors that have directly influenced this outcome?

For example, in identifying the proximate causes for a suicide, a team might conclude that the causes include

- failure to follow policies on precaution orders, involving *human factors;*
- a faulty initial assessment process which did not include an immediate psychiatric consultation, involving *process factors;* and
- a nonfunctional paging system that delayed communication with the client's physician, involving an *equipment factor.*

The probing continues. The team again asks Why? Why did that proximate cause happen? What systems and processes underlie proximate factors? The goal of asking questions at this stage is to identify the underlying causes for the proximate causes. Underlying causes may involve special-cause variation, common-cause variation, or both. It is critical at this point for the team to clearly define the issues regarding the sentinel event and be sure that team members share a common understanding of the issues. No matter how obvious the issues may seem, each team member may not understand them in the same way.

Brainstorming to identify all possible or potential contributing causes may be a useful technique for teams at this stage of the root cause analysis. Following traditional brainstorming ground rules such as There is no bad idea and ensuring that team members do not express reactions or provide commentary as ideas are expressed are critical to success. The team leader will want to keep team members focused on processes, not people, while asking questions to uncover causes. By repeatedly asking Why? the team can continue working until it feels it has exhausted all possible questions and causes. The importance of this stage cannot be overstated. It provides the initial substance for the root cause analysis without which a team cannot proceed.

Because the underlying causes of proximate causes in the health care environment may relate to care or other processes, the team might explore questions such as the following:

- What are the steps in the process?
- What steps were involved in or contributed to the event?
- What is currently being done to prevent failure at this step?
- What is currently being done to protect against a bad outcome if failure is occurring at this step?
- What other areas or services are affected?

Various tools can be helpful at this stage. Constructing a flowchart is a useful way to visualize the response to What are the steps in the process? Cause-and-effect diagrams; change analysis; and failure mode, effect, and criticality analysis are useful techniques in analyzing the response to What steps were involved in or contributed to the event? Fault tree analysis can be used to study what is currently being done to prevent failure at this step. Barrier analysis can be helpful in looking at what is currently being done to protect against a bad outcome if failure is occurring at the given step, and failure mode and effect analysis can be a useful tool in examining what other areas or services are being affected. Benefits and how-to information on each of these techniques appear later in this chapter.

After sorting and analyzing the cause list with the appropriate tools, the team may begin determining which process or system each cause is a part of and whether it is a special or common cause in that process or system. Being special or common is not an inherent characteristic of the cause itself. Rather, the distinction describes the relationship of the cause to a specific process or system. It is possible for the same cause to be a special cause in one process and a common cause in another. For example, as mentioned in Chapter 1, page 16, frequent assaults by staff against clients indicate a problem with the organization's hiring and training practices. Human resources practices should be examined for common-cause problems involving the personnel screening and interview processes. A flowchart of the processes at this stage may be very helpful.

For a special cause in a process, teams should search for the common cause in the system of which the process is a part. It is the larger system and its managers, not the process or process owners, that will need to be responsible for the redesign that will reduce the likelihood of future sentinel events. Again, in most cases, a special cause of variation in one process will be found to be the result of, or permitted by, a common cause of variation in a larger system of which the process is a part. Identifying a special cause is only an initial step in a full evaluation.

## Collecting and Assessing Data on Proximate and Underlying Causes

To advance further toward discovering root causes, teams need to explore in depth proximate and underlying causes. This exploration involves collecting and assessing relevant data. Various statistical and nonstatistical tools can help an organization uncover the root causes of a particular outcome in a process. Understanding causes is essential if the organization is to create lasting improvements. Tools include brainstorming, flowcharts, cause-and-effect diagrams, Pareto charts, indicators, scatter diagrams, affinity diagrams, barrier analysis, change analysis, failure mode and effects analysis, and fault tree analysis. The tools are designed to help root cause analysis team members understand processes and factors that contribute to both good and problematic performance. They are also designed to be used by any group studying a process. These tools are among the most popular and persuasive of performance improvement. None of the tools requires a statistical background (although Pareto charts and scatter diagrams are quantitative tools).

## Designing and Implementing Interim Changes

Even at this early stage, some quick or immediate "fixes" may be offered. For example, in the suicide case described on page 217, the organization could conduct mandatory in-service training for all staff on suicide risk assessment. Or, the organization could place all consumers with psychiatric or substance abuse diagnoses on suicide precautions. In addition, the organization could install a paging system with a wider range.

Teams conducting root cause analysis need not wait until they finish their analysis to begin designing and implementing changes. During the process of asking Why? potential interventions emerge. Intermediate changes may not only be appropriate, but necessary. First, they may be needed to reduce an immediate risk. For example, an unsecured window may need to be repaired and secured, and an intoxicated employee should be removed from the environment right away. Second, they may also uncover additional causes that were previously masked but are critical to the search for the root cause. Finally, intermediate changes can be part of a Plan-Do-Study-Act (PDSA) cycle to test process redesign before implementing it organizationwide. For example, an organization may wish to test the use of new bathroom hardware in one room before changing hardware organizationwide.

Altman calls the process of sorting through causes for the root cause "identifying the web of causation. The key point is to identify the web of causation and to intervene on as many levels as possible in this web. It is important to recognize that the deeper one progresses in the chain or web of causation, the closer one gets to underlying, structural (root) causes."[1] Hence, although the team may make intermediate improvements along the way, it should not stop the root cause analysis process before the root cause has been identified and corrective action taken. Where intermediate actions are planned, the team should identify

- *who* is responsible for implementation;
- *when* the actions will be implemented—including any pilot testing; and
- *how* the effectiveness of the actions will be evaluated.

Again, however worthy short-term solutions may be, the organization must not stop after implementing these, but rather must continue probing more deeply to arrive at the root causes and possible long-term solutions.

## Identifying the Root Causes

Root causes are the most fundamental causal factors of an event. As such, their origin lies in common-cause variation of organization systems. (A discussion of variation can be found in Chapter 1, pages 15 through 17.) In addition, common-cause variation of organization systems may lead to special-cause variation in dependent processes. Getting to the root cause of a sentinel event or potential sentinel event takes a lot of time and effort. It involves asking Why? at least three to five times and then exploring the ramifications of each response. Root causes of a sentinel event in a health care organization can be categorized according to the important organization functions or processes performed by the organization. These include

- human resource processes;
- information management processes;
- environmental management processes; and
- leadership processes, embracing corporate culture, encouragement of communication, and clear communication of priorities.

In addition, factors beyond an organization's control should be considered a separate category. However, organizations need to exercise caution in assigning factors to this category. Although a causative factor may be beyond an organization's control, protection of clients from the effects of the "uncontrollable factor" is within the organization's control in most cases and should be addressed as a risk-reduction strategy.

Concrete questions about each of the aforementioned functions can help team members reach the essence of the problem—the systems that lie behind or underneath problem-prone processes. At this stage, questions can be worded in the form of To what degree...? Follow-up questions for each could be Can this be improved, and if so, how? and What are the pros and cons of expending the necessary resources to improve this? See Sidebar 5–1, page 172-173, for a full itemization of possible questions.

Other questions may emerge in the course of an analysis. All questions should be fully considered. In the client suicide example, the team found that systems dealing with human resources, information management, environmental management, and leadership issues were root causes of the sentinel event. In the human resources area, age-specific staff competence had not been assessed adequately and staff needed additional training in management of suicidal clients. In the information management area, information about the client's past admission was not available. Communication delays resulted in failure to implement appropriate preventive actions. In the environmental management area, the team found that access to the appropriate unit for the client was denied because of a 99% occupancy rate. Hence, human resources, information management, and environmental management issues were determined to be root causes.

The root causes identified by 20 organizations that experienced a death of an individual who was physically restrained appear in Sidebar 5–2 (page 173). The

**Sidebar 5–1:** *Root Cause Analysis Questions*

The following questions may be used to probe for systems problems underlying problem-prone processes.

Questions concerning *human resource* issues may include the following:

- To what degree are staff members properly qualified and currently competent for their responsibilities? Can the status quo be improved, and if so, how? What are the pros and cons of expending the resources necessary to improve the status quo?

- How does actual staffing compare with ideal levels? Can staffing be improved and, if so, how? What are the pros and cons of expending the resources necessary to improve staffing?

- What are the plans for dealing with contingencies that would tend to reduce effective staffing levels? Can this situation be improved and, if so, how? What are the pros and cons of expending the resources necessary to improve the current situation?

- To what degree is staff performance in the operant processes addressed? Can staff performance be improved and, if so, how? What are the pros and cons of expending the resources necessary to improve staff performance?

- How can orientation and in-service training be improved? What are the pros and cons of expending the necessary resources to improve such training?

Questions concerning *information management issues* may include the following:

- To what degree is all necessary information available when needed? To what degree is the information accurate and complete? To what degree is the information unambiguous? Can these factors be improved and, if so, how? What are the pros and cons of expending the resources necessary to improve in this area?

- To what degree is the communication of information among participants adequate? Can the situation be improved and, if so, how? What are the pros and cons of expending the resources necessary to improve communication of information?

Questions concerning *environmental management issues* may include the following:

- To what degree was the physical environment appropriate for the processes being carried out? Can the physical environment be improved and, if so, how? What are the pros and cons of expending the resources necessary to improve the physical environment?

- To what degree are systems in place to identify environmental risks? Can this system be improved and, if so, how? What are the pros and cons of expending the resources necessary to improve identification of environmental risks?

- What emergency and failure-mode responses have been planned and tested? Can these responses be improved and, if so, how? What are the pros and cons of expending the resources necessary to improve response capabilities?

Questions concerning *leadership issues* may include the following:

- To what degree is the culture conducive to risk identification and reduction? Can the existing culture be improved and, if so, how? What are the pros and cons of expending the resources necessary to create a culture more conducive to risk identification and reduction?

- What are the barriers to communication of potential risk factors? Can these barriers be reduced and, if so, how? What are the pros and cons of expending the resources necessary to improve, reduce, or eliminate existing barriers?

- To what degree is the prevention of adverse outcomes communicated as a high priority?

*(continued on next page)*

---

**Sidebar 5–1:** *Root Cause Analysis Questions (continued)*

How is this priority communicated? Can communication processes be improved and, if so, how? What are the pros and cons of expending the resources necessary to improve the situation?

Questions concerning *uncontrollable factors* may include the following:

- What can be done to protect against the effects of uncontrollable factors? What are the pros and cons of expending the resources necessary to improve protection against such factors?

---

root causes for inpatient suicides identified by 65 organizations that experienced a patient suicide appear in Sidebar 5–3 (page 174). Graphs of the frequency of root causes of medication errors, inpatient suicides, and restraint deaths reported to and reviewed by the Joint Commission between 1996 and 1998 appear as Figures 5–3 through 5–5 (pages 176 and 178).

How does your organization know whether and when it has identified all of the true root causes of a sentinel event? Patrice Spath suggests using a checklist for determining whether those causes identified are indeed root causes. The checklist appears as Sidebar 5–4 (page 175).

## How to Organize a Root Cause Analysis

A framework for conducting a root cause analysis is provided in Figure 5–6 (pages 179-181). This framework provides an aid in organizing the steps in a root cause analysis, determining appropriate actions as part of a risk-reduction strategy, and identifying how the effectiveness of those actions will be measured. It is intended only to provide general guidance, not to prescribe any particular model or approach. The approach that a team uses will ultimately depend on the nature

---

**Sidebar 5–2:** *Root Causes Identified for Restraint-Related Deaths*

Twenty organizations that experienced restraint-related deaths and reported such deaths to the Joint Commission between 1996 and 1998 conducted root cause analyses and identified the following root causes:

- Patient assessment, such as incomplete medical assessment or incomplete examination of the individual (for example, failure to identify contraband, such as matches);

- Inadequate care planning, such as alternatives not fully considered, restraint devices used as punishment, and inappropriate room or unit assignment;

- Lack of patient observation procedures or practices;

- Staff-related factors, such as insufficient orientation or training, competency review or credentialing, or insufficient staffing levels; and

- Equipment-related factors, such as use of split-side rails without side rail protectors, use of two-point rather than four-point restraint devices, use of a high-neck vest, incorrect application of a restraining device, or a monitor or an alarm not working or not being used when appropriate.

*Source:* Joint Commission: Sentinel Event Alert, Issue Eight, Nov 1998.

---

**Sidebar 5–3:** *Root Causes Identified for Inpatient Suicides*

Sixty-five organizations that experienced inpatient suicides and reported such deaths to the Joint Commission between 1996 and 1998 identified the following root causes:

- The environment of care, such as the following: presence of non-breakaway bars, rods, or safety rails; lack of testing of breakaway hardware; and inadequate security;

- Patient assessment methods, such as incomplete suicide risk assessment at intake, absent or incomplete reassessment, and incomplete examination of the individual (for example, failure to identify a contraband);

- Staff-related factors, such as insufficient orientation or training, incomplete competency review or credentialing, and inadequate staffing levels;

- Incomplete or infrequent patient observations;

- Information-related factors such as incomplete communication among caregivers and information being unavailable when needed; and

- Care planning, such as assignment of the patient to an inappropriate unit or location.

*Source:* Joint Commission: *Sentinel Event Alert*, Issue Seven, Nov 1998.

---

of the event itself, the characteristics of the organization, and the experience and preferences of the people involved in the analysis.

Each column of the framework can be expanded. Even deeper levels of causality that should be explored and additional processes and systems to be analyzed may exist. The questions included in the framework are generic and are presented only to stimulate additional, more specific questioning.

## Planning Improvement: A Focus of Its Own

Once an organization has a solid hypothesis about one or more root causes, what should the next step be? After the root cause analysis team has determined the most likely root causes of a sentinel event, a team can begin devising and implementing improvement strategies to help ensure that faulty systems are improved for the future. The team may comprise the same members as during the early stages of the root cause analysis, or new members might be brought on board as required by the recommended improvements. Planning and implementing improvement are integral and critical steps in the root cause analysis process. In fact, no root cause analysis is complete until the following questions have been answered: So what are we going to do with the problematic systems now that we've identified them? What improvement strategies should be implemented? and How will we monitor these strategies to ensure their success? In fact, the implementation and assessment stages of the process are so important that they are the focus of Chapter 6, pages 203 through 223.

## Characteristics of a Root Cause Analysis

Teams conducting a root cause analysis, particularly those conducting one for the first time, will have many questions about whether their work has been thorough enough and whether it will be credible to all authorities, both internal and external.

We offer the following guidance for specific characteristics of a thorough, credible, and acceptable root cause analysis.

To be *thorough*, the root cause analysis must include

- a determination of the human and other factors most directly associated with the sentinel event, and the processes and systems related to its occurrence;
- analysis of the underlying systems and processes through a series of why questions to determine where redesign might reduce risk;
- for any event in one of the categories currently identified in the matrix of minimum requirements for root cause analysis, inquiry into each identified area for that category of event sufficient in depth to determine that there is, or is not, an opportunity within the associated systems, processes, or functions to redesign or otherwise take action to reduce risk;
- identification of risk points and their potential contributions to this type of event; and

---

**Sidebar 5–4:** *Checklist to Use in Determining Whether the Root Cause(s) of the Sentinel Event Have Been Found*

| **Test Questions** | **Yes/No** |
|---|---|
| 1. You ran into a dead end when asking What caused the proposed root cause? | _____ |
| 2. All conversation has come to a positive end. | _____ |
| 3. Everyone involved in the investigation feels good, is motivated, and uplifted emotionally. | _____ |
| 4. Everyone involved in the investigation agrees it is the root cause that keeps the problem from resolving. | _____ |
| 5. The root cause fully explains why the problem exists from all points of view. | _____ |
| 6. The earliest beginnings of the situation have been explored and understood. | _____ |
| 7. The root cause is logical, makes sense, and dispels all confusion. | _____ |
| 8. The root cause is something that can be influenced, controlled, and dealt with realistically. | _____ |
| 9. Finding the root cause has given people hope that something constructive can be done to prevent a reoccurrence of the incident. | _____ |
| 10. Suddenly workable solutions, not outrageous demands, that deal with the majority of the symptoms begin to appear. | _____ |
| 11. A stable, long-term, once-and-for-all resolution of the situation now appears feasible. | _____ |

*Source:* Spath PL: *Investigating Sentinel Events: How to Find and Resolve Root Causes.* Forest Grove, OR: Brown-Spath & Associates, 1997.

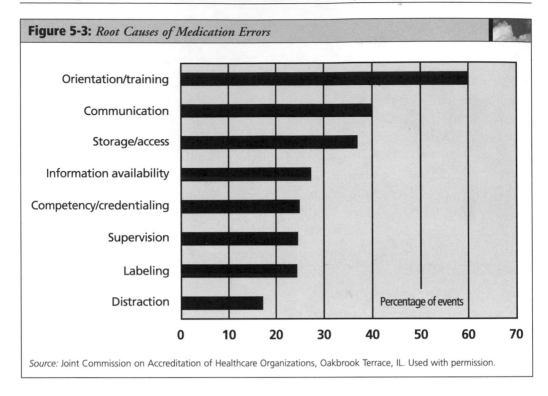

**Figure 5-3:** *Root Causes of Medication Errors*

Source: Joint Commission on Accreditation of Healthcare Organizations, Oakbrook Terrace, IL. Used with permission.

- a determination of potential improvements in processes or systems that would tend to decrease the likelihood of such events in the future, or a determination, after analysis, that no such improvement opportunities exist.
   To be *credible*, the root cause analysis must
- include participation by the leadership of the organization and by the individuals most closely involved in the processes and systems under review;
- be internally consistent, for example, not contradict itself or leave obvious questions unanswered; and
- provide a rationale for any conclusion that a relevant process, system, or function is not applicable to the event or offers no opportunity for risk reduction; and
- include consideration of any relevant literature.
   A root cause analysis will be considered *acceptable* by the Joint Commission if it
- focuses primarily on systems and processes, not individual performance;
- progresses from special causes in clinical processes to common causes in organization processes;
- repeatedly digs deeper by continuously asking Why? until the root cause has been thoroughly identified; and
- identifies changes that could be made in systems and processes—either through redesign or development of new systems or processes—that would reduce the risk of such events occurring in the future.
   A summary of key tips for conducting a root cause analysis appears in Sidebar 5–5, page 182. The minimum scope of a root cause analysis for specific types of sentinel events is identified in Sidebar 5–6, page 184.

## Tools for Root Cause Analysis

This section provides information on how to use selected tools during root cause analysis and the benefits of each tool. The tools are designed to help individuals and teams understand processes and factors that contribute to both good and problem-filled performance.

### Flowcharts

A flowchart is a graphic representation of the path a process follows from start to finish. Flowcharts are designed to help teams understand all steps in a process through the use of common, easily recognizable symbols. Clear understanding of a process is essential if improvement is to take place. Flowcharts can illustrate the actual path a process takes or the ideal path it should follow. When the root cause of an event is being analyzed, the flowchart should illustrate the actual path the process took. Only later might it be useful to design a new, improved "ideal" path.

Flowcharts are widely used to identify problems and plan solutions. They should be used whenever a team needs to identify the path that a product or service follows to spot problem areas and opportunities for improvement. Flowcharts help identify inefficiencies, misunderstandings, redundancies, and areas of neglect while providing insight into how a given process should be performed. By providing a clear picture of all components of the process, flowcharts give the people involved at the various steps a complete understanding of the process.

It is essential that flowcharts be constructed by the individuals actually performing the work being charted. A chart created by a manager or an administrator illustrating

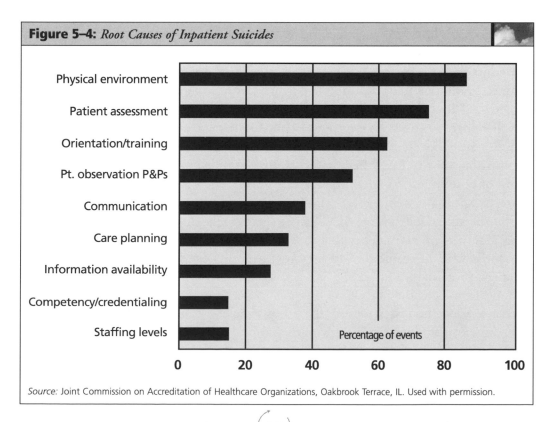

**Figure 5–4:** *Root Causes of Inpatient Suicides*

*Source:* Joint Commission on Accreditation of Healthcare Organizations, Oakbrook Terrace, IL. Used with permission.

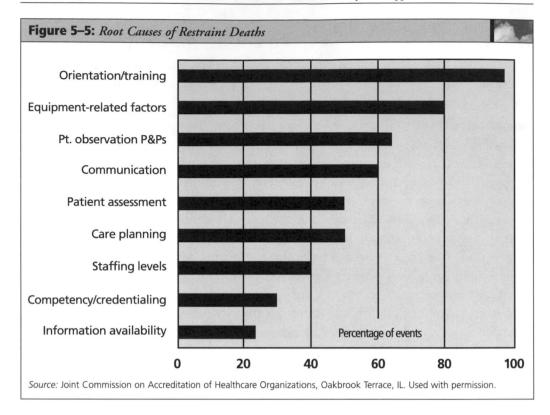

**Figure 5–5:** *Root Causes of Restraint Deaths*

*Source:* Joint Commission on Accreditation of Healthcare Organizations, Oakbrook Terrace, IL. Used with permission.

what is supposed to happen during a process often differs significantly from a chart created by those performing the process in real life.

Creating a flowchart can be a time-consuming endeavor. Keep in mind that difficulties probably reflect confusion in the process being charted and work through them. The following steps should help move a team toward creating a successful flowchart:

■ Define the process to be charted. This step helps contain the chart within manageable boundaries. One of the most common problems teams encounter in trying to create flowcharts is that they find themselves examining a system rather than a process within the system. Once team members begin to create a flowchart, they may find themselves with a process that seems dauntingly confusing. In this case, they should create a simple high-level flowchart containing only the most basic components. Such a chart may help them see that they are tackling a system rather than a process and also help identify the process that needs to be addressed. Once a process is chosen, specific boundaries of that process should be identified. When the flowchart is complete, it can then be held alongside the larger system to understand the impact of the system on the process.

■ Brainstorm activities and decision points in the process. Look for specific activities and decisions necessary to keep the process moving to its conclusion. This should be done by those most familiar with the various parts of the process, with assistance as necessary from people outside the team. One pitfall that teams encounter at this stage is trying to include too much detail in the analysis; be wary of obscuring the basic process with too many minor components.

**Figure 5–6:** *A Framework for a Root Cause Analysis and Action Plan in Response to a Sentinel Event*

| Level of Analysis | | Questions | Findings | Root cause? | Ask "Why?" | Take action? |
|---|---|---|---|---|---|---|
| **What happened?** | Sentinel event | What are the details of the event? (Brief description) | | | | |
| | | When did the event occur? (Date, day of week, time) | | | | |
| | | What area/service was impacted? | | | | |
| **Why did it happen?** | The process or activity in which the event occurred | What are the steps in the process, as designed? (A flow diagram may be helpful here) | | | | |
| What were the most proximate factors? (Typically "special cause" variations) | | What steps were involved in (contributed to) the event? | | | | |
| | Human factors | What human factors were relevant to the outcome? | | | | |
| | Equipment factors | How did the equipment performance affect the outcome? | | | | |
| | Controllable environmental factors | What factors directly affected the outcome? | | | | |
| | Uncontrollable external factors | Are they truly beyond the organization's control? | | | | |
| | Other | Are there any other factors that have directly influenced this outcome? | | | | |
| | | What other areas or services are impacted? | | | | |

This three-page template is provided as an aid in organizing the steps in a root cause analysis. Not all possibilities and questions will apply in every case, and there may be others that will emerge in the course of the analysis. However, all possibilities and questions should be fully considered in your quest for "root causes" and risk reduction.

As an aid to avoiding "loose ends," the three columns on the right are provided to be checked off for later reference:

"Root cause?" should be answered "yes" or "no" for each finding. A root cause is typically a finding related to a process or system that has a potential for redesign to reduce risk. If a particular finding that is relevant to the event is not a root cause, be sure that it is addressed later in the analysis with a Why? question. Each finding that is identified as a root cause should be considered for an action and addressed in the action plan.

"Ask Why?" should be checked off whenever it is reasonable to ask why the particular finding occurred (or didn't occur when it should have) – in other words, to drill down further. Each item checked in this column should be addressed later in the analysis with a Why? question. It is expected that any significant findings that are not identified as root causes will have check marks in this column. Also, items that are identified as root causes will often be checked in this column, since many root causes themselves have "roots."

"Take action?" should be checked for any finding that can reasonably be considered for a risk reduction strategy. Each item checked in this column should be addressed later in the action plan. It will be helpful to write the number of the associated Action Item on page 3 in the "Take Action?" column for each of the Findings that requires an action.

*(continued on next page)*

*Source:* Joint Commission on Accreditation of Healthcare Organizations, Oakbrook Terrace, IL. Used with permission.

**Figure 5–6:** *A Framework for a Root Cause Analysis and Action Plan in Response to a Sentinel Event (continued)*

| Level of Analysis | Questions | Findings | Root cause? | Ask "Why?" | Take action? |
|---|---|---|---|---|---|
| **Why did that happen? What systems and processes underlie those proximate factors?** (Common cause variation here may lead to special cause variation in dependent processes.) | | | | | |
| Human resource issues | To what degree are staff properly qualified and currently competent for their responsibilities? | | | | |
| | How did actual staffing compare with ideal levels? | | | | |
| | What are the plans for dealing with contingencies that would tend to reduce effective staffing levels? | | | | |
| | To what degree is staff performance in the operant process(es) addressed? | | | | |
| | How can orientation and in-service training be improved? | | | | |
| Information management issues | To what degree is all necessary information available when needed? accurate? complete? unambiguous? | | | | |
| | To what degree is communication among participants adequate? | | | | |
| Environmental management issues | To what degree was the physical environment appropriate for the processes being carried out? | | | | |
| | What systems are in place to identify environmental risks? | | | | |
| | What emergency and failure-mode responses have been planned and tested? | | | | |
| Leadership issues: Corporate culture | To what degree is the culture conducive to risk identification and reduction? | | | | |
| Encouragement of communication | What are the barriers to communication of potential risk factors? | | | | |
| Clear communication of priorities | To what degree is the prevention of adverse outcomes communicated as a high priority? How? | | | | |
| Uncontrollable factors | What can be done to protect against the effects of these uncontrollable factors? | | | | |

*(continued on next page)*

**Figure 5–6:** *A Framework for a Root Cause Analysis and Action Plan in Response to a Sentinel Event (continued)*

| Risk Reduction Strategies | Measures of Effectiveness |
|---|---|
| Action Item #1: | Measure: |
| Action Item #2: | Measure: |
| Action Item #3: | Measure: |
| Action Item #4: | Measure: |
| Action Item #5: | Measure: |
| Action Item #6: | Measure: |
| Action Item #7: | Measure: |
| Action Item #8: | Measure: |

For each of the findings identified in the analysis as needing an action, indicate the planned action, expected implementation date, and associated measure of effectiveness, OR...

If, after consideration of such a finding, a decision is made not to implement an associated risk reduction strategy, indicate the rationale for not taking action at this time.

Check to be sure that the selected measure will provide data that will permit assessment of the effectiveness of the action.

Consider whether pilot testing of a planned improvement should be conducted.

Improvements to reduce risk should ultimately be implemented in all areas where applicable, not just where the event occurred. Identify where the improvements will be implemented.

Cite any books or journal articles that were considered in developing this analysis and action plan:

**Sidebar 5–5:** *Summary of Key Tips for Conducting a Root Cause Analysis*

- Assign a team to assess the sentinel event. This team should include staff at all levels closest to the issues and those with decision-making authority.

- Establish a way of communicating your progress and findings to senior leadership. Keep your senior leaders informed.

- Create at least a high-level work plan that includes target dates by which you want to accomplish specific objectives so that you have a tool against which to guide and measure your progress.

- Clearly define the issue(s) regarding the sentinel event and be sure that the team shares a common understanding of the issue(s).

- Brainstorm all possible or potential contributing causes. Focus on processes, not people, until you believe you have exhausted all possible questions and causes.

- Sort and analyze your cause list. Constructing a cause-and-effect diagram can be helpful in this sorting process. Once a specific important proximate cause is placed on a branch of the diagram, begin a new diagram in which that cause is made the result to be prevented. This is a pictorial way of asking Why? repeatedly to drill down into the root cause.

- Begin determining which processes or systems each cause is a part of and whether it is a special or a common cause in that process or system. It is possible for the same cause to be a special cause in one process and a common cause in another. Flowcharting processes at this stage may be very helpful.

- For a special cause in a process, search for the common cause(s) in the system(s) of which the process is a part. The larger system and its managers, not the process or process owners, will need to be responsible for the redesigns that will reduce the likelihood of future sentinel events.

- Do not wait until you "finish" your root cause analysis to begin designing and implementing changes. Intermediate changes may not only be appropriate but necessary.

- Periodically assess your progress. Take a "snapshot" of where you are and determine whether you need to make any adjustments.

- Repeat certain activities as necessary, such as brainstorming if you get stuck or creating a cause-and-effect diagram to better identify parts of a process to target for improvement.

- Be thorough. Although you may make intermediate improvements along the way, do not stop your analysis before you identify the root cause and take corrective action.

- Focus improvement efforts on the larger systems. Only the larger systems can be redesigned to eliminate the common cause of the variation. Fixing the component process cannot prevent a special cause from recurring.

- Redesign to eliminate the root cause. This may involve changes in training, policies, procedures, forms, equipment, and so on.

- Measure and assess to evaluate whether the redesign produced the expected results.

- Determine the sequence of activities and decision points. Some activities may appear to occur simultaneously, whereas others may seem disconnected; certain decisions may cause steps to be repeated. Initially, teams can use adhesive notes placed on a wall to experiment with sequence until the appropriate one is determined.

■ Use the information to create the flowchart. Place each activity in a box and place each decision point in a diamond. Connect these with lines and arrows to indicate the flow of the process. Figure 5–7, page 185, shows common symbols used in flowcharting.

■ Analyze the flowchart. Look for unnecessary steps, redundancies, black holes, barriers, and any other difficulties. Make sure that every feedback loop has an escape. Make the chart the basis for designing an improved process, using spots where the process works well as models for improvement. The team may want to create a separate flowchart that represents the ideal path of the process, and then compare the two charts for discrepancies.

Figure 5–8, page 186, shows a detailed flowchart depicting how the intensive treatment unit of a behavioral health care center uses leather restraint devices.

## Cause-and-Effect Diagrams

Cause-and-effect diagrams show the many causal relationships between various actions or events leading to a specific outcome. Also called *Ishikawa diagrams* (for their inventor) or *fishbone diagrams* (because of their shape), cause-and-effect diagrams are helpful in the improvement process because they present a clear picture of the relationships between various factors and their outcomes. These diagrams are designed to identify and display large numbers of possible causes for each outcome or problem a team targets for improvement (such as equipment failures or medication errors).

Cause-and-effect diagrams are used to identify problems or specific parts of a process to target for improvement. They may also be used any time a team wants to know why specific problems or conditions occur; therefore, they are often among the first tools used in doing a root cause analysis of an adverse sentinel event. When used in connection with other tools, they are also helpful in data analysis. The diagram's appearance helps team members and others quickly visualize how various components relate to one another. Cause-and-effect diagrams lead teams to conclusions about specific causes and help teams develop solutions to problems.

Creating a cause-and-effect diagram may proceed quickly or may take considerable time. The key is to identify as many causes as possible. Team members' experience and expertise are the most valuable resources for developing the content. The following steps outline the process for creating a cause-and-effect diagram:

■ Identify the outcome or problem statement—the sentinel event. This statement defines the effect for which the team will identify possible causes. Place the outcome on the right side of the page, halfway down, and then, from the left, draw an arrow horizontally across the page, pointing to the outcome. The arrow will focus attention on the outcome and provide the main axis of the diagram.

■ Determine general categories for the causes. Common categories include work methods, personnel, materials, and equipment. Represent these on the diagram by connecting them with diagonal lines branching off from the main horizontal line. A generic cause-and-effect diagram is shown in Figure 5–9, page 187.

**Sidebar 5-6:** *Minimum Scope of Root Cause Analysis for Specific Types of Sentinel Events*

| Event type | Required areas of investigation |
|---|---|
| *Inpatient suicide* | Psychiatric (including suicide risk) assessment process<br>Medical assessment process<br>Physical environment<br>Staffing levels<br>Patient observation procedures<br>Communication among staff members<br>Orientation and training of staff<br>Competency assessment/credentialing process<br>Security systems and processes |
| *Medication error* | Control of medications: storage/access<br>Labeling of medications<br>Information availability<br>Communication among staff members<br>Factors distracting staff<br>Supervision of staff<br>Orientation and training of staff<br>Competency assessment/credentialing process<br>Adequacy of technological support |
| *Delay in treatment* | Communication among staff members<br>Communication with patient/family<br>Availability of information<br>Supervision of staff<br>Orientation and training of staff<br>Competency assessment/credentialing process |
| *Death in restraint* | Patient assessment process<br>Care planning process<br>Staffing levels<br>Patient observation procedures<br>Communication among staff members<br>Communication with patient/family<br>Management of the restraint equipment |
| *Elopement death* | Psychiatric (including suicide risk) assessment process<br>Medical assessment process<br>Physical environment<br>Security systems and processes<br>Staffing levels<br>Patient observation procedures<br>Communication among staff members<br>Orientation and training of staff<br>Competency assessment/credentialing process |
| *Assault/rape/homicide* | Physical environment<br>Security systems and processes<br>Staffing levels<br>Patient observation procedures<br>Orientation and training of staff<br>Competency assessment/credentialing process |

*Source:* Joint Commission on Accreditation of Healthcare Organizations, Oakbrook Terrace, IL. Used with permission.

- List proximate causes related to each general category. Brainstorm to come up with the important proximate causes. Place each proximate cause on a horizontal line connected to the appropriate diagonal line.

- List underlying causes related to each proximate cause. Team members should ask Why? or How? at least five times to get at these underlying causes. Not every major proximate cause will have an underlying cause, but try to find any relevant underlying causes that contribute to the important proximate causes. Use smaller diagonal lines to connect them to the proximate causes.

- When an important proximate or underlying cause is identified, it can become the outcome or problem statement for a new cause-and-effect diagram. This process will eventually lead to the underlying causes of the underlying causes— the root causes.

- Evaluate the diagrams. When all ideas have been noted, the team should study the diagrams to determine obvious areas for improvement, causes that are readily solved or eliminated, and areas needing study so that they can be better understood.

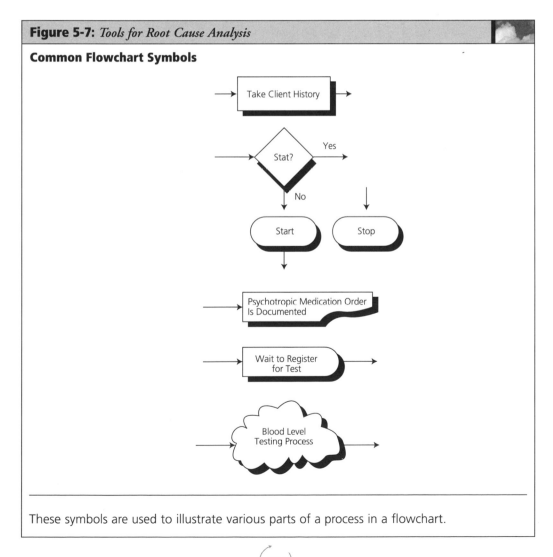

**Figure 5-7:** *Tools for Root Cause Analysis*

**Common Flowchart Symbols**

These symbols are used to illustrate various parts of a process in a flowchart.

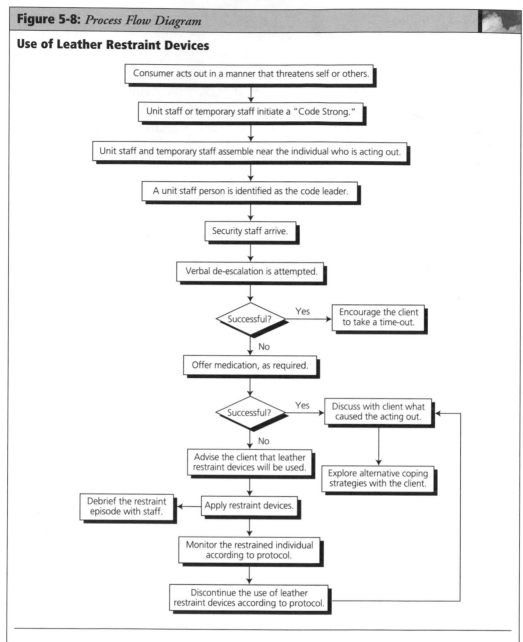

**Figure 5-8:** *Process Flow Diagram*

**Use of Leather Restraint Devices**

This flowchart presents a process flow diagram depicting how the intensive treatment unit at a behavioral healthcare facility may use leather restraint devices.

*Source:* Joint Commission on Accreditation of Healthcare Organizations, Oakbrook Terrace, IL. Used with permission.

■ The cause-and-effect diagram in Figure 5–10, page 188, was created by an organization following a patient suicide in a mental health unit. The causes are divided into the following major categories: patient, personnel, environment, and work methods. Figure 5–11, page 189, identifies the reasons for increased use of leather restraint devices at a behavioral health center.

## Pareto Charts

A Pareto chart is a special form of vertical bar graph that is used to compare events, problems, or causes according to their relative frequency or magnitude. The chart displays the relative importance of all the data, with elements arranged in descending order from left to right. The Pareto principle holds that the majority of effects are the result of a few causes. The purpose of a Pareto chart is to show which events or causes are most frequent and therefore have the greatest effect. This information helps a team determine which problems to solve and in what order.

A Pareto chart is a natural follow-up to a cause-and-effect diagram and can easily be constructed from data collected on a check sheet. By constructing a Pareto chart of proximate causes of a sentinel event, it is possible to identify those deserving the most attention. A Pareto chart of the underlying causes for the chosen proximate causes can then help identify the root causes that deserve the most attention. By creating subsequent Pareto charts using the original factors, team members can also do before-and-after comparisons to measure the changes that occur as they move through the improvement process.

The following steps guide a team to successful creation and use of a Pareto chart:

- Decide on a topic of study. The topic can be any outcome for which a number of potential causes has been identified. If the team is working from a cause-and-effect diagram, the topic will be the effect that has been targeted for improvement.

- Select causes or conditions to be compared. Identify the factors that contribute to the outcome—the more specific the better. This is where the cause-and-effect diagram is particularly helpful.

- Set the standard for comparison. In many cases, this is frequency. Factors also may be compared based on their cost or quantity.

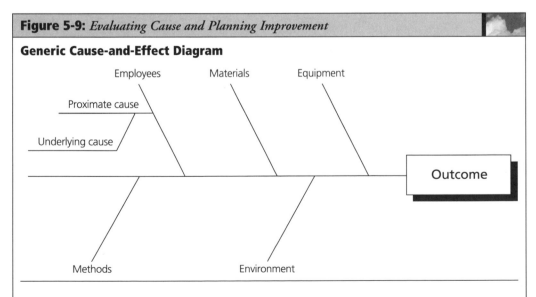

**Figure 5-9:** *Evaluating Cause and Planning Improvement*

**Generic Cause-and-Effect Diagram**

This figure shows the basic features of a cause-and-effect diagram: a central axis pointing toward an outcome, with proximate and underlying causes—separated into groups—that potentially lead to that outcome.

**Figure 5–10:** *Tools for Root Cause Analysis*

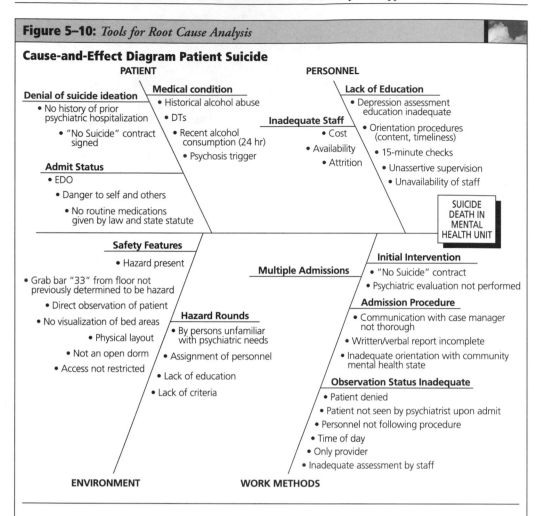

**Cause-and-Effect Diagram Patient Suicide**

This figure illustrates how the generic diagram can be adapted to specific needs. This detailed diagram breaks down the contributory factors that led to a sentinel event—the suicide of a patient in a mental health unit. By analyzing the proximate and underlying causes listed, staff members can identify and prioritize areas for improvement. DT, delirium tremens; EDO, emergency detention order.

*Source:* Joint Commission on Accreditation of Healthcare Organizations, Oakbrook Terrace, IL. Used with permission.

- Collect data. If this has not been done already, determine how often each factor occurs (or the cost or quantity of each, as appropriate). Use a check sheet to help with this task.
- Make the comparison. Based on the data collected in the previous step, compare the factors and rank them from most to least prevalent.
- Draw the chart's vertical axis. On the left side of the chart, draw a vertical line and mark the standard of measurement in increments.
- List factors along the horizontal axis. Place the name of each factor across the bottom of the chart. Factors should be arranged in descending order, with the highest-ranking factor at the far left.

- Draw a bar for each factor. The bars represent how often each factor occurs, the cost of each factor, or its quantity, as applicable.
- Include additional features, if desired. By making a few simple additions to the Pareto chart, a team can show the cumulative frequency, cost, or quantity of the categories in percentages. To do this, add a vertical percentage scale to the right side of the chart, where 100% is opposite the total frequency shown on the left and 50% is opposite the halfway point in the raw data. Be sure these are drawn to scale. Next, add a line that moves upward from left to right to represent how far toward the cumulative total each factor reaches. This can help team members see when the causes account for the majority of outcomes.

## Tips for Success:

### Pareto Charting

- When selecting factors for comparison, beware of grouping several distinct problems together, which can skew the rank order. Refer to the cause-and-effect diagram, and use the most specific causes and factors possible.
- Be sure to mark the chart clearly to show the standard of measurement. Do the numbers represent frequency, dollar amounts, quantity, or percentages?

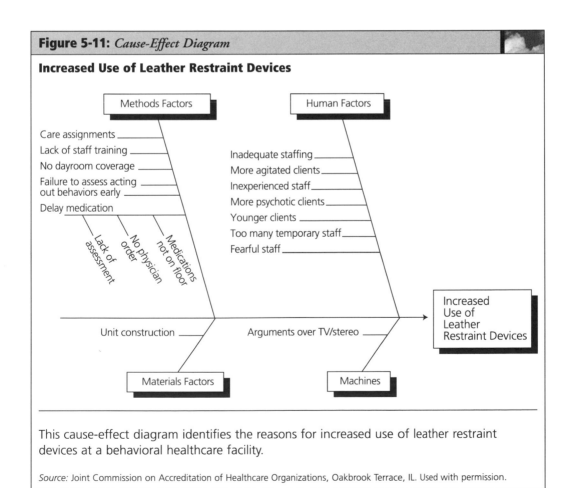

**Figure 5-11:** *Cause-Effect Diagram*

**Increased Use of Leather Restraint Devices**

This cause-effect diagram identifies the reasons for increased use of leather restraint devices at a behavioral healthcare facility.

*Source:* Joint Commission on Accreditation of Healthcare Organizations, Oakbrook Terrace, IL. Used with permission.

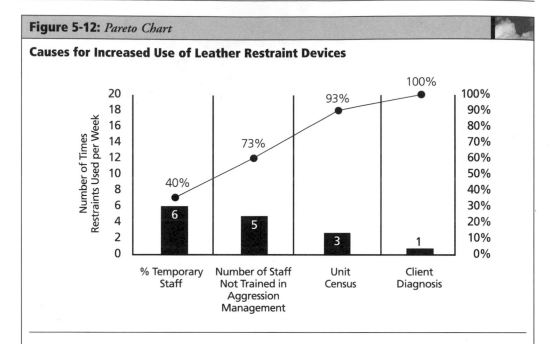

**Figure 5-12:** *Pareto Chart*

**Causes for Increased Use of Leather Restraint Devices**

This Pareto chart illustrates the main causes for the increased use of leather restraint devices at a behavioral healthcare facility.

*Source:* Joint Commission on Accreditation of Healthcare Organizations, Oakbrook Terrace, IL. Used with permission.

■ When analyzing your chart, keep in mind that numbers do not always tell the whole story. Sometimes two severe complaints deserve more attention than 100 other complaints.

Figure 5–12 (above) shows a Pareto chart illustrating the main causes for an increased use of leather restraint devices at a behavioral health facility.

### Barrier Analysis*

As the name implies, barrier analysis is the study of the safeguards that can prevent or mitigate (or could have prevented or mitigated) an unwanted event or occurrence. It offers a structured way to visualize the events related to system failure or the creation of a problem. It describes an issue in terms of protective barriers that are in place, are missing, could fail, or have failed. Barrier analysis identifies the barriers and controls that

■ will remove or reduce hazards (for example, providing prepackaged unit doses of medications for nurses to administer);

■ enforce compliance with procedures (for example, using structured forms for physicians to document medication orders); and

■ make targets invulnerable to hazards (for example, having emergency equipment readily available wherever hazards may occur).

Barriers might be physical requirements, special procedures, or routine activities such as training.

---

* This section is adapted from Wilson PF, et al: *Root Cause Analysis: A Tool for Total Quality Management.* Milwaukee: ASQC Quality Press, 1993.

Barrier analysis can be used reactively to solve problems, investigate sentinel events, or identify missing safeguards or proactively to evaluate existing barriers or identify additional barriers that should be considered to prevent recurrence of unwanted events. In either case, it defines the basic factors involved in a sentinel event or other problem. These factors include the following:

- *Targets.* Targets are those things of value that can be harmed by threats. With sentinel events occurring in health care facilities, targets are generally the people, either individually or collectively, who can be damaged or harmed by an unwanted incident. However, targets can also be material things such as buildings and equipment; nonmaterial things such as goodwill, friendship, and status; or the environment.

- *Threats.* Threats are those hazards or potential problems that cause harm or an adverse outcome or have the potential to do so. Threats involve the transfer of energy in such a way as to influence targets or things of value in unexpected or unwanted ways.

- *Barriers.* Barriers are those things that separate threats from a target, thereby preventing or minimizing harm or damage to the target. As preventive measures, barriers can include either a potential target or a potential threat. For example, surgical gloves are a protective barrier to the threat of HIV infection; insulation is an effective barrier that encases dangerous electrical wires. Barriers may be physical, such as gloves, doors, and warning signals, or administrative, such as work procedures, practice guidelines, supervision, codes, and so on. Administrative barriers are only as effective as the personnel who implement them. Hence, engineered, "hard" physical barriers that are more difficult to overlook or go around are generally preferable to "soft" administrative barriers, whenever possible. All barriers have limitations, however. They may fail partially or totally because of unforeseen circumstances.

- The *trace.* The trace is the path by which the threat reaches the target. At times, a single event will breach a barrier and create an unwanted event. Other times, a problem may result from a sequence of minor events that might not have much significance individually but collectively could produce a sentinel event or problem. Barrier analysis may be performed by following these steps:

- Define the target. Identify what has been damaged or could have been damaged by the threat. Remember that this list may include multiple items. List all the potential targets initially and let follow-up analysis eliminate those not affected by the event.

- Identify the threat. This will be the issue or condition that harmed the target or could have done so.

- Identify the barriers. These will be the elements that should have prevented or could prevent the undesired event.

- Analyze the barriers. This involves analyzing the adequacy of the barriers by asking questions about their performance. For example, you may ask the questions Were barriers in place to minimize threats to the target? Were such barriers adequate? That is, were they capable of handling the threat? and Were there backups for each barrier?

- Identify apparent or proximate causes and the root cause. List all the proximate causes. Each less-than-adequate barrier can be attributed to a different proximate

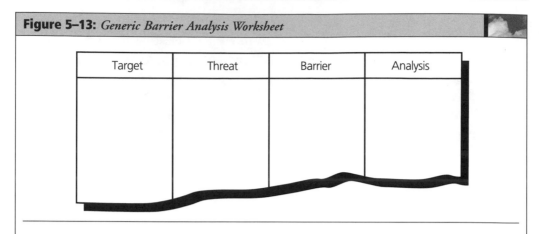

**Figure 5–13:** *Generic Barrier Analysis Worksheet*

| Target | Threat | Barrier | Analysis |
|--------|--------|---------|----------|
|        |        |         |          |

This generic worksheet shows a simple way of listing and comparing information for barrier analysis. The worksheet is arranged in columns to lead logically from the target to threat(s), barrier(s), and analysis. The same format can be used for a change analysis by marking columns for events, nonevents, differences, and analysis.

*Source:* Wilson PF, Dell LD, Anderson GF: *Root Cause Analysis: A Tool for Total Quality Management.* Milwaukee: ASQC Quality Press, 1993, p 147. Used with permission.

cause. The root cause can be identified as the cause that appears most often in explaining inadequate barriers or the cause that, if eliminated, would preclude the event from happening.

- Devise and recommend corrective or preventive actions.
- A simple worksheet, such as the one shown in Figure 5–13 (above), may be used for barrier analysis. A barrier analysis performed by a psychiatric hospital that experienced a sentinel event when a patient committed suicide appears as Figure 5–14, page 193.

## Change Analysis

Change analysis focuses on differences between the expected and actual performance of a process. Change analysis involves determining the root cause of an event by examining the effects of change and identifying causes. During change analysis, the questioner compares the present state of the system (the real, nonfunctioning situation) with either its prior state (when it was working properly) or the way the process was designed to work. Comparing a flowchart of the designed or former process with one of the present processes can help identify any differences. The goal is to identify what has changed in the system between the time it worked and the time it failed. Analyzing these changes will determine whether they had a significant effect.

Like other tools described here, change analysis may be performed reactively, by analyzing unwanted events or problems, or proactively, by identifying the potential effects of changes before they are actually implemented. In a reactive mode, it answers the question What has changed? or What is different? to probe what might have directly caused or indirectly precipitated the situation. In a proactive mode, change analysis answers the question What might change?

**Figure 5–14:** *Suicide Risk Barrier Analysis*

| BARRIERS | CONTROLS |
|---|---|
| Patient rights state that patients have the right to have personal items | 1. Utilized Suicide Risk Assessment Tool to identify patients with a high risk for suicide, and<br>2. Policy and procedure identifies which personal articles patient may keep and which items must be used with direct supervision. |
| Patient rights state that patients have a right to privacy | Patients will be directly supervised by staff in accordance with the Managing Suicidal Patients Risk Reduction Guidelines Policy and Procedure. |
| Identifying patients who are at a high risk for suicide | 1. Utilize Suicide Risk Assessment, and<br>2. Utilize information received from referral sources, needs assessment, nursing assessment, social services assessment, creative arts assessment, and psychiatric evaluation. |
| Patients who are intent on suicide and purposely do not disclose their plans to staff | 1. Utilize the Suicide Risk Assessment to help better identify high-risk patients,<br>2. Provide in-service training to sensitize staff regarding patients who may be intent on suicide but are careful not to disclose their plans to staff or other patients, and<br>3. Attempt to place patients at risk for suicide in a room with another patient and not in a room by themselves. |
| No past history or knowledge of the patient | Complete Suicide Risk Assessment by Needs Assessment Department. |
| Patients at risk for suicide may be placed in a room by themselves | Try to place patient at risk in a room with another patient. |
| Patients need razors for shaving and other needed personal articles that make it possible for patients to harm themselves or others | Utilize Managing Suicidal Patients, Risk Reduction Guidelines to indicate when patients need direct supervision with personal articles. |
| Patients bring contraband into the hospital which may be used to harm themselves or others | Nursing Services searches patient belongings on admission and documents articles in valuables list; all dangerous articles are placed in patient effects room. |
| Visitors sometimes bring contraband into the hospital that may be used by patients to harm themselves (matches, lighter, etc.) | Nursing Services monitors visitors when they are on the unit. Observations also look for possible contraband after visitation sessions. |
| Patients might hide their suicidal intentions on purpose; actions may indicate a significant improvement | Staff are in-serviced to be sensitive to patients who seem to suddenly improve. This may be a cover for a serious intent for suicide. |

This two-column version of a barrier analysis lists the barriers to implementing a patient suicide risk assessment protocol and the corresponding controls implemented by the organization to overcome them.

Source: Joint Commission on Accreditation of Healthcare Organizations, Oakbrook Terrace, IL. Used with permission.

Once a change analysis has been performed, additional questions must be asked to determine how the changes were allowed to happen. It is important to continue the questioning process into the organization's systems. Both barrier analysis and change analysis are commonly used for structuring the questioning process in a root cause analysis.

Not all changes create problems; rather, change can be viewed as a force that can either positively or negatively affect the way a system, process, or individual functions. Change can be planned, as is the case when needed improvements are implemented, or it can be unplanned and happen gradually. Change can be implemented in a timely and complete fashion or it can be implemented too slowly, too quickly, or incompletely. Change analysis involves identifying all changes, either perceived or observed, and all the possible factors related to the changes.

Change analysis may be performed by following these steps:

- Identify the problem, situation, or sentinel event. Try to describe it as accurately and in as much detail as possible. Include in the description who was involved in the event, what was involved in the event, where the event took place, when it took place, and what might have been a factor in causing it. Be as complete as possible and don't eliminate any potential factors or causes at this point.
- Describe an event-free or no-problem situation. Again, try to describe the situation without problems in as much detail as possible. Include the who, what, where, when, and how information.
- Compare the two descriptions. Take a close look at the event and nonevent descriptions and try to detect how these situations differ.
- List all the differences.
- Analyze the differences. Carefully assess the differences and identify possible underlying causes. Describe how these affect the event. Does each difference or change explain the result?
- Integrate information and specify root cause. Identify the cause that, if eliminated, would have led to a nonevent situation.

As with barrier analysis, a simple worksheet can facilitate the analysis (see Figure 5–13, page 192). For change analysis, the column headings would be changed to "Event," "Nonevent," "Differences," and "Analysis."

## Failure Mode, Effect, and Criticality Analysis*

Failure mode, effect, and criticality analysis (FMECA) is a systematic way of examining a design prospectively for possible ways in which failure can occur. It assumes that no matter how knowledgeable or careful people are, errors will occur in some situations and may even be likely to occur. The focus is on what, rather than who, allowed the error to occur.

The technique involves an analysis to identify potential mistakes before they happen and determine whether the consequences of those mistakes would be tolerable or intolerable. Potential failures are identified in terms of failure "modes" or symptoms, as opposed to causes. When potential effects are intolerable, actions

---

* This section is adapted from Juran JM: *Juran's Quality Control Handbook.* New York: McGraw-Hill, 1988.

**Figure 5-15:** *Generic Process for Failure Mode, Effect, and Criticality Analysis (FMECA)*

① Item _____          ② Analysis Engineer _____

③ Function _____          Date _____

| Mode of Failure | Mechanism and Cause of Failure | Effects of Failure | Frequency of Occurrence | Degree of Severity | Chance of Direction |
|---|---|---|---|---|---|
| ④ | ⑤ | ⑥ | ⑦ | ⑧ | ⑨ |

| Risk Priority Number | Design Action | Design Validation |
|---|---|---|
| ⑩ $= ⑦ \times ⑧ \times ⑨$ | ⑪ | ⑫ |

**Failure Mode and Effects Analysis Form Entry Explanation**

1. Item—Item to which analysis applies.

2. Analysis Engineer—An engineer in charge of design project.

3. Function—Function of the item as user perceives it. This description should be as broad as possible.

4. Mode of Failure—A mode in which the item will fail as perceived by user.

5. Mechanism and Cause of Failure—What causes failure to occur?

6. Effects of Failure—What effects will this failure have on the user or nearby person or nearby property?

7. Frequency of Occurrence (l-l0)—How often is this failure expected to occur? This column is subjectively rated on a 1 to 10 basis.
   l—Rare occurrence
   l0—Almost certain occurrence

8. Degree of Severity (1-10)—How severe is the effect of this failure on the user or anything else? This column is subjectively rated on a 1 to 10 basis.
   l—Insignificant loss to user
   l0—Product inoperable or major replacement cost or safety hazard

9. Degree of Detection (l-l0)—Can problem be detected by the user before it does the damage? This column too is subjectively rated on a 1 to 10 basis.
   l—Certain detection before failure
   l0—No detection possible before failure

10. Risk Priority Number (1-1000)—Order of problem-solving priority is given by multiplying numbers in columns 7, 8, and 9.

11. Design Action—Action to reduce risk priority number.

12. Design Validation—Method to verify the design motion.

This chart shows a step-by-step process for performing failure mode, effect, and criticality analysis.

*Source:* Juran JM: *Juran's Quality Control Handbook.* New York: McGraw-Hill, 1988. Used with permission.

are taken to eliminate the possibility of error, stop an error before it reaches people, or minimize the consequences of an error. For each mode, the effect on the total system is studied. Then the action or actions being taken (or planned) to minimize the probability or effect of failure are reviewed.

Various approaches can be used to show the criticality of the failure modes. For example, a risk priority number may be calculated as the product of ratings on frequency of occurrence, severity, and likelihood of detection. The risk priority number establishes priorities for further investigations of different failure modes.

Derived from the engineering world, this type of analysis is generally proactive, although reactive analysis is also possible. Potential failures are first identified in terms of failure modes. For each mode, the effect on the total system is then studied. Finally, actions (planned or already taken) are reviewed for their potential to minimize the probability of failure or the effects of failure. Performing FMECA involves three steps:

- List the failure modes for the proposed or actual situation or design;
- Describe the effect of each failure mode on other components or systems; and
- For each failure mode, rate the likelihood of occurrence, accessibility, and detectability to determine risk priority. The higher the likelihood of occurrence and severity, the higher priority the failure mode should be assigned.

A chart that can be used in performing FMECA appears in Figure 5–15, page 195.

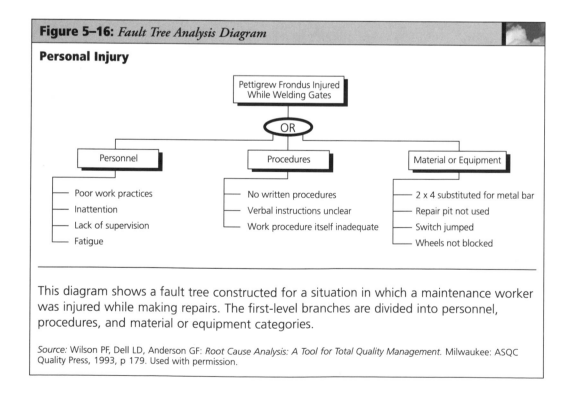

**Figure 5–16:** *Fault Tree Analysis Diagram*

**Personal Injury**

This diagram shows a fault tree constructed for a situation in which a maintenance worker was injured while making repairs. The first-level branches are divided into personnel, procedures, and material or equipment categories.

*Source:* Wilson PF, Dell LD, Anderson GF: *Root Cause Analysis: A Tool for Total Quality Management.* Milwaukee: ASQC Quality Press, 1993, p 179. Used with permission.

**Figure 5-17:** *Root Cause Analysis: Tools and Techniques*

## Tool Matrix

| Tools | Proximate | Root | Changes | Improvement |
|---|---|---|---|---|
| Affinity diagram | X | X | X | |
| Benefits and barriers exercise | X | | | X |
| Box plot | | X | | |
| Brainstorming | X | | X | |
| Brainwriting | X | | X | |
| Check sheets | | X | | X |
| Contingency diagram | X | | X | X |
| Control charts | | X | | X |
| Cost-of-quality analysis | X | | | |
| Critical-to-quality analysis | X | | | |
| Decision matrix | | X | X | |
| Deployment flowchart | X | | X | X |
| Effective-achievable matrix | | X | X | |
| Fishbone diagram | X | | | |
| Flowchart | X | | X | X |
| Force field analysis | X | | X | X |
| Graphs | | X | | X |
| Histogram | | X | | |
| Is–is not matrix | | X | | |
| Kolmogorov-Smirnov test | | X | | X |
| List reduction | | X | X | |
| Matrix diagram | | X | X | X |
| Multivoting | | X | X | |
| Nominal group technique (NGT) | X | | X | |
| Normal probability plot | | X | | X |
| Operational definitions | | X | X | X |
| Pareto chart | | X | X | |
| PDCA (plan-do-check-act) cycle | | | | X |
| PMI (plus, minus, interesting) | | X | X | |
| Relations diagram | X | X | X | |
| Run chart | | X | | X |
| Scatter diagram | | X | | |
| Storyboard | | | X | X |
| Stratification | | X | | |
| Top-down flowchart | X | | X | X |
| Tree diagram | X | | X | X |
| Why-why diagram | X | | | |
| Workflow diagram | X | | X | X |

Source: Joint Commission on Accreditation of Healthcare Organizations, Oakbrook Terrace, IL. Used with permission.

## Fault Tree Analysis*

Fault tree analysis is also a systematic way of prospectively examining a design for possible ways in which failure can occur. Fault tree analysis differs from FMECA in the following ways:

- Only those negative outcomes considered serious enough to warrant further analysis are studied; FMECA studies all potential modes of failure.

- Situations can be analyzed in which the negative event will not occur unless several subevents first occur.

- Relationships between events that have an interaction with each other can be shown more clearly.

As in FMECA, a fault tree analysis begins with a listing of potential failure modes. A solution must be designed for these failure modes (or other undesired events), and each mode on the list requires analysis. The analysis considers the possible direct proximate causes that could lead to the event and seeks their origins. Once this is accomplished, ways to avoid these origins and causes must be identified. Fault tree analysis is, in fact, proactive root cause analysis. The branching out of origins and causes is what gives this method its name: fault "tree" analysis. The approach is the reverse of FMECA, which starts with origins and causes and looks for any resulting bad effects.

Like FMECA, tree analysis derives from the engineering world and can be performed reactively, to analyze accidents or adverse events, or proactively, to prevent design oversights or accidents. The Department of Energy and the nuclear power industry routinely use fault tree analysis to investigate accidents.

A tree diagram, the chief tool of the analysis, provides a graphic display of an event and systematically describes each of the event's contributing factors. Tree diagrams use basic symbols—rectangles, gates, triangles, and so on—to visualize events, factors, constraints, and the relationships between them. Performing fault tree analysis involves the following steps:

- Define the top event of interest. This event or accident is the central subject of the analysis.

- Construct the fault tree for the top event. List the major contributory factors under the top event as the first-level branches. Generally, the contributory factors can be grouped under such headings as personnel, material or equipment, procedures/processes, and so on.

- Continue the branching process by adding a third level to the tree. These are the factors that might have accounted for the second-level factors. For example, sub-branches under the personnel branch might include fatigue, lack of supervision, inattention, or poor work practices. Sub-branches under the procedures branch might include no written procedures, unclear instructions, and inadequate work procedures.

- Add additional levels of branching, as necessary. Provide additional detail under each third-level branch.

- Validate the tree diagram. Review the visualized events for accuracy and com-

---

* This section is adapted from Juran JM: *Juran's Quality Control Handbook.* New York: McGraw-Hill, 1988, and Wilson PF, et al: *Root Cause Analysis: A Tool for Total Quality Management.* Milwaukee: ASQC Quality Press, 1993.

pleteness. Follow each of the paths through the tree for their "fit" with the facts of the sentinel event or accident. Is each factor plausible? Test and retest the tree diagram to "prune" the tree.

- Modify the diagram, as necessary. Retest the modified diagram.
- Analyze the tree diagram. Identify possible problem scenarios.
- Select the scenario that best fits the fact of the sentinel event or problem. The selection will be the scenario most likely to have resulted in the problem in terms of probability and/or the known facts of the particular situation.
- Determine the root cause of the event. The root cause can be identified based on the inadequacies (causes) identified when listing possible scenarios.
- Recommend corrective and/or preventive actions. These should be based on the event and root cause determination.
- Document the analysis and its results.

Figure 5–16, page 196, provides an example of a fault tree diagram involving a personal injury.

### Tools and Techniques Matrix

A tools and techniques matrix, providing information on selected tools and techniques that can be used to identify proximate and root causes, necessary changes, and improvement opportunities, appears as Figure 5–17, page 197.

## Reference

1. Altman DG: Strategies for community health intervention: Promises, paradoxes, pitfalls. *Psychosom Med* 57(3):226–233, 1995.

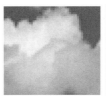

*Chapter Six*
**Conducting a Root Cause Analysis, Part 2— Planning, Implementing, and Assessing Systems Improvement**

*Chapter Six*
# Conducting a Root Cause Analysis, Part 2— Planning, Implementing, and Assessing Systems Improvement

*Chapter Six*
# Conducting a Root Cause Analysis, Part 2— Planning, Implementing, and Assessing Systems Improvement

In previous chapters, we discussed identifying the root causes of a sentinel event and setting priorities and objectives for improvement in these areas. The final and perhaps most important stage of the root cause analysis process involves developing and implementing improvement strategies. Your organization's search for the root causes of a sentinel event has unearthed opportunities for improvement in organizational systems. Now what? This chapter explores this question and provides a sample root cause analysis of an adolescent suicide with an evaluation of its credibility, thoroughness, and acceptability to the Joint Commission.

## Planning, Designing, and Redesigning for Improvement
Developing a plan to address medication-related problems. Implementing a new restraint protocol. Creating and implementing a suicide assessment training program. No single activity, process, or function in a health care organization is an end in itself; rather, each is a necessary component of a larger whole. Each should be planned, designed, or redesigned to fulfill a specific objective.

### Functions and Processes
When addressing what to design or redesign, think in terms of the everyday work of your organization and the systems deficiencies and opportunities for improvement highlighted during the early stages of your root cause analysis. Work can be defined in terms of functions or processes. A *function* is a group of processes with a common goal, and a process is a series of linked, goal-directed activities. Any new process design or redesign must pay careful attention to the customer-supplier relationships inherent in the process. The design should facilitate the greatest efficiency in these relationships, coordinating and integrating the activities to produce desirable outcomes.

Improvement actions should be directed primarily at processes. As stated earlier in this book, process improvement holds the greatest opportunity for significant change, whereas changes related to an individual's performance tend to have limited effect. Good people often find themselves carrying out bad processes.

## Defining Goals

What goals does your organization have in implementing necessary improvements related to a sentinel event? By asking the following four questions, your organization should be able to set appropriate goals for improvement efforts.

*What dimensions of performance will be most affected by the change?* To understand the potential effects of the improvement activity, the organization must determine which dimension of performance—efficacy, appropriateness, availability, timeliness, effectiveness, continuity, safety, efficiency, or respect and caring—will be affected. At times, the relationship between two or more dimensions must be considered. Redesign in response to a sentinel event will most often focus on safety, but may affect any or all of the other dimensions.

*How do we expect, want, and need the improved process to perform?* The team carrying out the effort should set specific expectations for performance resulting from the design or improvement. These expectations can be derived from staff expertise, consumer expectations, experiences of other organizations, recognized standards, and other sources. Without these expectations, the organization will not be able to determine the degree of success of the efforts.

*How will we measure to determine whether the process is actually performing at the level we expect?* The organization or group will need specific tools to measure the performance of the newly designed or improved process in order to determine whether expectations are met. These measures can be taken directly or adapted from other sources or newly created, as appropriate.

*Who is closest to this process and should therefore "own" the improvement activity?* To a great extent, the success of an improvement effort hinges on involving the right people from all disciplines, services, and offices involved in the process being addressed.

## Involving the Right People

As with other phases of the root cause analysis, involving the right people is essential. The process for taking action consists of several stages, each of which may have different players.

*Designing the action.* In general, the group that participated in the root cause analysis should have the necessary expertise to recommend improvements and may be in the best position to design or redesign the improvements. This group should include those who carry out or are affected by the process.

*Approving recommended actions.* When substantial resources are involved and the potential effects are significant, the organization's leaders will usually have to approve the action. This will most certainly be the case with improvements recommended following a sentinel event. If a group has obtained the necessary input and buy-in while devising an improvement, the approval should come readily.

*Testing the action.* Testing should occur under "real world" conditions involving staff who will actually be carrying out the process. Effects can be measured with the same methods used to establish a performance baseline.

*Implementing the action.* Although full-scale implementation of a process change should have positive results, any change can create anxiety. Therefore, care should be taken to prepare people for change and explain the reason for the change in an educational, nonthreatening way. Cooperation is essential for changes to succeed, but it will not occur if people believe a change is being forced on them without good reason. An effective team should have already acquired much of the necessary buy-in during earlier phases of the improvement process or during the early stages in the root cause analysis.

Leaders and managers must take an active role in overseeing and setting priorities for design and redesign. Generally, managers are responsible for processes within their areas; design or redesign of processes with a wider scope may be overseen by upper management or by a team of managers. Leaders must ensure that the people involved have the necessary resources and expertise. Furthermore, their authority to make changes should be commensurate with their responsibility for process improvements. Although regular feedback and contact with management are important, rigid control can stifle creativity.

The group that creates the process should include the people responsible for the process, the people who will carry out the process, and the people affected by the process. As appropriate, the group members could include staff from different units, different branch offices or teams, different services, different disciplines, and different job categories. When the group needs a perspective not offered by its representatives, it should conduct interviews or surveys outside the group or invite new members into the work group.

## Designing or Redesigning

To create a new design for client care, management, or support processes, or redesign an existing one in response to a root cause analysis, organizations should consider the following guidelines:

- Design a systematic method to determine the process's effect on the organization's mission, vision, plans, customers, resources, and so forth. Surveys, informal discussions, focus groups, environmental assessments, and consensus techniques are useful tools.
- Base decisions on valid, reliable data. Historical data and comparative information are key to developing accurate design or redesign specifications and to assessing the effectiveness of the design or redesign.
- Involve the right people, as already discussed. Other important customers and suppliers to consider are purchasers, payers, physicians, referral sources, accreditors, regulators, and the community as a whole.
- Obtain a variety of information on the subject. Examine the professional literature, advice of professional societies or trade associations, and practices of other organizations. A view of other organizations' practices and experiences can help avoid mistakes and inspire creative thinking.
- Consider the availability of resources. Sentinel events frequently shake up the organization's notions of the resources that should be expended in particular areas. Organizations contemplating a design or redesign effort will certainly weigh the availability of resources against the potential benefits for clients, customers, and the organization.

## Tools and Methods for Improvement and Innovation

Once the goals for improvement have been established, the organization can begin planning and carrying out the improvements. A systematic method for design or improvement of processes can help organizations pursue identified opportunities. A standard, yet flexible, process for carrying out these changes should help leaders and others ensure that actions address root causes, involve appropriate people, and result in desired and sustained changes. Depending on an organization's mission and improvement goals, any of the processes described here may be used to implement a process improvement.

### The Scientific Method

The fundamental components of any improvement process are
- planning the change,
- testing the change,
- studying its effects, and
- implementing changes determined to be worthwhile.

Many readers will readily associate the activities listed—plan, test, study, implement—with the scientific method. Indeed, the scientific method is the fundamental, inclusive paradigm for change, and includes these steps:
- Determine what we know now (about a process, problem, topic of interest);
- Decide what we want to learn, change, or improve;
- Develop a hypothesis about how the change can be accomplished;
- Test the hypothesis;
- Assess the effect of the test; compare results "before versus after" or "traditional versus innovative;" and
- Implement successful improvements or rehypothesize and conduct another experiment.

This orderly, logical, inclusive process for improvement will serve organizations well as they attempt to assess and improve performance.

### The Plan-Do-Study-Act Cycle

A well-established process for improvement that is based on the scientific method is the plan-do-study-act (PDSA) cycle. (This method is also called the PDCA cycle, with the word *check* replacing the word *study*). This process is attributed to Walter Shewhart, a quality improvement pioneer with Bell Laboratories in the 1920s and 1930s, and is also widely associated with W. Edwards Deming, a student and later a colleague of Shewhart. Deming made the PDCA cycle central to his influential teachings about quality. The cycle is compelling in its logic and simplicity. A brief explanation of this process should help readers not already familiar with the cycle to understand it and its use (see Figure 6–1, page 209).

During the *planning* step, an operational plan for testing the chosen improvement action is created. Small-scale testing can help determine whether the improvement actions are viable, whether they will have the desired result, and whether any refinements are necessary before putting them into full operation. The list of proposed improvement actions should be narrowed to a number that can be reasonably tested—perhaps between two and four, but generally not more.

**Figure 6–1:** *Conducting a Root Cause Analysis, Part 2—Planning Systems*

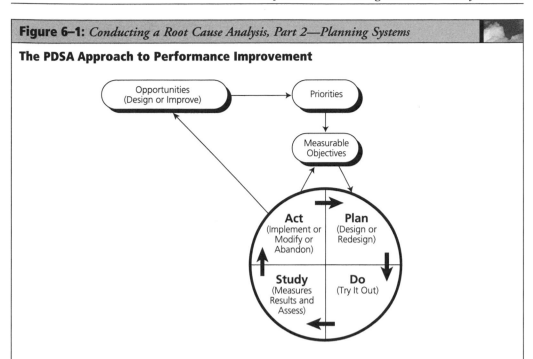

**The PDSA Approach to Performance Improvement**

The plan-do-study-act (PDSA) approach to performance improvement includes identifying design or redesign opportunities, setting priorities for improvement, and implementing the improvement project.

Source: Joint Commission on Accreditation of Healthcare Organizations, Oakbrook Terrace, IL. Used with permission.

During the planning stage, several issues should be resolved:
- Who will be involved in the test?
- What do they need to know to participate in the test?
- What are the testing timetables?
- How will the test be implemented?
- Why is the idea being tested?
- What are the success factors?
- How will the process and outcomes of the test be measured and assessed?

The *do* step involves implementing the pilot test and collecting actual performance data.

During the *study* (or *check*) step, data collected during the pilot test are analyzed to determine whether the improvement action was successful in achieving the desired outcomes. To determine the degree of success, actual test performance is compared to desired performance targets and baseline results achieved using the established process.

The next step is the *act* step—to take action. If the pilot test is not successful, the cycle repeats. Once actions have been shown to be successful, they are made part of standard operating procedure. The process does not stop here. The effectiveness of the action will continue to be measured and assessed to ensure that improvement is maintained.

| **Table 6–1:** *Components of the PDSA Cycle* | |
|---|---|
| **Plan** | ■ Develop or design a new process or redesign or improve an existing process;<br>■ Determine how to test the new or redesigned process;<br>■ Identify measures that can be used to assess the success of the strategy and whether the objective was reached;<br>■ Determine how to collect the measures of success; and<br>■ Involve the right people in the development and testing. |
| **Do** | ■ Run the test of the new or redesigned process, preferably on a small scale; and<br>■ Collect data on the measures of success. |
| **Study** | ■ Assess the results of the test;<br>■ Determine whether the change was successful; and<br>■ Identify any lessons learned. |
| **Act** | ■ Implement the change permanently;<br>■ Modify the change and run it through another testing cycle; or<br>■ Abandon the change and develop a new approach to test. |

Source: Joint Commission on Accreditation of Healthcare Organizations, Oakbrook Terrace, IL. Used with permission.

The components of the four-step PDSA cycle as they relate to designing and improving processes appear as Table 6–1 (above).

A single initiative can involve a number of different testing phases or different change strategies and therefore requires the use of consecutive PDSA cycles.

To help teams and individuals involved in design or improvement initiatives apply the method effectively, your organization may, depending on the nature of your improvement project, want to consider the following questions at each step of the method.

## Plan

- How did you select a design or improvement strategy to test?
- Does knowledge-based information (for example, from the literature, other organizations, or other external sources) exist that supports the new or improved process?
- What issues in the external environment (such as economy, politics, customer needs, competitors, regulations) will affect the performance of the new or improved process?
- What issues in the internal environment will affect the performance of the new or improved process?
- Who is the customer of the process?
- What is the current process?
- What is the desired process?
- Who are the suppliers of the process?
- What changes will have the most impact?
- Is there a plan for testing the design or improvement?
- Is there a time line for testing?

- What data will be collected so that you can decide whether the test was successful (that is, whether the objective was met)?
- How do we know that the measures actually address the issue we want to study?
- Can the measures we will use actually track performance?
- How will we collect data?
- Who will collect data?
- Are systems in place to support planned measurement?
- Is benchmarking feasible for this initiative?
- Are the right people involved?
- What resources are needed to design or redesign the process? What resources are available?

## Do

- Was the testing plan followed?
- Were needed modifications discussed with the appropriate people?
- Was data collection timely?
- Was data collection reliable?

## Study

- How will the test data be assessed—what process should we use?
- Who should be involved in data analysis?
- What methods or tools should we use to analyze data?
- Is training needed on data analysis methods and tools?
- Are comparative data (internal or external) available?
- Does data analysis lead to an understanding of problem areas?
- Is data analysis timely—that is, are the results available soon enough to take needed actions?
- Did the test data indicate that the design or improvement was successful?
- What lessons were learned from the test?
- How will we decide whether to implement the tested design or improvement on a permanent basis?
- How and to whom will the results of assessment activities be communicated?

## Act

- Do we need to recommend changes to others (for example, for purchasing equipment or implementing specific processes)?
- How will these changes be communicated to the appropriate people?
- Is any education or training needed?
- How do we maintain the gain and prevent backsliding?
- What measures will we use to assess the performance of the new or improved product or process?
- Should any of the measures identified be included in ongoing measurement activities?

## Critical Paths

One type of process design/redesign that can be used in health care, particularly in response to a sentinel event in a hospital setting, is the development of a *critical path* (also referred to as clinical path and clinical or critical pathway). The primary objective of critical pathways is to reduce common-cause variation, thereby reducing the risk of special-cause variation (sentinel events) in dependent processes. Critical paths offer a systematic, flexible guide for standardization of patient care that can start, for example, before admission and follow the patient across all care settings. They are designed by those involved in the process—clients, clinicians, nurses, pharmacists, and others—who come together to offer their unique perspectives and expertise.

A critical path is an excellent way to redesign an existing clinical process that needs change. One advantage of a critical path is the opportunity to start fresh, cast aside traditional but not particularly effective procedures, and research and implement the best practices. To date, many critical paths have been developed by numerous organizations, including professional societies, government agencies, and health care organizations. These may provide guidance.

A summary of the steps involved in critical path development and implementation follows.

*Selecting the process.* The initial step in creating a critical path is choosing a process to standardize. The first part of the root cause analysis will have identified the relevant process(es) that needs redesign.

*Defining the diagnosis, condition, or procedure.* An appropriately defined process and patient population will simplify critical path development. A process that is too broadly defined will result in a path that is either too complex or too vague; conversely, a process that is too narrowly defined can result in a path that applies in only a limited number of cases.[1,2]

*Forming a team.* The group that creates the critical path must represent all disciplines involved in the process. The scope of the process will help determine team members. Another valuable perspective comes from clients and their families or caregivers, customers, and others. The team should elicit information from the people the process is designed to benefit. Similarly, if other parties are involved but are not team members, their input will also need to be elicited.

*Identifying or creating the critical path.* Team members will need to reach consensus on the key activities involved in each stage of the care process. Members can draw on personal experience and knowledge, existing clinical literature and practice guidelines, and patient perspectives. When varying styles or methods of care arise—as they inevitably will—the team should not panic. The resulting discussion can yield important knowledge about patient care. If varied practice patterns are such that the group cannot reach consensus, the path should not dictate one approach over the other; separate paths can be developed when necessary.[2] Subsequent outcome measurement may demonstrate an advantage of one path over the other. The path need not be limited to just clinical activities; it can also include activities that surround the clinical process, such as transportation to the radiology department. Critical paths should also include descriptions of expected outcomes.

Despite the complexity of the processes involved, teams should attempt to make their paths as concise as possible—one page is ideal—so they can be used as practical tools in daily practice.

The time needed to develop a critical path may vary from two hours to four months.[3] Organizations should be prepared for a significant commitment of time.

*Results.* At all stages of the care process, organization staff can refer to critical paths. They should be available to all involved personnel in all the relevant work areas and office locations. Critical paths are also valuable for clients; they can increase clients' knowledge and sense of partnership with providers.[1-3]

### Additional Improvement Tools

The tools used for measurement and assessment (mentioned in Chapter 5, page 197) are also useful for taking action to improve processes. For example,

- *brainstorming* can be used to create ideas for improvement actions;
- *multivoting* and *selection grids* can help a group decide among various possible improvement actions;
- *flowcharts* can help a group understand the current process and how the new or redesigned one should work;
- *cause-and-effect diagrams* can indicate which changes might cause the desired result or goal;
- *Pareto charts* can help determine which changes are likely to have the greatest effect in reaching the goal;
- *run charts* and *control charts* can measure the effect of a process change or variation in processes and outcomes; and
- *histograms* can show how much effect each change has had.

## Measuring and Assessing Improvement Efforts

A previous section described how to design or redesign a function or process, where the improvement cycle often begins. Once a function or process is under way, an organization should collect data about its performance. Measurement is the process of collecting and aggregating these data, a process that helps assess the level of performance and determine whether further improvement actions are necessary. Specifically, measurement can be used as an integral technique throughout the PDSA cycle to

- assist in process design or redesign (the plan step);
- test whether process design or redesign is implemented properly (the do step);
- assess the results of the test (the study step);
- provide assistance in implementing the improvement (the act step); and
- maintain the improvement and determine whether the improvement should be part of the organization's ongoing monitoring process (repeat of the PDSA cycle).

Measurement also helps determine whether improvement has occurred and is sustained.

Measurement provides a baseline when little objective evidence exists about a process. Specific indicators for a particular outcome or a particular step in a process may be used for ongoing data collection. Once assessed, these data can help management and staff determine whether a process is ineffective and needs more intensive analysis. Data about costs, including costs of faulty or ineffective processes, may also be of significant interest to organization leaders and can be part of ongoing performance measurement.

Measurement also is used to gain more information about a process chosen for assessment and improvement. For example, perhaps a performance rate varies significantly from the previous year, from shift to shift, or from the statistical average. Such findings may cause an organization to focus on a given process to determine opportunities for improvement. Detailed measurement would then be necessary to gather data about exactly how the process performs and about factors affecting that performance.

Finally, measurement helps determine the effectiveness of improvement actions. Measurement can also be used to demonstrate that key processes (for example, the preparation, delivery, and administration of medications) are in control. Once a process has been stabilized at an acceptable level of performance, measures may be taken periodically to verify that the improvement has been sustained.

## Who Performs the Measurement?

The people responsible for performing measurement activities will differ depending on the goals of the measurement. Measurement for a specific improvement effort is more detailed than routine screening. When an organization has decided to improve a particular process—from adverse drug reaction reporting to staff education about restraint use and therapeutic holds—it may empower a specific group to study the process and recommend changes. This group could be an existing team or a special team composed of those involved in the process studied. This team will usually be responsible for designing and carrying out the measurement activities necessary to determine how the process performs. After making changes to improve the process, the team should continue to apply some or all of its measures to determine whether the change has had the desired effect.

Organizations have various experts who can help design measurement activities, including experts in information management, quality improvement, and the function to be measured.

Information management professionals and those responsible for carrying out the process being measured will be key players in data collection. The people involved will vary widely depending on the specific organization, on the function being measured, and on the measurement process. Organizations should make every effort to coordinate any ongoing measurement with data collection already taking place as part of everyday activities.

## Types of Measurement

Organizations carry out two basic types of measurement:

- Ongoing measurement about selected outcomes or aspects of the process; and
- Measurement about priority issues chosen for improvement.

The first type is considered a quality control measure. The second is part of a more intensive assessment and improvement effort, which may have been initiated based on the results of ongoing measurement, such as client/staff feedback, increased errors, or the occurrence of a sentinel event.

## Measurement and Joint Commission Requirements

One important factor to consider when choosing processes to measure continuously is standards or requirements from regulating or accrediting bodies, including the Joint Commission. With a new program called the ORYX Initiative, the Joint

Commission's triennial survey process is increasingly driven by measurement and assessment of outcome data. Organizations of all types are required to include performance measurement data in the survey evaluation process.

## Assessing Data and Information

Once data are collected as part of measurement, whether for ongoing measurement such as with the ORYX or other initiatives or to address priority issues, they must be translated into information that organizations can use to make judgments and draw conclusions about performance. This assessment forms the basis for further actions taken to improve performance and improvement initiatives.

When an organization designs a new process or redesigns an existing one as part of a root cause analysis, it should measure its performance and compare the resulting data with design specifications to determine whether the process is performing up to expectations. If not, the organization must decide exactly how it can be improved.

It should assess whether the process is stable, what its capabilities are, and whether its outcomes are consistent with expectations. Assessment of data can identify the types of undesirable variation. Even if a process is stable, assessment might reveal possible opportunities for improvement.

After an organization takes action to improve performance, it must continue to assess data to determine whether improvement occurred, that is, whether undesirable variation was reduced or eliminated or whether the capability of the process was improved.

Assessment is not confined to information gathered within the walls of a single organization. To better understand its level of performance, an organization will want to compare its performance against reference databases, professional standards, trade association guidelines, and other sources.

### Who Performs the Assessment?

Intensive assessment ordinarily includes the people closest to the process being addressed: those who carry out or are affected by the process. Service, discipline, or office location barriers cannot be allowed to limit participation in improvement efforts. When a process involves more than one service, the group improving the process should reflect all services. By including process participants, the organization not only taps the necessary expertise, but also helps ensure the necessary buy-in for the recommended changes.

### Assessment Techniques

Numerous techniques can be used to assess the data collected. Most types of assessment require comparing data to a point of reference. When a root cause analysis is conducted, these reference points may include

- internal comparisons;
- aggregate external reference databases;
- practice guidelines/parameters; and
- desired performance targets, specifications, or thresholds.

*Internal comparisons.* An organization can compare its current performance with its past performance by using run charts and control charts. These charts show changes over time, variation in performance, and the stability of performance.

*Aggregate external reference databases.* In addition to assessing its own historical patterns of performance, an organization can compare its performance with that of other organizations. Expanding the scope of comparison helps an organization draw conclusions about its own performance and learn about different methods to design and carry out processes. Aggregate external databases take various forms. Aggregate, risk-adjusted data about specific indicators help each organization set priorities for improvement by showing whether its current performance falls within the expected range.

*Practice guidelines or parameters.* Practice guidelines or parameters, critical paths, and other standardized patient care procedures are very useful reference points for comparison. Whether developed by professional societies or in-house practitioners, these procedures represent an expert consensus about the expected practices for a given diagnosis or treatment. Assessing variation from such established procedures can help an organization identify how to improve a process.

*Desired performance targets.* Organizations may also establish targets, specifications, or thresholds for evaluation against which they compare current performance. Such levels can be derived from professional literature or expert opinion within the organization.

One method of comparing performance is *benchmarking.* Although a benchmark can be any point of comparison, most often it is a standard of excellence. Benchmarking is the process by which one organization studies the exemplary performance of a similar process in another organization and, to the greatest extent possible, adapts that information for its own use. Or the first organization may wish to simply compare its results with those of other organizations or with current research or literature.

Studying the patterns of care or service in another institution often results in an infusion of new ideas—ideas that never would arise if the assessment remained within one facility's walls. The organization serving as the benchmark can benefit as well. By discussing the process in question—by re-examining each step and its rationale—that organization may also gain new insights.

## Assessment Tools

Many tools can be used to identify issues for design or improvement, diagnose causes, and develop and study remedies or solutions. Three statistical quality control tools are especially helpful in comparing performance with historical patterns and assessing variation and stability: run charts, control charts, and histograms. A number of tools are helpful for determining the root causes of current performance: flowcharts, cause-and-effect diagrams, scatter diagrams, and Pareto charts. Two specific tools can be used to set priorities for improvement: selection grids and multivoting. A number of resources describe how to use these tools and manage teams, including Joint Commission publications and external publications from the Juran Institute, Goal/QPC, Joiner & Associates, and others. The Selected Bibliography (pages 225 through 231) lists many helpful resources.

# Sample Root Cause Analysis of an Adolescent Suicide

A framework for a root cause analysis and action plan for an adolescent suicide case appears as Figure 6–2, pages 218 through 220. This root cause analysis is *not* an example of a "good" root cause analysis, and as such, should *not* be used as a model. Rather, it is presented to assist readers in understanding the process of root cause analysis and how the organization could have improved the analysis and use of the framework.

## The Event

The key points of the sentinel event are as follows:

*At 11 PM a 13-year-old female arrived in the emergency department (ED) of an acute care teaching hospital with mild dyspnea (difficulty breathing), color was gray, skin cold to the touch, and she was sweating profusely. Her pulse was rapid and thready, and her blood pressure was 94/60. She had a vial labeled with a current prescription for amoxycillin. The friends who brought her to the ED indicated that she had allergies. An IV line was started and she was seen by both the ED physician and an on-call pediatric resident. The patient's parents were contacted but were unable to come to the hospital immediately. They gave permission to treat over the phone. The patient's attending physician did not respond to her page, and the on-call physician for the group practice was not familiar with the patient's history.*

*The patient was admitted to the pediatric unit for observation at 2 AM. The nursing assessment revealed that she had recently been admitted for a suicide attempt. At approximately, 3 AM, she appeared to be very nervous and acting out loudly, wanting to take her IV out and go home. The on-call pediatric resident was called. He prescribed a sedative prn and decided to wait until morning to continue efforts to reach the attending physician.*

*The pediatric resident left a note for the relieving resident to follow up on the case. At 11 AM the attending was contacted and a psychiatric consultation was ordered.*

*At 1 PM the patient had visits from her family and friends. Relations between the family members and the patient's friends appeared strained. The parents did not want the friends to be allowed to visit. The nursing supervisor was called, but no immediate action was taken as the friends were well-behaved and cooperative when approached. The patient wanted her friends to remain. Staff decided that everyone should leave until the psychiatric consultation was completed.*

*The psychiatric resident saw the patient at 2 PM and recommended admission to the child psychiatric unit as soon as a bed became available. The psychiatric resident paged the attending physician, but received no response. He left verbal orders to increase precautions and wrote the transfer order. He asked the nurse to reach the attending physician to notify her of the transfer.*

*The patient's family and friends returned in separate groups. Her friends left at 5 PM and the patient began to pace nervously and became boisterous and disruptive. She was given a sedative. She calmed down. A note that the patient became lethargic was entered in the chart.*

*At approximately 7 PM, a bed became available in the psychiatric unit. When the nurse came to get the patient, she was found unconscious with labored breathing. Her IV had been pulled out. Her blood pressure was 90/58. Shortly after the nurse called for assistance, the patient went into cardiac arrest. Resuscitation efforts were unsuccessful and the patient was pronounced dead at 7 PM.*

**Figure 6–2:** *Sample Framework for a Root Cause Analysis and Action Plan in Response to a Sentinel Event*

| Level of Analysis | | Questions | Findings | Root cause? | Ask "Why?" | Take action? |
|---|---|---|---|---|---|---|
| **What happened?** | Sentinel event | What are the details of the event? (Brief description) | Suicide of a 13-year-old in an acute care teaching hospital | | | |
| | | When did the event occur? (Date, day of week, time) | | | | |
| | | What area/service was impacted? | Pediatric unit. | | | |
| **Why did it happen?** | The process or activity in which the event occurred | What are the steps in the process, as designed? (A flow diagram may be helpful here) | Admission process. Initial assessment. Treatment planning. | | | |
| What were the most proximate factors? (Typically "special cause" variations) | | What steps were involved in (contributed to) the event? | Admission process resulted in inappropriate placement of the patient on the pediatric unit rather than the psychiatric unit. | | | 3 |
| | | | Initial assessment did not include an immediate psychiatric consultation in the emergency department. | | | 3 |
| | | | Patient's physician could not be reached by paging system. | | | 4 |
| | | | Delay in requesting psychiatric consultation after need for consultation was established. | | | 3 |
| | | | Patient could not be transferred to psychiatric unit because system indicated "no beds" even though beds were available. | | | 5 |
| | | | Verbal orders for "precautions" not entered into the medical record nor communicated to PM nursing staff. | | | 3,6 |
| | | | Verbal order for increased precautions not followed. | | | 7 |
| | | | Confusion over terms: "precautions" and "suicide watch" not accurately defined. | | | 7 |
| | | | Resident did not want to "bother" the attending physician with another call that evening. | | | 8 |
| | Human factors | What human factors were relevant to the outcome? | Resident failed to diagnose suicidal behavior and admit as such. | | | 9 |
| | | | Nurse failed to appropriately take action when past suicide attempt was noted. | | | 1 |
| | | | Nurse failed to follow through on precaution orders. | | | 1 |
| | | | Admissions office did not allocate beds properly. | | | 2 |
| | Equipment factors | How did the equipment per-formance affect the outcome? | Paging system was not working. | | | 4 |
| | | | Computerized bed tracking system did not indicate correct bed status. | | | 5 |
| | Controllable environmental | What factors directly affected the outcome? | N/A | | | |
| | Uncontrollable external factors | Are they truly beyond the organization's control? | N/A | | | |
| | Other | Are there any other factors that have directly influenced this outcome? | Nonresponse of parents resulted in delay of hospital personnel receiving critical information. | | | 9 |
| | | What other areas or services are impacted? | All patient care areas. | | | |

This three-page template is provided as an aid in organizing the steps in a root cause analysis. Not all possibilities and questions will apply in every case, and there may be others that will emerge in the course of the analysis. However, all possibilities and questions should be fully considered in your quest for "root causes" and risk reduction.

As an aid to avoiding "loose ends," the three columns on the right are provided to be checked off for later reference:

"Root cause?" should be answered yes or no for each finding. A root cause is typically a finding related to a process or system that has a potential for redesign to reduce risk If a particular finding that is relevant to the event is not a root cause, be sure that it is addressed later in the analysis with a Why? question. Each finding that is identified as a root cause should be considered for an action and addressed in the action plan.

"Ask Why?" should be checked off whenever it is reasonable to ask why the particular finding occurred (or didn't occur when it should have) – in other words, to drill down further. Each item checked in this column should be addressed later in the analysis with a Why? question. It is expected that any significant findings that are not identified as root causes will have check marks in this column. Also, items that are identified as root causes will often be checked in this column, because many root causes themselves have "roots."

"Take action?" should be checked for any finding that can reasonably be considered for a risk reduction strategy. Each item checked in this column should be addressed later in the action plan. It will be helpful to write the number of the associated Action Item on page 3 in the "Take Action?" column for each of the Findings that requires an action.

*(continued on next page)*

Source: Joint Commission on Accreditation of Healthcare Organizations, Oakbrook Terrace, IL. Used with permission.

**Figure 6-2:** *Sample Framework for a Root Cause Analysis and Action Plan in Response to a Sentinel Event (continued)*

| Level of Analysis | | Questions | Findings | Root cause? | Ask "Why?" | Take action? |
|---|---|---|---|---|---|---|
| **Why did that happen? What systems and processes underlie those proximate factors?** (Common-cause variation here may lead to special cause variation in dependent processes.) | Human resource issues | To what degree are staff properly qualified and currently competent for their responsibilities? | All involved nursing staff were properly trained and competent for their assigned duties. | | | |
| | | How did actual staffing compare with ideal levels? | Staffing levels appropriate for patient load and mix of patients on this unit that day. | | | |
| | | What are the plans for dealing with contingencies that would tend to reduce effective staffing levels? | Actual, planned, flex, and resident loads are assigned on a coordinated basis, stressing learning as an outcome of this function. | | | |
| | | To what degree is staff performance in the operant process(es) addressed? | Annual staff evaluations were complete and showed all involved to be exceptional practitioners, nurses, and residents. However, annual evaluations do not currently provide for age-specific competency assessment for emergency department staff. | | | 10 |
| | | | Attending may not have heard beeper because of multiple priorities, fatigue, personal problems. | | | 11 |
| | | How can orientation & in-service training be improved? | Re: obtaining urgent psychiatric consults, recording verbal orders, management of suicidal patients. | | | 7 |
| | Information management issues | To what degree is all necessary information available when needed? accurate? complete? unambiguous? | Information about the patient's past admission was not available. | | | 9 |
| | | To what degree is communication among participants adequate? | Communication delays resulted in not implementing appropriate steps that may have prevented the event. | | | 4,6,8 |
| | Environmental management issues | To what degree was the physical environment appropriate for the processes being carried out? | Pediatric psychiatry patient was placed in the pediatric unit for a prolonged time. | | | 3,5,7 |
| | | What systems are in place to identify environmental risks? | Need to enlarge psychiatric unit. Unit routinely runs at 99% occupancy. | | | 12 |
| | | What emergency and failure-mode responses have been planned and tested? | | | | |
| | Leadership issues: Corporate culture | To what degree is the culture conducive to risk identification and reduction? | | | | |
| | Encouragement of communication | What are the barriers to communication of potential risk factors? | Reluctance to "bother" on-call and attending staff during night hours. | | | 8 |
| | Clear communication of priorities | To what degree is the prevention of adverse outcomes communicated as a high priority? How? | Unclear chain of communication between nursing, residents, and attendings. | | | 7 |
| | Uncontrollable factors | What can be done to protect against the effects of these uncontrollable factors? | | | | |

*(continued on next page)*

219

**Figure 6–2:** *Sample Framework for a Root Cause Analysis and Action Plan in Response to a Sentinel Event (continued)*

| | Risk-Reduction Strategies | Measures of Effectiveness |
|---|---|---|
| For each of the findings identified in the analysis as needing an action, indicate the planned action, expected implementation date, and associated measure of effectiveness, OR.... | **Action Item #1:** Nurse placed on probation. Evaluation plan instituted. | **Measure:** Evaluated at 90-day intervals. |
| | **Action Item #2:** Admission clerk reassigned. New admission clerk hired and trained. | **Measure:** |
| If, after consideration of such a finding, a decision is made not to implement an associated risk reduction strategy, indicate the rationale for not taking action at this time. | **Action Item #3:** a. Residents and nursing staff will have mandatory in-service on suicide risk assessment. b. To be included in new staff orientation: Proper precautions for suicide-risk patients Documenting verbal orders Obtaining timely consultations | **Measure:** All participants will achieve a score of 90 or better on the post-training test. To be implemented in a 60-day time frame. |
| Check to be sure that the selected measure will provide data that will permit assessment of the effectiveness of the action. | **Action Item #4:** a. Install paging system with wider range. b. Notify medical staff and others utilizing paging system of system limitations. c. Memo to all MS to leave phone number when potentially out of range of pager system. | **Measure:** IT to conduct review and make recommendations in 30 days. |
| Consider whether pilot testing of a planned improvement should be conducted. | **Action Item #5:** Ensure that accurate data are entered in a timely manner for the bed tracking system. | **Measure:** |
| | **Action Item #6:** All patients with psychiatric or substance abuse diagnoses will be placed on suicide precautions until discontinued by written order from attending or consulting psychiatrist. | **Measure:** |
| Improvements to reduce risk should ultimately be implemented in all areas where applicable, not just where the event occurred. Identify where the improvements will be implemented. | **Action Item #7:** Review and revise hospital policy and procedure manual. a. Clarify precautions to be taken when a patient is identified to be at risk for suicide. b. Clarify terms: "suicide precautions," "Suicide Watch." c. Visitor policy for patients on "precautions" to be revised and enforced. d. Maximum emergency department hold time and transfer policy for psychiatric patients. e. Define chain of communication between nursing, residents, and attendings. | **Measure:** To be completed in a 60-day time frame. |
| | **Action Item #8:** a. Emphasize residents' responsibility to contact attending physicians whenever needed. b. Work with Medical Staff to ensure responsiveness without intimidation or rudeness. | **Measure:** |
| | **Action Item #9:** Computer program to be developed to facilitate access to medical records from prior admissions. | **Measure:** |
| | **Action Item #10:** Age-specific competency assessment to be included in all emergency department staff evaluations. | **Measure:** |
| | **Action Item #11:** a. Support group formed by group practice. b. Peer review of physicians conducted. | **Measure:** |
| | **Action Item #12:** Evaluate options for enlarging psychiatric unit. | **Measure:** |
| Cite any books or journal articles that were considered in developing this analysis and action plan: | | |

## The Proximate Causes

Careful study of this narrative indicates at least 12 things, or *proximate* causes, that "went wrong" in this case. They demonstrate the "cascade of failure" phenomenon that can occur in closely coupled systems, especially the series of events immediately following the initially incorrect clinical impression. They are as follows:

1. Commitment to an incorrect presumptive diagnosis (vial labeled amoxycillin + history of allergies = probable allergic reaction).
2. Staff were unable to contact the patient's attending physician by pager.
3. Patient's past medical history was not available.
4. Patient was admitted to a pediatric unit rather than the psychiatric unit.
5. Staff did not respond to the finding of a prior suicide attempt.
6. Patient was treated with sedatives.
7. Staff decided to defer efforts to reach the attending physician until morning.
8. Transfer of the patient to the psychiatric unit was delayed.
9. Attending physician still did not respond when paged.
10. Verbal (rather than written) orders for precautions were issued.
11. Unrestricted and unsupervised visitors were allowed, even after precautions were ordered.
12. No observation/reassessment of patient was performed for two hours after lethargy was noted.

Another useful technique at this early stage is to list all the individuals (by title or job) who were involved. This is done not to point fingers or assign blame but rather to double-check that additional process variations, especially omissions, have not been left out. The individuals identified in this scenario are as follows: ED physician, on-call pediatric resident, attending physician, on-call physician for the group practice, nurse on the pediatric unit, relieving pediatric resident, nursing supervisor, and psychiatric resident.

Page 1 of the framework indicates that the organization completing the root cause analysis missed a number of the proximate factors, namely causes 1, 3, 6, 7, and 12. It is also helpful to identify items listed as proximate factors that actually are intermediate or root causes. The item is a root cause if it directly identifies a specific process, step of a process, or component of a system that can be redesigned to reduce the risk of an error or failure in the future.

The next step is to ask Why? about each of the 12 process variations outlined earlier in this section. The columns on the right-hand side of the framework can be used to categorize the findings and direct the next steps in the analysis. All findings in a root cause analysis should provoke a subsequent why question, be identified as a root cause with consideration of an action to reduce risk, or both. Root causes can themselves have roots.

## The Root Causes

Page 2 of the framework illustrates the organization's findings regarding root causes. The top section on "human resource issues" reveals internal inconsistency. In the first box, the organization wrote, "All involved nursing staff were properly trained and competent for their assigned duties." However, in the fourth box from the top of the page, the organization wrote, "Annual evaluations do not currently provide for age-specific competency assessment for ED staff." This inconsistency would be noted by the Joint Commission during its assessment of the credibility of the root cause analysis. Also, mention of resident supervision should be addressed in the human resources section.

The section on "information management issues" indicates that the organization did not follow up on the finding that the "computerized bed tracking system did not indicate correct bed status." This case illustrates reliance on an unreliable computer system. The system depended on human input and did not have checks for missing information. This fact should raise questions about how such systems are designed, who has input into the design, how the system is tested, and so forth. The overall question is, "What is the nature of the planning process and how can it be improved?"

The section on "leadership issues" is not filled out completely. Although findings about corporate culture can be quite threatening, they can be made less so by asking about the leadership *functions*, rather than the leaders.

Other why questions that might have been asked during this stage include the following:

■ Why didn't the computerized bed tracking system provide the correct information?
■ Why was the initial diagnosis incorrect? Can anything be done to raise the "index of suspicion" in such cases?
■ Why wasn't the paging system working? Is there an equipment management problem here?
■ Why weren't the precautions effective in protecting the patient?

## The Action Plan

Page 3 of the framework outlines the organization's action plan, including risk-reduction and measurement strategies. Each of the findings identified as root causes should be addressed in the action plan. The organization outlines different types of risk-reduction strategies. They involve

■ punitive actions (items 1 and 2);
■ retraining, education, and counseling (items 3, 7, and 10);
■ policy and procedures changes (item 7); these changes only become a process change when the plan also addresses communication, implementation, and verification of the changes reflected in the revised policies and procedures;
■ redundant process creation (item 4c);
■ fail-safe process redesign (item 6);
■ technical system enhancements (items 5 and 9); and
■ culture change (item 8).

Of the suggested strategies, system enhancements and culture change are likely to be the most effective in the long run.

The measurement strategies outlined by the organization are not sufficiently objective and quantitative to adequately assess the effectiveness of the risk reduction strategies. Process measures or intermediate outcome measures should be used when assessing the effectiveness of actions designed to prevent sentinel events.

# References

1. Bower KA: Developing and using critical paths. In Lord JT (ed): *The Physician Leader's Guide.* Rockville, MD: Bader & Associates, Inc, 1992, pp 61–66.

2. Zander K: Critical pathways. In Melum MM, Sinioris MK (eds): *Total Quality Management: The Health Care Pioneers.* Chicago: American Hospital Publishing, Inc, 1992, pp 305–314.

3. Weber DO: Clinical pathways stretch patient care but shrink costly lengths of stay at Anne Arundel Medical Center in Annapolis, Maryland. *Strategic Healthcare Excellence* 5(5):1–9, 1992.

# Selected Bibliography

## Articles

AAS: National suicide statistics. American Association of Suicidology, June 1997.

Altman DG: Strategies for community health intervention: Promises, paradoxes, pitfalls. *Psychosom Med* 57(3):226–233, 1995.

APA Online: APA task force reports: Seclusion and restraint. Washington, DC: American Psychiatric Association, 1998.

Barker KN, Allan EL: Research on drug-use-system errors. *Am J Health Syst Pharm* 52(4):400–403, 1995.

Bates DW, et al: Evaluation of screening criteria for adverse events in medical patients. *Med Care* 33(55):452–462, 1995.

Bates DW, et al: Incidence of adverse drug events and potential adverse drug events. *JAMA* 274(1):29–34, 1995.

Beck SA et al: Multiagency outcome evaluation of children's services: A case study. *Behav Health Serv Res* 25(2):163–176.

Belkin L: How can we save the next victim? *New York Times Magazine* June 15, 1997, Section 6.

Bindler R, Boyne T: Medication calculation ability of registered nurses. *Image* 23:221–224, 1991.

Blumenthal D: Making medical errors into medical treasures. *JAMA* 272(23):1851–1857, 1994.

Bower KA: Developing and using critical paths. In Lord JT (ed): *The Physician Leader's Guide.* Rockville, MD: Bader & Associates, Inc, 1992, pp 61–66.

Bradbury K, et al: Prevention of medication errors: Developing a continuous-quality-improvement approach. *Mt Sinai J Med* 60(5):379–386, 1993.

Brennan TA, et al: Identification of adverse events occurring during hospitalization. *Ann Intern Med* 112(3):221–226, 1990.

Brennan TA, et al: Incidence of adverse events and negligence in hospitalized patients. *N Engl J Med* 324(6):370–376, 1991.

Chen TL: Using automation to reduce medication errors. *Health Data Manage,* July 1997, pp 74–83.

Christensen JF, Levinson W, Dunn PM: The heart of darkness: The impact of perceived mistakes on physicians. *J Gen Intern Med* 7(4):424–431, 1992.

Cohen MR: Drug product characteristics that foster drug-use-system errors. *Am J Health Syst Pharm* 52(4):395–399, 1995.

Coleman RL, Hunter DE: Contemporary quality management in mental health. *Am J Med Qual* 10(3):120–6, Fall 1995.

Colling R: Protect your patients: Hire with care. *Jt Comm Envir of Care News,* July/Aug 1998, pp 10–11.

Cooper JB: Is voluntary reporting of critical events effective for quality assurance? *Anesthesiology* 85(5):9061–9064, 1996.

Cooper JB, Cullen DJ, Eichhorn JH, et al: Administrative guidelines for response to an adverse anesthesia event. *J Clin Anesth* 1993; 5:79.

Cooper JB, Gaba DM: A strategy for preventing anesthesia accidents. In Lebowitz PW (ed): *International Anesthesiology Clinics.* Boston: Little Brown, 1989, pp 148–152.

Cooper JB, et al: Preventable anesthesia mishaps: A study of human factors. *Anesthesiology* 49(6):399–406, 1978.

Cooper JB, Newbower RS, Ritz RJ: An analysis of major errors and equipment failures in anesthesia management—Considerations for prevention and detection. *Anesthesiology* 60(1):34–42, 1984.

Cooper MC: Can a zero defects philosophy be applied to drug errors? *J Adv Nurs* 21(3):487–491, 1995.

Cullen D, et al: The incident reporting system does not detect adverse drug events: A problem for quality improvement. *Jt Comm J Qual Improv* 21(10):541–548, 1995.

Dew JR: In search of the root cause. *Qual Prog* 24(3):97–102, 1991.

Ferner RE: Is there a cure for drug errors? *BMJ* 311(7003):463–464, 1995.

Firestone T: Physical restraints: Meeting the standards/improving the outcomes. *Med Surg Nurs* 7(2)121–123.

Fleming ST: Complications, adverse events, and iatrogenesis: Classifications and quality of care measurement issues. *Clin Perform Qual Health Care* 4(3):137–147, 1996.

Food and Drug Administration: Safe use of physical restraint devices. *FDA Backgrounder,* July 1992.

Foreman JT: HealthReach Home Care. In Joint Commission on Accreditation of Healthcare Organizations Quality Improvement in Home Care. Oakbrook Terrace, IL: Joint Commission, 1993, pp 125–137.

Fox GN: Minimizing prescribing errors in infants and children. *Am Fam Physician* 53(4):1319–1325, 1996.

Gaba DM: Human error in anesthetic mishaps. In Lebowitz PW (ed): *International Anesthesiology Clinics.* Boston: Little Brown, 1989, pp 137–147.

Gaba DM, DeAnda A: The response of anesthesia trainees to simulated critical incidents. *Anesth Analg* 68(4):444–451, 1989.

Gaucher EJ, Coffey RJ: A case study of quality improvement. In *Total Quality in Healthcare: From Theory to Practice*. San Francisco: Jossey-Bass, 1993, pp 397–440.

Gawande A: When doctors make mistakes. *The New Yorker*, Feb 1, 1999, pp 40, 42–44, 48–51, 53–55.

Geraci JM, et al: Predicting the occurrence of adverse events after coronary artery bypass surgery. *Ann Intern Med* 118(1):18–24, 1992.

Goren S, Abraham I, Doyle N: Reducing violence in a child psychiatric hospital through planned organizational change. *J Child Adolesc Psychopharmacol* 9(2):27–37.

Goren S, Curtis WJ: Staff members' beliefs about seclusion and restraint in child psychiatric hospitals. *J Child Adolesc Psychoparmacol* 9(4):7–14, Oct/Dec 1996.

Granville RL, et al: Some characteristics of Department of Defense medical malpractice claims: An initial report. *Legal Medicine Open File*, Washington, DC: U.S. Government Printing Office, 1992, pp 1–10.

Hackel R, Butt L, Banister G: How nurses perceive medication errors. *Nurs Manage* 27(1):31–34, 1996.

Hilfiker D: Facing our mistakes. *N Engl J Med* 310(2):118–122, 1984.

James BC: Establishing accountability for errors: Who, how, with what impact? Presented at the Examining Errors in Health Care Conference, Rancho Mirage, CA: Oct 13–15, 1996.

Joint Commission: Inpatient suicides: Recommendations for prevention. *Sentinel Event Alert*, Issue 7, Nov 6, 1998.

Joint Commission: Preventing restraint deaths. *Sentinel Event Alert*, Issue 8, Nov 1998.

Joint Commission: Rationale guiding the evaluation of sentinel events. *Jt Comm Perspectives* 16(3):6–7, 1996.

Kelly WN: Pharmacy contributions to adverse medication events. *Am J Health Syst Pharm* 52(4):385–390, 1995.

Kessler DA: Introducing MedWatch: A new approach to reporting medication and device adverse effects and product problems. *JAMA* 269(21):2765–2768, 1993.

Keyes C: Responding to adverse events. *Forum* 18(1):2–3, Apr 1997.

Kravitz RL, Rolph JE, McGuigan K: Malpractice claims data as a quality improvement tool: Epidemiology of error in four specialties. *JAMA* 266(15):2087–2092, 1991.

Leape LL: Error in medicine. *JAMA* 272(23):1851–1857, 1994.

Leape LL, et al: The nature of adverse events in hospitalized patients: Results of the Harvard Medical Practice Study. *N Engl J Med* 324(6):377–384, 1991.

Leape LL, et al: Preventing medical injury. *Qual Rev Bull* 19:144–149, 1993.

Leape LL, et al: Systems analysis of adverse drug events. *JAMA* 274(1):35–43, 1995.

Levinson W, Dunn PM: A piece of my mind: Coping with fallibility. *JAMA* 261(15):2252, 1989.

Lilley LL, Guanci R: Med errors: Applying systems theory. *Am J Nurs* 95(11):14–15, 1995.

Localio AR, et al: Identifying adverse events caused by medical care: Degree of physician agreement in a retrospective chart review. *Ann Intern Med* 125(6):457–464, 1996.

Marek CL: Avoiding prescribing errors: A systematic approach. *JADA* 127(5):617–623, 1996.

McPhee SJ, et al: Practical issues in disclosing medical mistakes to patients. Presented at the Examining Errors in Health Care Conference, Rancho Mirage, CA: Oct 13–15, 1996.

Mion LD, et al: Physical restraint use in the hospital setting: Unresolved issues and directions for research. *Milbank Q* 74(3):426.

Moray N: Error reduction as a systems problem. In Bogner MS (ed): *Human Error in Medicine.* Hillsdale, NJ: Lawrence Erlbaum Associates, 1994, pp 70–71.

O'Leary DS: Relating autopsy requirements to the contemporary accreditation process. *Arch Pathol Lab Med* 120(8):763–766, 1996.

Pepper GA: Errors in drug administration by nurses. *Am J Health Syst Pharm* 52(4):390–395, 1995.

Peterson LA, et al: Does housestaff discontinuity of care increase the risk for preventable adverse events? *Ann Intern Med* 121(11):866–872, 1994.

Rasmussen J, Jensen A: Mental procedures in real-life tasks: A case study of electronic troubleshooting. *Ergonomics* 17(3):293–307, 1974.

Reason J: Human and organizational factors: Lessons from other domains. Presented at the Examining Errors in Health Care Conference, Rancho Mirage, CA: Oct 13–15, 1996.

Reichheld FF: Learning from customer defections. *Harv Bus Rev* 74(2):56–69, 1996.

Roseman C, Booker JM: Workload and environmental factors in hospital medication errors. *Nurs Res* 44(4):1226–1230, 1995.

Rupp RO, Russell JR: The golden rules of process redesign. *Qual Prog* 27(12):85–90, 1994.

Sagduyu K, Hornstra RK, Munro S et al: A comparison of the restraint and seclusion experiences of patients with schizophrenia or other psychotic disorders. *Missouri Med,* June 1995, p 303–307.

Sanborn KV, et al: Detection of intraoperative incidents by electronic scanning of computerized anesthesia records. *Anesthesiology* 85(5):977–987, 1996.

Schiff GD: Commentary: Diagnosis tracking and health reform. *Am J Med Qual* 9(4):149–152, 1994.

Schwid HA, O'Donnell D: Anesthesiologists' management of simulated critical incidents. *Anesthesiology* 76(4):495–501, 1992.

Senders JW: Detecting, correcting, and interrupting errors. *J Intraven Nurs* 18(1):28–32, 1995.

Spath P: Add root-cause analysis to your PI armament. *Hosp Peer Rev*, Apr 1998.

Spath P: Avoid panic by planning for sentinel events. *Hosp Peer Review*. June 1998, pp 112–117.

Spath P: Manage sentinel events by fixing root causes. *Hosp Peer Rev*, Dec 1997.

Spath PL: Performance measurement in behavioral health. Brown-Spath & Associates, July 1998.

Tommasello T: Do substance abuse and dependence contribute to errors in health care? Presented at the Examining Errors in Health Care Conference, Rancho Mirage, CA: Oct 13–15, 1996.

Trick OL: Adverse drug reactions: Establishing a hierarchy of definitions for adjustment of report rates. *Hosp Pharm* 31(12):1593–1595, 1996.

Trostorff DL: Medical staff privileging: How to avoid pitfalls in the administrative process. *QRB*, June 1987, pp 198–203.

Troutman B, Myers K, Borchardt C et al: Case study: When restraints are the least restrictive alternative for managing aggression. *J Am Acad Child Adolesc Psychiatry* 37(5):554, May 1998.

Turnbull JE, Garrett SENTINEL EVENT: Hospital develops methods for uncovering underlying causes of error in health care. *QRC Adv* 14(3), Jan 1998.

U.S. General Accounting Office: Medical device reporting: Improvements needed in FDA's systems for monitoring problems with approved devices. GAO/HEHS-97–21. Washington, DC: U.S. General Accounting Office, 1997.

Valentine DR: Case review process using a systems approach. *Int Anesthesiol Clin* 30(2):15–27, 1992.

Weber DO: Clinical pathways stretch patient care but shrink costly lengths of stay at Anne Arundel Medical Center in Annapolis, Maryland. *Strateg Healthcare Excellence* 5(5):1–9, 1992.

Weiss EM: A nationwide pattern of death. *The Hartford Courant,* Oct 11, 1998.

Willoughby D, Budreau G, Livingston D: A framework for integrated quality improvement. *J Nurs Care Qual* 11(3):44–53, 1997.

Witman AB, Hardin S: Patients' responses to physicians' mistakes. *Forum,* Apr 1997, pp 4–5.

Wolff AM: Limited adverse occurrence screening: Using medical record review to reduce hospital adverse patient events. *Med J Aust* 164(8):458–461, 1996.

Wu AW, et al: Do house officers learn from their mistakes? *JAMA* 265(16):2089–2094, 1991.

Wu AW, et al: How house officers cope with their mistakes. *West J Med* 159(5):565–569, 1993.

Wu AW, et al: To tell the truth: Ethical and practical issues in disclosing medical mistakes to patients. *Gen Intern Med* 12(12)770–775, Dec 1997.

Zander K: Critical pathways. In Melum MM, Sinioris MK (eds): *Total Quality Management: The Health Care Pioneers.* Chicago: American Hospital Publishing, Inc, 1992, pp 305–314.

## Books

Ammerman M: *The Root Cause Analysis Handbook.* New York, NY: Quality Resources, 1998.

Bogner MS (ed): *Human Error in Medicine.* Hillsdale, NJ: Lawrence Erlbaum Associates, 1994.

Cesarone D: *Assess for Success: Achieving Excellence with Joint Commission Standards and Baldrige Criteria.* Oakbrook Terrace, IL: Joint Commission, 1997.

Cousins DD: *Medication Use: A Systems Approach to Reducing Errors.* Oakbrook Terrace, IL: Joint Commission, 1998.

Davenport TH: *Process Innovation: Reengineering Work Through Information Technology.* Boston: Harvard Business School Press, 1993.

Joint Commission on Accreditation of Healthcare Organizations: *Framework for Improving Performance: From Principles to Practice.* Oakbrook Terrace, IL: Joint Commission, 1994.

Joint Commission on Accreditation of Healthcare Organizations: *A Guide to Performance Improvement in Behavioral Health Care Organizations.* Oakbrook Terrace, IL: Joint Commission, 1996.

Joint Commission on Accreditation of Healthcare Organizations: *Reducing Restraint Use in the Acute Care Environment.* Oakbrook Terrace, IL: Joint Commission, 1998.

Joint Commission on Accreditation of Healthcare Organizations: *Sentinel Events: Evaluating Cause and Planning Improvement.* Oakbrook Terrace, IL: Joint Commission, 1998.

Joint Commission on Accreditation of Healthcare Organizations: *Storing and Securing Medications.* Oakbrook Terrace, IL: Joint Commission, 1998.

Joint Commission on Accreditation of Healthcare Organizations: *Using Performance Measurement to Improve Outcomes in Behavioral Health Care.* Oakbrook Terrace: Joint Commission, 1998.

Juran JM, Gryna FM: *Juran's Quality Control Handbook.* New York: McGraw-Hill, Inc, 1988.

Paradies M, Unger L: TapRooT® *Incident Investigation System Manual.* Knoxville, TN: System Improvements, 1996.

Perrow C: *Normal Accidents: Living with High-Risk Technologies.* New York: Basic Books, 1984.

Reason J: *Human Error.* Cambridge, MA: Cambridge University Press, 1990.

Reason JT: *Managing the Risks of Organizational Accidents.* Aldershot, UK: Ashgate 1997.

Riegelman RK: *Minimizing Medical Mistakes: The Art of Medical Decision Making.* Boston: Little Brown, 1991.

Senders J, Moray N: *Human Error: Cause, Prediction, and Reduction.* Hillsdale, NJ: Lawrence Erlbaum Associates, 1991.

Sharpe VA: *Medical Harm: Historical, Conceptual, and Ethical Dimensions of Iatrogenic Illness.* Cambridge, MA: Cambridge University Press, 1998.

Spath PL: *Investigating Sentinel Events: How to Find and Resolve Root Causes.* Forest Grove, OR: Brown-Spath & Associates, 1997.

Tague NR: *The Quality Toolbox.* Milwaukee, WI: ASQC Quality Press, 1995.

Wilson PF, Dell LD, Anderson GF: *Root Cause Analysis: A Tool for Total Quality Management.* Milwaukee: ASQC Quality Press, 1993.

# Glossary of Terms

**Accreditation Watch**   An attribute of an organization's Joint Commission accreditation status. A health care organization is placed on Accreditation Watch when a reviewable sentinel event has occurred and has come to the Joint Commission's attention and a thorough and credible root cause analysis of the sentinel event and action plan have not been completed within a specified time frame.

**action plan** The product of the root cause analysis that identifies the strategies an organization intends to implement to reduce the risk of similar events occurring in the future. The plan should address responsibility for implementation, oversight, pilot testing as appropriate, time lines, and strategies for measuring effectiveness of the actions.

**active failure**   An error that is precipitated by the commission of errors and violations. These errors are difficult to anticipate and have an immediate adverse affect on safety by breaching, bypassing, or disabling existing defenses.

**adverse drug event (adverse drug error)**   Any incident in which the use of a medication (drug or biological) at any dose, a medical device, or a special nutritional product (for example, dietary supplement, infant formula, medical food) may have resulted in an adverse outcome in a patient.

**adverse drug reaction (ADR)**   An undesirable response associated with use of a drug that compromises therapeutic efficacy, enhances toxicity, or both.

**adverse event** An untoward, undesirable, and usually unanticipated event, such as the death of a patient, an employee, or a visitor in a health care organization. Incidents such as a patient falling or improper administration of medications are also considered adverse events, even if there is no permanent effect on the patient.

**aggregate data**   Data collected and reported by organizations as a sum or total over a given time period, for example, monthly or quarterly.

**barrier analysis** The study of the safeguards that can prevent or mitigate (or could have prevented or mitigated) an unwanted event or occurrence. It offers a structured way to visualize the events related to system failure or the creation of a problem.

**benchmarking**   Continuous measurement of a process, product, or service compared with those of the toughest competitor, those considered industry leaders, or similar activities in the organization in order to find and implement ways to improve it. Benchmarking is one of the foundations of both total quality management and continuous quality improvement. Internal benchmarking occurs when similar processes within the same organization are compared. Competitive benchmarking occurs when an organization's processes are compared with best practices within the industry. Functional benchmarking refers to benchmarking a similar function or process, such as scheduling, in another industry.

**causation**  The act by which an effect is produced. In epidemiology, the doctrine of causation is used to relate certain factors (predisposing, enabling, precipitating, or reinforcing factors) to disease occurrence. The doctrine of causation is also important in the fields of negligence and criminal law. Synonym: causality.

**change analysis**  A study of the differences between the expected and actual performance of a process. Change analysis involves determining the root cause of an event by examining the effects of change and identifying causes.

**circadian rhythm**  The rhythmic repetition of certain phenomena in living organisms at about the same time each day. Without cues provided by light, the human circadian cycle lasts 25.9 hours.

**clinical pathway**  A treatment regimen, agreed on by consensus, that includes all the elements of care, regardless of the effect on patient outcomes. It is a broader look at care and may include tests and x-ray scans that do not affect patient recovery. Synonyms: clinical path, critical pathway.

**cognitive psychology**  The branch of psychology that concentrates its studies on human perception, thinking, and learning.

**common-cause variation**  See variation.

**complication**  A detrimental patient condition that arises during the process of providing health care, regardless of the setting in which the care is provided. For instance, perforation, hemorrhage, bacteremia, and adverse reactions to medication (particularly in the elderly) are four complications of colonoscopy and its associated anesthesia and sedation. A complication may prolong an inpatient's length of stay or lead to other undesirable outcomes.

**coupled system**  A system that links two or more activities so that one process is dependent on another for completion. A system can be loosely or tightly coupled.

**epidemiology**  The field of medicine concerned with the determination of causes, incidence, and characteristic behavior of disease outbreaks affecting human populations. It includes the interrelationships of host, agent, and environment as related to the distribution and control of disease. Clinical epidemiology is a decision-making process applied by an individual practicing physician, where decisions are based on the likelihood of a patient having a given disease process given the patient's age, previous state of health, family history, the season, the previous appearance of similar diseases in the community, and other factors.

**error of commission**  An error that occurs as a result of an action taken. Examples include a drug being administered at the wrong time, in the wrong dose, or via the wrong route; surgeries performed on the wrong side of the body; and transfusion errors involving blood cross-matched for another patient.

**error of omission**  An error that occurs as a result of an action not taken. Examples include a delay in performing an indicated cesarean section, resulting in a fetal death; a nurse omitting a dose of a medication that should be administered; and a patient suicide that is associated with a lapse in carrying out frequent patient checks in a psychiatric unit. Errors of omission may or may not lead to adverse outcomes.

**fault tree analysis**  A systematic way of prospectively examining a design for possible ways in which failure can occur. The analysis considers the possible direct proximate causes that could lead to the event and seeks their origins. Once this is accomplished, ways to avoid these origins and causes must be identified.

**flowchart**  A pictorial summary that shows with symbols and words the steps, sequence, and relationship of the various operations involved in the performance of a function or a process. Synonym: flow diagram.

**FMECA** (failure mode, effect, and criticality analysis)  A systematic way of examining a design prospectively for possible ways in which failure can occur. It assumes that no matter how knowledgeable or careful people are, errors will occur in some situations and may even be likely to occur.

**human factors research**  The study of the capabilities and limitations of human performance in relation to the design of machines, jobs, and other aspects of the physical environment.

**iatrogenic**  1. Resulting from the professional activities of physicians, or, more broadly, from the activities of health professionals. Originally applied to disorders induced in the patient by autosuggestion based on a physician's examination, manner, or discussion, the term is currently applied to any undesirable condition in a patient occurring as the result of treatment by a physician (or other health professional), especially to infections acquired by the patient during the course of treatment. 2. Pertaining to an illness or injury resulting from a procedure, therapy, or other element of care.

**immediate cause**  See proximate cause.

**incident report**  The documentation for any unusual problem, incident, or other situation that is likely to lead to undesirable effects or that varies from established policies and procedures or practices. Synonym: occurrence report.

**indicator**  1. A measure used to determine, over time, performance of functions, processes, and outcomes. 2. A statistical value that provides an indication of the condition or direction over time of performance of a defined process or achievement of a defined outcome.

**latent failure**  An error that is precipitated by a consequence of management and organizational processes and poses the greatest danger to complex systems. Latent failures cannot be foreseen but, if detected, can be corrected before they contribute to mishaps.

**local trigger**  An intrinsic defect or atypical condition that can create failures.

**malpractice**   Improper or unethical conduct or unreasonable lack of skill by a holder of a professional or official position; often applied to physicians, dentists, lawyers, and public officers to denote negligent or unskillful performance of duties when professional skills are obligatory.

**mistake**   In law, an act or omission arising from ignorance or misconception which may, depending on its character or the circumstances, justify rescission of a contract or exoneration of a defendant from tort or criminal liability.

**negligence**   Failure to use such care as a reasonably prudent and careful person would use under similar circumstances.

**observation method**   An active method of error surveillance in which a trained observer watches the care delivery process.

**occurrence screening**   A system for concurrent or retrospective identification of adverse patient occurrences (APOs) through medical chart–based review according to objective screening criteria. Examples of criteria include admission for adverse results of outpatient management, readmission for complications, incomplete management of problems on previous hospitalization, or unplanned removal, injury, or repair of an organ or structure during surgery. Criteria are used organizationwide or adapted for departmental or topic-specific screening. Occurrence screening identifies about 80% to 85% of APOs. It will miss APOs that are not identifiable from the medical record.

**outcome**   The result of the performance (or nonperformance) of a function(s) or process(es).

**Pareto chart**   A form of vertical bar graph that displays information in such a way that priorities for process improvement can be established. It shows the relative importance of all the data and is used to direct efforts to the largest improvement opportunity by highlighting the "vital few" in contrast to the "many others."

**plan-do-study-act (PDSA) cycle**   A four-part method for discovering and correcting assignable causes to improve the quality of processes. Synonyms: Deming cycle, Shewhart cycle.

**process**   A goal-directed, interrelated series of actions, events, mechanisms, or steps.

**proximate cause**   An act or omission that naturally and directly produces a consequence. It is the superficial or obvious cause for an occurrence. Treating only the "symptoms," or the proximate special cause, may lead to some short-term improvements but will not prevent the variation from recurring.

**restraint**  Any method of physically restricting a person's freedom of movement, physical activity, and normal access to the body. This encompasses many physical devices, such as wrist restraints, jacket vests, and mitts.

**retrospective review**   1. A method of determining medical necessity or appropriate billing practice for services that have already been rendered. 2. In behavioral health, evaluative activities conducted when an individual being served is no longer in active treatment.

**risk containment** Immediate actions taken to safeguard patients from a repetition of an unwanted occurrence. Actions may involve removing and sequestering drug stocks from pharmacy shelves and checking or replacing oxygen supplies or specific medical devices.

**risk management** Clinical and administrative activities undertaken to identify, evaluate, and reduce the risk of injury to patients, staff, and visitors and the risk of loss to the organization itself.

**risk points** Specific points in a process that are susceptible to error or system breakdown. They generally result from a flaw in the initial process design, a high degree of dependence on communication, nonstandardized processes, and failure or absence of backup.

**root cause** The most fundamental reason for the failure or inefficiency of a process.

**root cause analysis** A process for identifying the basic or causal factor(s) that underlie variation in performance, including the occurrence or possible occurrence of a sentinel event.

**seclusion** Involuntary confinement of a person alone in a room where the person is physically prevented from leaving.

**sentinel event** An unexpected occurrence involving death or serious physical or psychological injury, or the risk thereof. Serious injury specifically includes loss of limb or function. The phrase "or the risk thereof" includes any process variation (see below) for which a recurrence would carry a significant chance of a serious adverse outcome. Such events are called "sentinel" because they signal the need for immediate investigation and response.

**special-cause variation** See variation.

**surveillance** Ongoing monitoring using methods distinguished by their practicability, uniformity, and rapidity, rather than by complete accuracy. The purpose of surveillance is to detect changes in trend or distribution to initiate investigative or control measures. Active surveillance is systematic and involves review of each case within a defined time frame. Passive surveillance is not systematic. Cases may be reported through written incident reports, verbal accounts, electronic transmission, or telephone hotlines, for example.

**taxonomy** The science of the classification according to resemblances and differences, with the application of names or other labels.

**underlying cause** The systems or process cause that allows for the proximate cause of an event to occur. Underlying causes may involve special-cause variation, common-cause variation, or both.

**variation** The differences in results obtained in measuring the same phenomenon more than once. The sources of variation in a process over time can be grouped into two major classes: common causes and special causes. Excessive variation frequently leads to waste and loss, such as the occurrence of undesirable patient health outcomes and increased cost of health services. Common-cause variation, also called endogenous-cause variation or systemic-cause variation, in a process is due to the process itself and is produced by interactions of variables of that process and is inherent in all processes, not a disturbance in the process. It can be removed only by making basic changes in the process. Special-cause variation, also called exogenous-cause variation or extrasystemic-cause variation, in performance results from assignable causes. Special-cause variation is intermittent, unpredictable, and unstable. It is not inherently present in a system; rather, it arises from causes that are not part of the system as designed.